THE ENCYCLOPEDIA OF
PREDICTION

THE ENCYCLOPEDIA OF
PREDICTION

DAVID V BARRETT

Book Express
Quality and Value in Every Book....

Dedicated to all those who are asking questions

© Bookmart Limited 1992

Specially produced for
Book Express, Inc.
Airport Business Center,
29 Kripes Road,
East Granby, Connecticut, USA.

North American Direct Sales rights in this edition
are exclusive to Book Express Inc.

Designed, edited and produced by
Anness Publishing Limited
Boundary Row Studios
1 Boundary Row
London SE1 8HP
United Kingdom

ISBN 1 873762 35 6

Editorial Director: Joanna Lorenz
Project Editor: Penelope Cream
Art Director: Peter Bridgewater
Designer: Simon Balley

Printed and bound in Hong Kong

Contents

Introduction

*D*o we really want to know what the future holds? The future can never be fixed and rigid, yet through the use of divinatory systems we can glimpse what it might produce. The art of prediction allows us to assess our lives and examine what paths we should follow.

People have attempted to predict the future from the earliest of eras: dream interpretation occurs in both the Old and New Testaments of the Bible, and has been practised by monks, scholars and clergy of different denominations for many centuries. The symbolism contained within systems such as Tarot embraces a wide range of Christian, pagan and Oriental religious references. The alphabets and letter systems of cultures from Scandinavia to China have taken on esoteric significance through the centuries, reaching beyond their original communication forms into the runes and *I Ching* of current usage.

Why are some forms of prediction so remarkably accurate and perceptive? Some people believe there is a guiding force directing the fall of cards, coins or runes, or the time and date of one's birth. Others suggest the psychoanalyst Carl Jung's system of synchronicity: everything in the universe is connected, including the pattern of stars at our birth and our personality, hence the way in which the Tarot cards fall and the information they provide, for example. Synchronicity incorporates what could be termed "meaningful coincidence".

Others think that the position of the stars, a selection of cards, or the appearance of the palms of our hands, for example, is completely random, entirely unconnected to anything else in the universe. Everything, they say, hangs on the interpretation and the ability of the interpreter. The best professional Tarot consultants, the best dream analysts and the most skilled astrologers and palm readers not only know the tools and rules of their trade inside out but are also probably highly sensitive to others' emotions. They can "read" the client as much as the cards, dreams or the palm of the hand.

It is possible that the means of divination or prediction covered within these pages is a means of extrapolation from character analysis. But then we meet the chicken and egg problem: where does character come from, and what shapes the individual personality? These are questions of metaphysics and it would be presumptuous to attempt to provide all the answers. Answers are as individual as the questions and do not always apply to other people: in fact, it is the questions that are more important than the answers. But the very act of questioning means that we open ourselves to self-analysis and learning. Divination allows you to push aside personal limitations through the constant exploration of future possibilities.

Overall, have respect for the powerful symbolism within the divinatory systems, but regard the ritual surrounding some systems with objectivity: if it works for you, use it; if it gets in the way, avoid it. Ritual behaviour can be extremely useful to some users on some occasions, but it is not essential and is peripheral to the main process of divination itself.

Interpretation is largely a matter of insight and intuition. We must find what is right for ourselves by asking questions, listening to the answers and examining the paths ahead.

Dreams & their Meaning

What are dreams? Where do they come from? What do they mean? Every historical period, and every culture around the world, has come up with a different answer to these questions, but on one thing they are all agreed – dreams are of vital significance, and their proper understanding can open up the hidden areas of man's psyche and soul.

Dreams are the time when we meet our neglected but honest other self: they are a window through which we can glimpse our truest, deepest feelings. By being able to analyse what happens in our dreams, and understanding their imagery and symbolism, we can get as close as possible to knowing our genuine concerns and attitudes. Dreams are the surest indicators of what we will do, how we will react, and when we will change. This knowledge is the key to the future.

Opposite: *While we sleep our unconscious mind throws up fantastically vivid and dramatic images, which more often than not appear to be totally unconnected with our everyday lives. Yet by learning more about the language and symbolism of the dream world, we can soon begin to analyse, interpret and understand these visions, and take heed of their messages about our deeper feelings and concerns. This dream-inspired picture,* Hope, *was painted by G.F. Watts in 1885.*

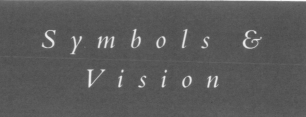

Symbols & Vision

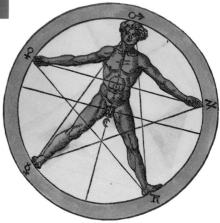

We all dream. Even those who claim they never dream have been shown to dream as much as the rest of us; they simply do not remember them as well.

Why some of us find it difficult to remember our dreams has still not been discovered; it is one of the many mysteries which make dreaming so fascinating. One longs for a headset or a skullcap with electrodes that can monitor exactly when we dream, and record the dreams on videotape to be played back later.

Perhaps one day the anxious scientists and dreamers, switching the video-recorder to playback, will be disappointed by the apparently unconnected jumble of images flashing across the screen. One of the numerous theories about dreams is that the coherent story we can sometimes remember so well is added later, when our conscious, waking mind attempts to impose some structure and sense on the otherwise arbitrary confusion of pictures and thoughts.

Above: Our dreams can be peopled with angels and demons. Mythological creatures, gargoyles, fantastic beasts and monsters surface as dream archetypes – visions from folklore and from what Jung first described as the "collective unconscious" shared by all.

Right: Sometimes our dreams throw up quite fantastic and impossible images, such as this two-headed androgynous figure. Seemingly ludicrous visions when interpreted and analysed can have very real and meaningful implications for our waking selves.

Above: Everything is related: within man, and all around him, are signs of the spiritual forces linking him with the cosmos. These symbols form the vocabulary of the language of dreams: it is the identification and understanding of these shared symbols that give our dreams meaning.

Or perhaps we will be able to watch, together, the fantastic (in its true sense) and colourful stories we call dreams. If we saw as waking visions half the things we see in our dreams we would think we were going mad. Jeanne d'Arc claimed she saw in daylight, many times, the Archangel Michael, and Saints Margaret and Catherine. Was she mad? Or deluded? Or lying? Did the saints truly appear to her? Or were what she called visions what we today would call hallucinations? Why do we feel so uncomfortable about "seeing things" by day that we take so much for granted by night? Visions and dreams: what are they, and where do they come from?

What is dreaming?

Perhaps as much as seven years of the average seventy-year life is spent in dreaming. This is something that happens to every human being on Earth, three, four or five times every night of our lives – and has done throughout recorded history and no doubt much longer – and yet we know surprisingly little about it.

Only in this century have we been able to tell for sure when someone is dreaming, and for how long. In 1952 Eugene Aserinsky, a young graduate research student at the University of Chicago,

noticed that babies' eyes appeared to move rapidly under their eyelids while they were asleep. They would move for a while, then be still, then start to move again. (Later research has shown that babies spend far more of their sleep time dreaming than do children or adults, who spend least of all.)

Aserinsky and his professor, Nathaniel Kleitman, used an electroencephalograph (EEG) to monitor the different brainwaves of sleeping people, and tied in the results with observation of their rapid eye movements (REMs). REMs correlated with faster brainwaves, and also with changes in the pulse rate, less regular breathing, and muscle movements. It is as if the eyes were following moving pictures projected on the inside of their lids.

The average pattern goes something like this: shortly after falling asleep we go into a deep sleep; after about ninety minutes we dream for perhaps ten minutes, before falling back into deep sleep again. There are other levels of sleep between, but it is only in the shallowest that we dream. Through the night we "surface" into dreaming between three and five times, with the dreaming periods becoming gradually longer, and the periods between them gradually shorter. This is why we are quite likely to be in the middle of a dream, or to have just finished dreaming, when we wake up.

But what is dreaming? Why do we dream? Is dreaming important? There are many theories

Left: *Artists of all eras and nationalities have been fascinated by the world of dreams: its depiction gives unlimited scope to the imagination. This dream image,* Queen Katherine's Dream, *is by the great mystic and poet William Blake.*

Below: *This romantic print by the nineteenth-century artist William Etty reflects the underlying Victorian preoccupation with eroticism: the dream image is used to provide the requisite distancing between sensuousness and reality.*

Right: *The Moon is a common dream image. It represents intrigue and mystery, but at the same time comfort and security. A full Moon in a cloudless sky is a very fortuitous symbol. This picture,* Full Orbed Moon, *was painted by A B Davies in 1901.*

Right: *Here dying and excitement are connected, this time in one of Holbein's prints on the theme of the Dance of Death. In this nightmare image the archetype of the skeleton, representing death, is seen to excite the dancers to a frenzy, while leading them to their graves. The medieval* danse macabre *existed in many cultures: it evolved into religious and pagan festivals, the celebration of which helped our ancestors to cope with the concept of dying, just as dreams help our conscious selves to cope with the stresses of events outside our control.*

Volunteers have allowed themselves to be "tortured" by being woken up every time their REM activity begins. When they fall asleep again, it takes less time to reach the REM period. Each time the period of deeper sleep before REM becomes shorter, until eventually the "victim" dives, as if desperately, straight into REM sleep.

If they are not allowed any REM sleep – if they are not allowed to dream at all – they begin to hallucinate when they are awake. (Hallucinations and other visions may be closely related to dreams, as we shall see.) If they are still denied their dreams, they become increasingly disorientated and may eventually suffer severe mental disturbance.

What do dreams do?

Clearly it is essential to dream, but scientists are no closer to saying why. What purpose, what function do dreams have? And what do they mean?

Around AD 405 Macrobius, a philosopher who held administrative office under Emperor Honorius, divided dreams into five types:
★ The dream: a symbolic scene or story which requires interpretation.
★ The vision: a clear view of a future event.
★ The ocular dream: a priest or god telling what is to come.
★ The insomnium: an ordinary, unimportant dream.
★ The phantasm: a disturbed, half-awake dream or nightmare.

attempting to answer the first two questions; the answer to the third is, emphatically, yes.

Researchers over the last forty years have conducted many experiments with sleepers and dreamers. They have found, for example, that if people are woken within a few minutes of their rapid eye movement ceasing, they will be very likely to remember the dream they have just had. If they are woken after more than about ten minutes, they will probably have forgotten it. Again this is why we can often remember the dream we were having just before we woke up. But if the alarm clock wakes us during a period of deep sleep, more than ten minutes after the last dream, we will not remember it.

Sleep deprivation has been a much-used torture over the centuries; as soon as the prisoner falls asleep he is woken up by his gaolers. After a few days and nights of this he begins to suffer mentally. Yet it now seems from sleep and dream research that it is not sleep deprivation that causes mental disturbance, but dream deprivation. The body needs sleep to recharge the batteries for the following day, though it can make do to quite a large extent with short snatches of rest between periods of activity, instead of actual sleep. But the mind cannot do without dreams.

This is a sound categorization, but there have been many other ideas over the years, usually expressed in terms reflecting developments in society, to explain what dreams are for and why they occur.

A likely current theory is the analogy of the brain to a computer. During the day it is assaulted by images provided by the five senses of sights, sounds, smells, tastes and touch, and also by our reasoning and emotions; not just loves and hates and joys and fears and frustrations and delights, but also absorption of new knowledge, puzzling things out, debating, learning and reaching conclusions.

All of these impressions are stored in short-term memory, but this gets very cluttered very quickly. Overnight, then, the equivalent of a sorting program sifts through the day's input, organizing, correlating, storing and rejecting data. Some of it we will need the following day: the name and appearance of the wonderful person we met at a party and desperately want to meet again. Some of it will be less important: how much change we received each time we bought a drink, how many people there were in our railway carriage or bus on the way home, and what colour hair each of them had.

The mind is not normally aware of this data processing; it goes on in the background, and the brain, like the computer, is incredibly fast at sifting information. But every now and then, according to this theory, the sleeper becomes aware of random images flung up from the mass of data. The conscious mind on waking attempts to impose a pattern, to make order out of chaos. And so a story-line is created, for example, out of an anonymous face, and a certain amount of change, the fact that someone asked for three spoonfuls of sugar in a cup of coffee, the irritating neon flicker of an advertising sign.

Another function of dreams is to help the mind to cope with the annoyances and frustrations of our waking life. Let's examine a typical day in one man's life: there was engineering work on the railway lines; one train was cancelled, the next delayed by an hour, and he had rushed to the station an hour early because he had been given the wrong timetable information. For several hours the frustration and anger and cold and hunger build up inside him.

Left: *Many of the predictive systems are connected, principally because they all rely to a greater or lesser extent on the understanding of the inner self and the personal and collective unconscious. These signs, from the Ptolemaic zodiac, are shown in this woodcut in an astrological context, but such images and symbols are also common in dreams.*

Eventually he arrives home, and goes to bed, and to sleep, still fuming. The next morning he remembers the previous evening: yes, it was annoying at the time, but the frustration and rage have gone now; he chalks it up to experience, and gets on with the new day.

During the night something has changed. The man's mind has dealt with whatever had been churning destructively inside him; it has removed some of the stress which might contribute to causing a stomach ulcer or high blood pressure or a heart attack, and has made things right again. Whether he remembers dreaming about the delayed trains or not – or whether his subconscious mind has used different images, different symbols for his anger and worry and disappointment – his sleeping self has dealt with the effects on him, and has repaired the damage.

Dreams save lives.

They can also reveal a great deal about us. Here is a dream recounted in a personal interview:

I'm in a huge hotel; I think it's made up of several large buildings knocked together, because I go through a door in a corridor and there's a short flight of stairs followed by another corridor. A long flight of stairs takes me to another floor, but if I try to get

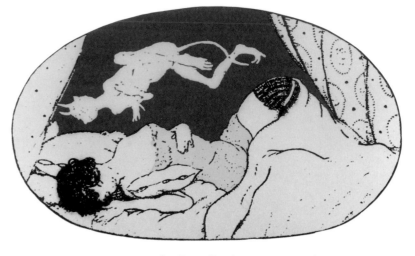

Above left: *In our dreams we are not necessarily limited by the moral strictures of our daily lives, and some of the fantasies we create can consequently be shocking to the conscious mind. In the late nineteenth century Freud began to investigate and codify for the first time the possible meanings of these dreams and to examine why such powerful and erotic images can be conjured up even by the most puritanical of people. In this picture, after the style of Fuseli's* The Nightmare, *a medieval woman imagines that the sensuousness of her vision is caused by an incubus squatting upon her sleeping form. The same image is interpreted in Sosmov's 1906 painting* Summer Dream (top, right).

back I get confused by all the corridors and stairs, and all the different levels.

I'm there for a conference or convention. Nobody else seems to have any difficulty finding their way around. I'm supposed to be going down to dinner, but I can't find my way to the right floor. Sometimes I think I'm on the right floor, but as I try to find the dining room I find I'm changing levels again, and lose my way.

When I eventually find it, everybody else is sitting down having dinner. The room is full; I can't see a space anywhere for me to join them.

I've had this dream, or variations on it, for many years.

This is a fairly standard anxiety dream: the dreamer is putting into it all his fears of rejection and isolation. He cannot cope with the complexities of life. He feels lost and confused. He feels he does not fit in, that he is always on the outside of any group.

Dreams of this sort both embody and act as a safety valve for fears that we may not consciously realize are troubling us; to admit to them would be to admit to failure and inadequacy. The frequent recurrence of the dream shows that these are very deep-seated fears with a long history, but recounting the dream to someone else is the first step towards dealing with them.

This technique, of using dreams as a window into the mind, and as an indicator of a subject's state of mental well-being, was developed by Sigmund Freud during the second half of the nineteenth century. It has been a crucial element of psychoanalysis and psychotherapy ever since.

Freud's protégé, and later, rival, Carl Jung took Freud's interpretive theories further by claiming that dreams also have a healing function. They attempt "to restore our psychological balance by producing dream-material that re-establishes, in a subtle way, the total psychic equilibrium."

Dream symbolism

Dreams are laden with symbolism, and oneiromancy, the interpretation of dreams, has been practised for thousands of years.

Pharaoh dreamed: and behold, he stood by the river. And behold, there came up out of the river seven well favoured kine, and fatfleshed; and they fed in a meadow. And, behold, seven other kine came up after them out of the river, ill favoured and leanfleshed, and stood by the other kine on the brink of the river. And the ill favoured and leanfleshed kine did eat up the seven well favoured and fat kine. So Pharaoh awoke.

And he slept and dreamed the second time: and behold, seven ears of corn came up upon one stalk, rank and good. And, behold, seven thin ears, and blasted with the east wind, sprung up after them. And the seven thin ears devoured the seven rank and full ears. And Pharaoh awoke, and, behold, it was a dream.

And it came to pass in the morning that his spirit was troubled; and he sent and called for all the magicians of Egypt, and all the wise men thereof: and Pharaoh told them his dream; but there was none that could interpret them unto Pharaoh . . .

Then Pharaoh sent and called Joseph . . .

And Pharaoh said unto Joseph, I have

dreamed a dream, and there is none that can interpret it: and I have heard say of thee, that thou canst understand a dream to interpret it . . .

(Genesis 41: 1–15)

It was, of course, Joseph's accurate interpretation of the Pharaoh's dream – that seven years of plenty would be followed by seven years of famine – and his consequent plan to store the bounty of the fruitful years (thus saving the people of Egypt) that endeared him to the Pharaoh, who made him ruler of Egypt.

Sigmund Freud and analytical interpretation

Freud was the father and founder – inventor, if you like – of psychoanalysis, and as such he has probably had a greater impact on our knowledge of the mind than any other human being, for good and for bad. He opened up the subconscious to scrutiny but like all too many scientists, he de-

veloped tunnel vision.

It is impossible to discuss all of Freud's theories adequately in a limited space, but the relevant aspects are these: we all have repressed memories, desires and impulses, most of them going back to our very young childhood. Because the rules of society are burned into us so deeply, we cannot admit these recollections and desires even to ourselves; we would find them too shameful, too disgusting, too disturbing and horrifying.

Freud theorized that a boy is resentful of his father's place in his mother's affections – and in her bed. At the extreme he fantasizes about wanting to kill his father; so that he can usurp his

A b o v e : Sigmund Freud, the father of psychoanalysis, published his book The Interpretation of Dreams *in 1899. It was at first viewed with suspicion – and even derision – but gradually the thesis that the interpretation of dreams, by providing a window into the unconscious, can be of vital benefit in the long-term treatment of mental disorders has come to be commonly accepted around the world.*

L e f t : This fifteenth-century woodcut charmingly illustrates Joseph interpreting Pharaoh's dream. The ancients had just as much faith as Freud in the meanings of dreams, though they sought more direct symbolical interpretations than Freud's more sophisticated analytical approach.

position as his mother's lover. This he termed the Oedipus complex, after the Greek mythological character who – inadvertently – killed his father and married his mother. As an adult, a man cannot possibly cope with the memory of these desires, so he buries them deep below the level of his consciousness.

This insight was not new to Freud; Plato had written of men's incestuous dreams of their mothers over two thousand years earlier. But it was Freud who perceived how violently the repression of these memories and desires could affect the mental health and behaviour of the adult male, resulting in neuroses and depression.

In our dreams, Freud said, these deeply repressed desires are able to surface safely. We can kill our fathers, we can make love to our mothers – or, equally horrifying, our daughters – with no legal or moral consequences. The fact that very few of us actually do dream of doing these things takes us into the heart of Freudian analysis: dream interpretation. Even our subconscious mind cannot visualize these acts directly; instead we allow our shameful, hidden urges to surface symbolically. Freud's breakthrough was in appreciating the value of these symbols: by learning to understand them he could reveal to patients the true, unfiltered, nature of their deeper anxieties – problems, worries or memories that they were either completely unaware of or had been repressing for decades. This "unlocking" formed the first part of the "cure" (a term never actually used in psychoanalytical circles), and clearly set the subject matter for the deep discussion which is at the heart of analysis.

Freud's symbol interpretation has, of course, taken its place as part of the everyday vocabulary of the twentieth century. For example, if a man dreams of sitting at a desk, writing a letter, and he is rolling the pen or pencil in his hands, he is ashamed of his sexuality; the pencil, being long and thin, is sexually symbolic.

Where Freud is attacked by his critics is in his obsession with just this one area of dream interpretation. To oversimplify, everything is seen as sexual, and everything is repressed. It is this narrowness of focus that caused rifts in Freud's school of thinkers even during his lifetime. No one felt Freud's theories were wrong, but many believed that dreams originated from so many

A b o v e : *Carl Jung was a pupil and protégé of Sigmund Freud. The two men parted partly because of personal rivalry and jealousy, but also because Jung disagreed with Freud's purely scientific approach to dreams and the unconscious, feeling instead that there was a mystical dimension to the world of the unconscious that Freud was categorically denying.*

other sources and contained so many more messages, that Freud's views were limiting.

Carl Jung and symbolism
....

Carl Jung contributed far more to the broader understanding of dreams than did Freud. Jung spent much of his life studying mythology and alchemy, and found over and over again similar symbolism in the myths of very different cultures. These mythic archetypes point to a unity in religious and magical beliefs across all ages and times, a universal consensus (though often expressed in different ways) which was overturned by the coming of Judaism, Christianity and Islam (three religions which share the same god but deny each other's truths).

A b o v e , l e f t : *William Blake's images – mainly inspired by religious iconography – stem very much from the preoccupations of his time and his own personal obsessions. Dreams of God or holy figures usually imply a desire on the part of the dreamer for self-improvement – an impulse which drove Blake, an artist who was never satisfied with his work, to struggle with self-doubt throughout his life.*

An archetype, or primordial image, in Jung's terminology, is "an irrepresentable, unconscious, pre-existent form that seems to be part of the inherited structure of the psyche."

Why should two or twenty or two thousand people in different cultures share common imagery and symbolism in their dreams? Jung coined the term "collective unconscious", with the idea that the combined experiences and wisdom of all people throughout history lie like a deep well below each individual's personal unconscious mind. Without conscious effort we draw from this well to populate our dreams.

A similar idea came from novelist and philosopher Arthur Koestler, who wrote in 1964 that dreaming could be seen as a "sliding back towards the pulsating darkness, of which we were part before our separate egos were formed."

External influences

Dreaming of a loud bell ringing, and waking up to hear the alarm clock is a common experience. For example, someone may dream of being a pupil at school, desperately struggling to finish an exam question, and the bell goes when he is only half way through. Or he is in an office or factory or shop, perhaps trying to do something complicated and important, and he has almost succeeded when the fire alarm goes off. Or a man may dream of having a secret liaison with his lover (perhaps

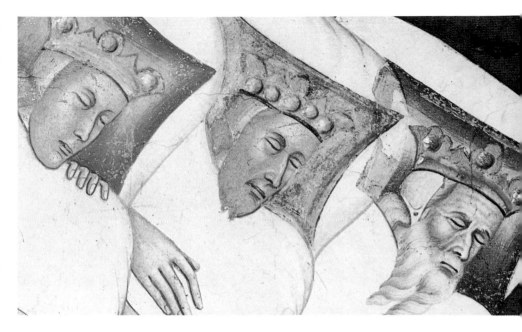

someone in real life with whom he has never actually been romantically involved); he is in a small empty store-room in an otherwise crowded building such as a shopping mall, and the fire bell sounds, meaning that they will be discovered as they rush out together. Or someone may dream of breaking into a building for what seem to be very important reasons, although knowing there will be serious trouble if he is discovered; he has nearly finished what he came to do or to find, when the burglar alarm splits the air.

In each of these there is a sense of worry, of battling against time, of fear of discovery; in each the dreamer very nearly achieves what he so desperately wants; and in each the harsh reality of the real world comes crashing in to spoil it.

Very rarely if ever does the bell announce the end of a victorious prize fight, or the final correct answer that wins the star prize in a television contest, though sometimes the dreamer might be "saved by the bell" from an embarrassing, frightening or life-threatening situation. But usually the bell breaks in to destroy a fantasy, to bring back unceremoniously and brutally the reality of a cold bedroom, a crowded bus ride, and a boring day at work. But no one has yet explained how the dream can have lasted for several minutes before the alarm clock presumably triggered it.

In one classic case, the nineteenth-century Frenchman Alfred Maury dreamed of being in the French Revolution. He saw the many horrors of those times, he spoke with revolutionaries, and eventually he himself was arrested, tried, and found guilty. He was led to the guillotine, made to

Above: A common Jungian archetype is that of the Wise Old Man – which can also appear in the form of a judge, master, or, as seen here, king. In Jungian terms such an image will represent not only a bringer of sense and order, but also an authority figure – very often the father of the dreamer. Jung researched civilizations all around the world and came to realize that such archetypes were common to so many peoples that some form of shared cultural memory – or, as he styled it, "collective unconscious" – must link all of humanity.

Left: A picture by Gustave Doré illustrating a monster seen by Dante during his trip to hell with Virgil, as described in the famous fourteenth-century allegorical poem, The Inferno. In the language of dreams, visits to the nether regions do not necessarily imply base desires or ambitions: such a trip is commonly a sign of a courageous search for the truth (in Jungian terms, for knowledge of the dark side of the self).

kneel down, and felt the blade fall on his exposed neck. He woke to find that the bed rail had fallen onto his neck.

Maury wrote of many tests where a dream was influenced from the outside: by sounds or smells or the dreamer being touched. But how does this account for a long, coherent narrative dream being triggered by something that happens right at the end of it?

One explanation is that the brain, struggling awake, tries to impose order on the confusion of images chasing around inside it: the familiar questions of "Where am I? What's happening?" lead to the creation of a logical story to explain the thoughts and feelings and mind-pictures of the previous few moments.

Another explanation is that time is different in dreams, as it is for Peter Pan, or for Alice down her rabbit hole, or for the children in CS Lewis's *Narnia* books, in the land beyond the wardrobe. Years can pass, and yet we return to the same moment that we left. It is a form of time travel, or at least time distortion. Perhaps it *is* possible to cram a long story into the second or two before the alarm clock is switched off.

JW Dunne proposed in *An Experiment with Time* (1927) that our subconscious mind has a different perception of time. It can look ahead, see that the bed rail is about to fall, or the alarm clock

to ring, and pass this information to our dreaming mind. This, Dunne argued, also explains how precognitive dreams work.

Precognitive dreams

Hundreds of people claim to have had dreams warning that John F Kennedy and, five years later, his brother Robert, would be assassinated. Decades earlier, dozens of people claimed they didn't travel on the *Titanic* because they had dreamed of its sinking.

Dreams, it has been believed for thousands of years, can give warnings of danger in the future. If we include visions as well – they could be called waking dreams – we have the whole lore of prophets and soothsayers to draw on.

"Beware the Ides of March!" did Julius Caesar little good; he died as foretold. So did both Kennedys.

This leads to the whole question of whether the future that is sometimes glimpsed is fixed, or if it is one of many possible futures: if fixed, then all our actions are predetermined, and dream-warnings can merely prepare us for the inevitable worst; but if the vision is of a possibility, even a likelihood, but is of only one of the many paths that time may take, we can perhaps change our actions to avoid the disaster that has been foretold.

Left: *One explanation for precognitive dreams is that, as for Lewis Carroll's Alice, time is fractionally distorted, so that what appears to be the future is either the present, or has actually already taken place. Some scientists now believe that what has been described as precognition – particularly in the form of déjà vu – can be explained by the different speeds of perception of the two sides of the brain.*

Below, left: *After the assassination of the much-loved but ill-fated President John Kennedy in Dallas in November 1963, hundreds of Americans claimed to have foreseen the shooting in their dreams. But whether their foresight was genuine, a retrospective self-delusion, or merely a statistical probability, is open to argument.*

Left: *Rudyard Kipling (1865–1936) once experienced a very strong precognitive dream experience. He was not a particular believer in the psychic world, but during his many years in India and the British imperial colonies he encountered hundreds of extraordinary mystical phenomena.*

Far left: *Jung's theory of the collective unconscious awareness of archetypes is reinforced by the fact that the planets, old gods, stars, mythological images, astrological signs, pagan rituals and similar symbolism appears in the dreams even of those who have no formal or classical education. This old woodcut, in the style of an English Shepherd's Calendar from the fifteenth century, depicts the Sun, ruler of the astrological sign of Leo.*

Multiple time paths branching out from the present moment are a favourite theme in science fiction; Fritz Leiber's *The Big Time* (1958) and Michael G Coney's *The Celestial Steam Locomotive* (1983) are just two of many excellent examples. The potential paradoxes of time travel provide a wonderful adventure playground for authors.

The nature of time is yet another of life's unsolved mysteries. Doctoral theses have been written on it, and a host of books from the scientific to the silly, but we are no nearer to understanding it.

Rudyard Kipling, no believer in psychic phenomena, mentions a precognitive dream in his autobiography. The dream and its fulfilment were hardly spectacular, but they had quite an effect on Kipling. "How, or why," he wrote, "had I been shown an unreleased roll of my life film?"

But what of all those who dreamed of the Kennedy deaths? Unfortunately, as so often happens in this field, well-documented cases are far rarer than the hundreds who claim to have had a precognitive dream. Whether we believe that precognitive dreams actually happen or not, it is as

well to take a look at the arguments levelled against them by sceptics.

First, the overwhelming majority of precognitive claims are revealed *after* the event. "You know," someone says at the end of November 1963, "it's really weird. I dreamt JFK was going to get shot. I saw the car, the motorcade, the lot." It would be far more convincing if they had told the tale at the beginning of the month. The person is not necessarily fabricating (though some undoubtedly do); what is far more likely is that he or she is misremembering the dream. Maybe the dream actually was about smart cars on a long road, or about someone dying; but after the event, vaguely remembering this, the mind adds details which were not in the original dream. Of course it was Kennedy – who else could it have been? Alternatively, the dream could have been dreamt the night after the assassination, when the mind was full of images; that would be entirely natural. But by a few days later, the dream is "remembered" as having occurred before the event.

Even those who genuinely did dream about the President being killed before it happened can

A b o v e: *Few men have been more down-to-earth than Samuel Clemens – "Mark Twain" – the ultimate prophet of straight-talking good sense and folk wisdom. Yet even he admitted to having had a powerful precognitive dream vision accurately predicting his brother's death.*

easily be explained away, if one wishes. The population of the United States at the time was over two hundred million. In just the week before 22 November, 1963, at an average of, say, four dreams per person per night, well over five billion dreams were dreamt in the USA. Considering that from time to time, everyone dreams of someone being violently killed, and everyone dreams of someone famous, and everyone dreams of big expensive cars, some of those dreams will be of someone famous being violently killed, and in some, that person is likely to be in a car; in some, the famous person will be Kennedy.

Out of five billion dreams in that week it would be extremely surprising – in fact, utterly unlikely – if none of them were to do with Kennedy being assassinated. In fact the White House receives letters every day from citizens who have had a precognitive dream of the death of the President, and feel it is their patriotic duty to duly warn him.

Two other famous cases that are often cited are Samuel Clemens (Mark Twain)'s dream of his brother's body laid out in the living room, and Abraham Lincoln's dream, just days before he was killed, of a death at the White House.

Clemens's dream and his brother Henry's death happened in 1858; but Clemens did not write of it until his *Autobiography*, published several decades later. An old man's memories can become confused, embroidered, or even totally invented; we cannot say.

Lincoln apparently told some friends of his dream in April 1865 (he was shot on 14 April):

> " 'Who is dead at the White House?' I deman-
> ded of one of the soldiers. 'The President,' was his
> answer; 'he was killed by an assassin!' "

No one, of course, wrote it down at the time; why should they? In fact the story did not appear in print for thirty years, until Ward Hill Lamon (one of those whom Lincoln had told of the dream) wrote his *Recollections of Lincoln*. Thirty years is a little too long for credibility, but in any case, even if the story is accurate, all political leaders must worry occasionally about being assassinated, and perhaps dream of it.

The only way to test the accuracy of pre-cognitive dreams is for the dreamer to write them

down at the time in as much detail as possible ("I dreamt someone was shot" is too imprecise), seal them in a dated envelope, and deposit them with an official disinterested party. It is essential, of course, that "dud" dreams be counted as well when all the envelopes are opened.

Unfortunately, when experiments of this kind have been carried out, they have not shown any consistent successes, although this does not in itself disprove precognitive dreaming. Most laboratory-type testing of psychic or paranormal abilities is inconclusive, but there is little doubt that such abilities may exist, and that such phenomena do occur. It may simply be that the paranormal does not take well to being graded and tested. (A possibly related phenomenon is the large number of gifted, creative or successful adults who always scored poorly in tests when they were at school; genius – as opposed to skill and hard work – cannot always be measured on a score card.)

Few mediums, prophets, clairvoyants or others who claim paranormal abilities, are prepared to guarantee their results. Those who do should be regarded with some suspicion; they may not be charlatans, but they are not being realistic.

The same applies to precognitive dreams none of which can as yet be utterly proven. Having looked at some of the doubts, now let's examine a couple of well-attested cases.

The British Prime Minister

Great Britain is some way behind the USA in assassinations; Spencer Perceval is the only British Prime Minister to have been assassinated, although murder attempts have been made on many others.

In 1812 a provincial banker called John Williams dreamt several times in one night that "a small man, dressed in a blue coat and white waistcoat" in the lobby of the House of Commons was shot by a man in a "snuff-coloured coat with metal buttons"; in the dream he was told that the victim was Spencer Perceval. Williams told his wife about the dreams that night, and also told several friends over the next few days.

About ten days later Perceval was shot by John Bellingham in the Commons; both were dressed as Williams had seen them. It could be coincidence, but this one has the ring of truth.

Betting on the horses

Everyone who has ever thought about being able to see into the future, whether by dreams, visions, automatic writing or by any other means, must have given some thought to the possibilities for making a bit of money out of it. After all, if you can read the racing results in tomorrow's paper, it seems a waste not to place a bet.

In 1946 and 1947 John Godley, later to become Lord Kilbracken, was able to do exactly that. On several occasions he dreamed of reading the racing results, and told a few friends; they all placed bets, and won, though the details he dreamt were not always entirely accurate. For example, he dreamt that his first two winners, Bindal and Juladin, were at odds of 7–1, though neither of the horses (at two different meetings) was at this price. On other occasions he had to search to find a horse with a similar name to one he had dreamt. Tubermore was actually Tuberose, and Monumentor was Mentores, but with a bit of detective work Godley and his friends were able to make a few profitable bets. In one case he missed the name of the horse, but saw the jockey's colours and face, and was able to track it down successfully from these. On that occasion he wrote down the information, dated and witnessed, and sealed it in an envelope. The horse won.

A b o v e *One of the most exciting elements of prediction is the thought of the fortune that could be made by gambling if it were possible to tell the future reliably. One man, Lord Kilbracken, proved he could make money by betting on horses he had dreamed would win: and he repeated the feat several times in front of witnesses. He even shared his dream tips with his gambling friends.*

L e f t : *The only British Prime Minister ever to have been assassinated was Spencer Perceval, in 1812. His death was accurately foretold by John Williams, with several witnesses to corroborate that Williams had told them about his precognitive dream before the killing took place.*

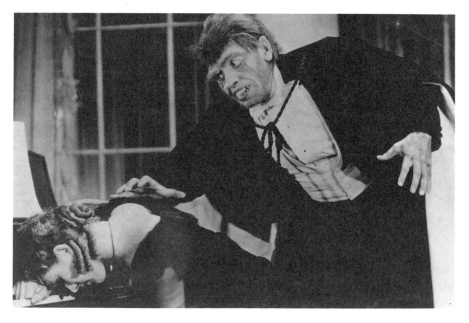

Creative dreams

Writing dreams down is vitally important, and not just for evidence of precognitive dreams.

How often have you woken in the middle of the night from a particularly interesting or weird dream and thought, "I must remember this one, it's wonderful!" – only to wake again in the morning to find it gone? Dreams vanish rapidly: a notepad and pen by the bed can catch many of them before they fade.

Record all of your dreams, not just those which seem to be precognitive. Keeping a dream diary can teach you much about yourself. Dreams can contain the answers to problems that have been besetting you, and can also provide the inspiration for creative work.

One of the best-known stories is of the nineteenth-century German chemist, Friedrich von Kekulé. In 1865, after several years of racking his brains to figure out the molecular structure of benzene, he dreamt one night:

> " . . . *the atoms were juggling before my eyes . . . larger structures of different forms and in long chains, many of them close together; everything was moving in a snake-like and twisting manner. Suddenly, what was this? One of the snakes got hold of its own tail and the whole structure was mockingly twisting in front of my eyes. As if struck by lightning, I awoke . . . "*

Kekulé realized that the carbon and hydrogen atoms in benzene were arranged in a closed ring; the ancient mythological symbol of a snake swallowing its own tail had given him the answer.

Some of our best-known literary works have

sprung from dreams. Mary Shelley's *Frankenstein: or, the Modern Prometheus* was inspired by a dream in which she saw "the hideous phantasm of a man stretched out, and then, on the working of some powerful engine, show signs of life, and stir with an uneasy, half vital motion." So was born not just Frankenstein's monster but, according to Brian W Aldiss, the entire genre of science fiction.

Samuel Taylor Coleridge's experience with the fickle inconstancy of inspiration has bequeathed a bitter phrase to the English language, "The Man from Porlock". His opium dreams gave him a vision of the palace of Kubla Khan; he woke with the poem complete in his head, and began to write.

The poem should have been two or three hundred lines long, a glorious and inspired description of the palace. But Coleridge had scarcely begun to write it down when he was interrupted by "a person on business from Porlock" calling at his cottage. By the time Coleridge was able to get back to his work, the perfect clarity of the dream was gone, leaving him with only "some vague and dim recollection of the general purport of the vision."

Robert Louis Stevenson had better luck with his dreams. He had the rare ability to dream serially, as if, night after night, he were watching episodes of a soap opera. Awake, he would write down the stories told to him by "the Little People", as he called them.

Stevenson's classic *The Strange Case of Dr Jekyll and Mr Hyde* was also inspired by his dreams. "I dreamed the scene at the window, and a scene afterwards split in two, in which Hyde, pursued for some crime, took the powder and underwent the change in the presence of his pursuers." Having been "given" this much, he was able to write the rest of the book.

The Dutch-Canadian writer Charles de Lint has used this idea in his fantasy *Yarrow*. His character Cat Midhir, also a fantasy writer, steps each night into a dream world of gnomes and harpers and standing stones, and wakes each day to write her dreams into her novels.

Dream inspiration is not limited to the written word. The eighteenth-century Italian violinist and composer Giuseppe Tartini lacked an ending to a sonata he was writing. Racking his brains, he went to bed and fell asleep. He dreamt that the

Devil appeared, and offered to finish his sonata in exchange for his soul. Tartini agreed, and the Devil picked up a violin and began to play. When he had finished, Tartini woke up and wrote down what he had heard. The trill at the heart of *The Devil's Sonata* is unusual and otherworldly; one only hopes for Tartini's sake that he managed to avoid the rest of the agreement.

Coleridge took opium, as did his contemporary Thomas de Quincey and many others in the eighteenth and nineteenth centuries, to open the doors of perception, a phrase later made famous as the title of Aldous Huxley's classic work on the effects of the Mexican Indian drug, mescalin. Huxley took the quotation from William Blake:

"If the doors of perception were cleansed, everything will appear to man as it is, infinite."

Since the 1960s countless thousands have taken LSD for the same purpose. So-called "trips" and visions come from the same place as dreams: our unconscious mind.

The creative aspect of dreams is at its most powerful when we are not quite asleep, in that strange hinterland before we drop off, or as we slowly surface. Some people see hypnagogic images, very sharp, clear pictures flashing through their mind, just before they fall asleep; or hypnopompic images, much the same, as they are awakening. These are perhaps nearer to visions than to dreams, and can occur when you are wide awake but relaxed, or alternatively when you are under great stress.

Sometimes, quite without warning, a particular smell, an exact tone of light, or a combination of sounds can trigger a flash of pictorial memory so vivid that you can actually feel yourself there for a moment, and experience the other senses, and even feel the emotions of happiness, expectation, worry or boredom, and think the thoughts you had at that original time. This is a far more common experience for some people than for others; it also tends to come in waves, perhaps one flash a day for a week or so, then perhaps none for several months.

Seers and prophets throughout history often fasted or "mortified the body", sometimes putting themselves through great physical discomfort to encourage their visions. Without going this far, it is sometimes possible, when falling asleep, to deliberately direct your hypnagogic images, and even to choose your dreams.

Lucid dreaming and shared dreams

As mentioned, Robert Louis Stevenson was able not only to recall his dreams well enough to write them into stories, but to dream serially, which means (unless you believe his dreams were given to him by "Little People") having some control over what he dreamt. Controlled dreams have two elements: dreaming what you want to dream, and being able to control the progress of the dream as it happens: lucid dreaming.

The term was coined by psychologist Celia Green (*Lucid Dreams*, 1968), but the phenomenon has been studied for much longer. In lucid dreams, dreamers are aware that they are asleep and dreaming, but this knowledge does not wake them up. Instead, they are able to decide (not always with complete success) the direction of their dream.

"Direction" may well be the case. Many people who practise lucid dreaming find that in part of the dream they are flying; they are able to take control of their flight, soaring, diving, wheeling around the sky, and may be able to influence where they fly, for example to a mountain, or a meadow, or to a meeting with a specific person.

What happens when two lucid dreamers each decide to dream of meeting the other? There is plenty of anecdotal evidence that this can happen: that the dreamers can meet, and talk together. On waking, and writing down their individual dream

Left: *Aldous Huxley came from a very conventional background, but he became fascinated by the mind, and the possibilities of expanding the boundaries of thought and imagination. He was particularly interested in the effects of drugs, especially hallucinogens, on the mental processes, and wrote several books on the subject. Manipulation of the mind by drugs also provided the central theme for his most popular book,* Brave New World.

experiences and conversations, they find that they have similar accounts.

Is this a true meeting of souls on another plane? Is it a semi-conscious form of telepathy? Perhaps, though a more mundane explanation could be that the two people, awake, have agreed to try to meet in their dreams in a certain place at a certain time; the setting, and the fact that they have succeeded in meeting, are likely to form the basis of part of their conversation, and, if the two people know each other well, they are likely to talk about something they are both interested in: hence the similarity of accounts.

In one experiment three people agreed to meet in their dreams. Two of them actually dreamt of meeting each other; the third, who failed to dream the meeting, was not present in the dreams of the other two. Coincidence? Telepathy? Or something else? Much more research needs to be done in this fascinating area.

It is a fairly common experience to dream of someone you have not seen or spoken to for months or years, and the following day (or week) they phone you out of the blue, or you bump into each other in the street. Could the dream have caused the phone call, in that you telepathically contacted the person you dreamt of? Or was it precognitive, the unconscious mind seeing ahead to the consciously unforeseen meeting?

It can also happen that natural empathists pick up someone else's distress in their dreams. Usually, though not always, they are emotionally close to the other person who may be a lover, a parent or child, or a twin. There are many well-documented cases of people waking in the middle

Above: Waking visions have been witnessed by a number of people; the division between a day dream and a scene seen in sleep is often hard to distinguish. Some events which remain otherwise inexplicable have been termed psychic, religious or spiritual visions.

of the night with the strong conviction that someone close to them has died, or is dangerously ill, or has had a serious accident, and in the morning finding their dream-knowledge confirmed.

Sometimes the link is so strong that you actually dream someone else's dream, without intending to.

"I dreamed that I was present when a coffin was being opened. It was a very small coffin, for a child. It was very disturbing. In my dream I was very worried about what I would see when the coffin was opened: the decomposing body of a small child. But when it was opened, there was a lot of cloth, and clothing, and when we lifted out the bundle it was a doll, very much dressed up, not a child at all.

Both the story, and the whole feel of the dream, were totally unfamiliar to me. It didn't feel like one of my own dreams.

The following evening I phoned my girlfriend, who was suffering from depression. As always, I asked how she had slept the night before. She had had a very disturbed night, with little sleep. 'I had a strange night,' I said, and told her about my dream. At the end she gasped, then went silent. 'What's wrong?' I asked. 'That's my dream,' she said, and burst into tears because of what she'd put me through without meaning to."

(personal interview)

The dreamer, trying to find out the roots of his girlfriend's depression, later discovered that she longed to have his child, but could not, because she had been sterilized. The pain of this had poured into her dream and he, a powerful receiving empathist, had picked it up a hundred miles away.

Although it is sometimes possible to track down the triggers for nightmares in our own lives – worries, problems, fears – it might be that the strangest, most unfamiliar nightmares are other people's dreams to which we have somehow become receptive.

Reincarnation

Many people find in their dreams evidence of past lives. In their dreams they are in another body, not always of their own sex, in a foreign land, and clearly in another time. Often they are speaking fluently a language that their conscious mind, on waking, does not know; but in the dream it makes perfect sense. There are many accounts of people working out roughly where and when their dream was set, researching the place and the period, and finding that all sorts of details in their dreams are accurate.

The usual criticism of past-life dreamers is that they are remembering in their dreams information that their conscious mind had forgotten: a period film they had once seen, a book they had read years ago, a conversation overheard in another country. But in recent years there has

Below: A seventeenth-century scene showing the great god of alchemy Hermes supervizing the union of Sun and Moon. This Solar-Lunar conjunction presents a dream image which returns us in fantasy to the origins of time itself. Hermes Trismegistus was a mystery figure who was heralded as the inspiration of the Hermetic philosophers. They strove for universal oneness, here symbolized by the fusion of the Sun and the Moon.

been supporting evidence, often supplied by non-sceptical doctors and psychiatrists.

Hypnosis, which is simply a controlled form of deep relaxation, has been used to take thousands of people back into memories of past lives. Some of the accounts are amazingly convincing.

Are these just dreams that are related out loud to the hypnotherapist? Or are they really evidence

that we have lived before? Or, another possibility, if time is a tangled skein rather than one long thread, could dreamers and regressed hypnotic subjects be tuning in on the lives or picking up the memories of people who we think of as historical, but who might be living close by in some form of time-warp?

Primitive beliefs

Certainly primitive religions have a more flexible attitude to time than we have in our "civilized" modern Western world. The word "primitive" usually carries the value-judgement of "not-very-clever, not-very-sophisticated". When talking about primitive religious beliefs, though, the word has its true meaning of prime, or first, early, or even pure. Most religions today have developed over the centuries and millennia, absorbing beliefs and practices from many earlier faiths.

Primitive religions are the nearest we can get to those early, uncluttered, unvarnished belief-systems and what we find, very basically, is that men and women were in far closer touch with gods and the spiritual realm, with nature and their local environment, and with themselves, than we are today. Many of their myths are close to early versions of our own religious and folk stories; symbolism was a vital part of their everyday life, and so were dreams. In some tribal societies

Left: *Australian Aboriginal paintings onto bark and rock or cave walls have remained unchanged in style through the centuries, forming a continuous link between the present generation and their ancestors as strong as their Dreamtime beliefs.*

Right: *These North American Indians dance under the leadership of their medicine-man. In early cultures, dancing is used as a form of sympathetic magic, and to induce a trance-like frenzy – bringing the dancer closer to his or her unconscious "dream" state.*

people believed in the absolute reality of their dreams. If in a dream they committed some crime against their tribe, when awake they would confess this and make full repayment for the wrongdoing. If in a dream they were injured, or bitten by a snake, they would then seek healing in the waking world.

In many societies, the adults would interpret their children's dreams for them, and would tell the stories of their own dreams and discuss them. Much guidance was to be found in dreams, both individually and for the tribe as a whole.

Dreamtime is central to the beliefs of Australian aboriginals: the Dreamtime, or Alchera, is the remote past time when their ancestors created and walked on the Earth. Man was made out of clay, and the creator spirits are still there beneath the soil, which is why the aboriginals see white settlers as the despoilers of their sacred places.

All over the world, for the indigenous peoples

of North and South America, of Australia and of Asia, the shaman was the central figure for religion, teaching, healing and magic (which were all seen as aspects of the same thing). The shaman was usually, but not always, a man; the *aniteras* in the mountains of the Philippines, for example, are always women.

It was, and in some places in the world still is, the shaman's role to mediate between the different levels of reality, between the people and their gods. Using drugs, dancing, chanting and fasting they would go into a trance state in which they could talk to the spirits of animals or ancestors, bringing back messages and teachings for the tribe. The interpretation of their visions and dreams was essential to the well-being of the whole tribe, and the shaman – who in our sophisticated world we would probably lock up as a disturbed schizophrenic – was an honoured and powerful person.

Prophets and visionaries

It seems that the more "advanced" a civilization, the less credit it gives to its prophets and seers. Certainly today it is fashionable to scoff at them; believers, unless they are fired with evangelical enthusiasm, tend to keep quiet. Nor have they always been well received through history.

The Bible is full of dreams and visions, from Jacob's ladder to the revelation given to John on the island of Patmos. But the Old Testament prophets of doom had a fairly rough ride, and whatever kudos a prophet might have, there was a strong feeling of "not in my back yard": "A prophet is not without honour," said Jesus, "save in his own country, and in his own house." (Matthew 13:57)

Belief in Jeanne d'Arc's prophecies put Charles VII on the throne of France in 1429, but did Jeanne herself little good; the Burgundians sold her to the English, who burnt her as a heretic and sorceress in 1431.

Michel de Notredame, known to us as Nostradamus, lived in the first half of the sixteenth century. He published his first prophetic quatrains in 1555, and people have been trying to apply them to actual events ever since. This style is imprecise, and even those which seem a close fit are often slightly wrong (Hister for Hitler, for example). It is possible that he was being purposefully vague, to give himself more chance of getting them right.

The last few hundred years are littered with dates of the end of the world. Many prophets now seem to have learnt the lesson that generalities are a safer bet; of all those who allowed themselves to be pinned down to a specific date, none has so far got it right.

Dream travel

Where do prophets get their information from? Where does the shaman go while in his trance? And when you dream you are flying, where can you fly to? Dreaming, an everyday though mysterious phenomenon, here becomes caught up with the supernatural.

Distinctions should be drawn between astral projection, etheric projection and travel, and out of the body experiences (OOBEs).

OOBEs are usually involuntary; the classic case is floating above your own body in a hospital operating theatre, watching and hearing what is going on during the operation, while your body lies anaesthetized below you.

Left: *The sixteenth-century French seer Michel de Notredame, commonly known now as Nostradamus, published thousands of prophesies, many referring to events in the current century. Depending on the sympathies of the interpreter (the predictions are sometimes quite vaguely expressed) many of his prophesies are quite astonishingly accurate.*

There are too many accounts of this to dismiss the experience as imaginary, and the physiological/psychological explanation does not cover everything. True, we all know what an operating theatre looks like from films, and our ears are still capable of working even if our eyes are closed, so our unconscious brain can listen in and interpret what it hears. On the other hand, patients have described in clear detail nurses and doctors who have only been present during the operation itself, or equipment which is not usually in an operating theatre.

Similarly, OOBEs which (more rarely) happen whilst walking down the street or along a forest path can give the person information he or she would not otherwise have had: a red car about to shoot out of a concealed side street, or somebody walking on another path.

But OOBEs are usually brought on by some sort of crisis, and are involuntary. Etheric projection, which is often confusingly called astral travel, is quite a different matter. In etheric projection, whether in dreams, visions or a trance state, consciousness (the self) can be deliberately separated from the body: it can either be allowed to

Left: *Travel, journeys, and quests are common dream fantasies. One school of thought is that these are not just travels in the mind, but that part of the soul or psyche actually leaves the sleeping body to visit the exotic locations envisioned.*

wander at will, or be directed to a particular place. Sometimes on waking the "travellers" can re-member clearly where they have been; at other times they are left with a vague and misty im-pression, as in a fading dream.

Sometimes, etheric travellers can observe what is happening in another room or another town, while remaining unseen themselves: the "fly on the wall" or invisible observer. At other times – and again, there are many accounts of this happening – they themselves are actually seen by the people they are "visiting", and sometimes even hold conversations with them. This has occurred often enough for there to be a word for it in Scotland: a psychic projection of someone who will later be arriving physically is known quite matter-of-factly as a "forerunner".

As distinct from this, astral projection and travel is where the spirit or soul or consciousness visits another plane or dimension, in meditation or vision or dreams. This could be the land of the spirits or ancestors for the shaman or the Austra-lian aboriginal; for the Irish it is the land of faery; for the eighteenth- and nineteenth-century poet William Blake it was heavenly spheres.

Whether these places actually exist outside the imagination of the traveller, visionary or dreamer, cannot be proven. But even if they have no

objective reality, the world of the imagination should not be dismissed: creative use of the powers of the imagination is the basis of magic.

What is reality?

Some mystics and philosophers have held that the dream world is the *real* reality, and our everyday world a mere shadow:

"Apart from faith, no one has any assurance whether he is awake or asleep",

said the seventeenth-century philosopher Blaise Pascal, "Who knows that when we think we are awake, we may not be in slumber, from which slumber we awaken when we sleep?".

Three centuries before Christ the Chinese philosopher Chuang Tzu put it even more clearly: "Am I Chuang Tzu who dreamed that he was a butterfly, or a butterfly now dreaming that I am Chuang Tzu?"

Above: *The concept of astral travel is seductive. Some believe that we can choose where we go, and whom we meet. There are even documented cases of two people agreeing to meet in their dreams and doing so — even describing the exact location of the meeting. The thought of being able to nominate a destination — say a beautiful garden, as in this illustration — and determining the person you will visit — perhaps an old friend or lover — is so attractive that it is not surprising that people like to believe in the reality of such astral projections.*

Right: *A scene of divination from the Oracle at Delphi depicted in a nineteenth-century edition of Christian's* History of Magic. *The oracular pythoness, in order to answer questions about the future, has to throw herself into a dream-like trance.*

Dream Interpretation

There is no single, simple set of symbols. It is not possible to say that dreaming of a horse or a key or a tunnel always means the same thing; as with, say, Tarot readings, a single image cannot be taken in isolation; it must be taken in balance with everything else in the dream.

Also, the many books on interpreting dreams often give wildly different meanings. This often depends on the writer's background and influences: a scholar of Celtic mythology will probably ascribe different primary meanings to dream symbols than will an astrologer, or a Tarot expert, or a Freudian. At one time, it was believed that everything in dreams mirrored (in the sense of turning around) real life, so that dream events represented their opposites: death in a dream meant great joy and happiness, poverty meant richness to come, richness meant poverty, and so on.

Different interpretations

To take just one example: dreaming of a key can mean, according to different books:

★ failure in an important interview
★ love and marriage if a single key appears
★ prosperity but little affection if many keys are seen
★ finding a key: success in emotional life
★ losing a key: ill luck in emotional life
★ the key, or solution, to a problem
★ the key to happiness
★ the keys to the kingdom of heaven
★ being ready for the next step
★ finding the right partner

Many of these interpretations can be linked to each other, but all the same this demonstrates the difficulty and danger of depending on just one list of dream meanings.

Personal interpretation

Your dreams are *your* dreams, not anyone else's (with very rare exceptions), and must be interpreted for you personally. Although, as Jung showed, there will be a lot of overlap with others, your own dream symbolism is uniquely yours. For example, if you are a devoted cat lover, the common interpretation of treachery or deceit is less likely to be true for you; instead, dreaming of a cat might mean warmth, companionship, with a streak of wild independence.

Symbolism is not a dead thing; it develops and changes with society. But many lists or dictionaries of dream symbolism still depend wholly on the traditional meanings, which may have been codified hundreds, if not thousands of years ago. Symbols in your dreams, today, may mean something quite different.

Trust your instincts: if you feel strongly that a meaning in a dream list – even the one in this book – is wrong for you, then examine just what that dream object means for your life. Write it down, then write down everything else that comes to mind, and look for a meaningful association of ideas that has resonance for you. By doing this over a period of time you will build up a personal dictionary of dream symbols more relevant than any 'ready-made' version.

The vocabulary of the language of dreams consists of signs and symbols: some, like the images decorating these pages, are shared – drawn from what Jung described as the collective unconscious: visions like astrological and alchemical symbols, and mutually understood images such as the devil. Other images may be more personal: the figure of a friend; a recollection of a house once lived in, or an object once owned, which has a particular association. To understand the meaning of our dreams we need to learn to decipher this complex language. This is no easy matter, as can be seen from the example of the various meanings given for just one simple object, the key.

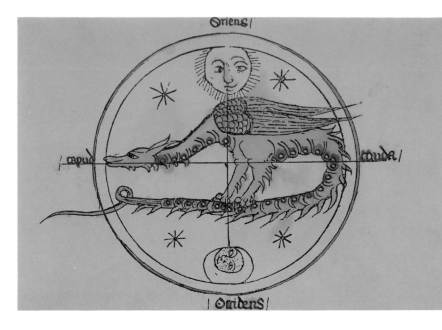

Should all dreams be interpreted?

As Macrobius said, some dreams are, well, just dreams; they might be replaying something you did or saw that day, they might be a scene from a film you have seen or a book you have read, they might be an obvious anticipation of something you will be doing the next day. A straightforward dream of a long car journey the night before you go on a touring holiday is unlikely to hold hidden messages.

Look for recurrent images and ideas, for differences from normality, for strangenesses. If you simply dream you are walking your dog in the country, that is a dream about contentment, companionship, loyalty. If your dog speaks to you, or if it is bright blue, or if the country lane develops briars and thistles, or if there are three trees, three bushes, three telegraph poles, and three paths leading off from a three-barred gate, you need to look more deeply.

Learn to listen to the moods in your dreams: joy, contentment, safety, worry, foreboding, terror. Just as with, for example, Tarot cards, if the main listed meaning of one of the symbols contradicts the prevailing mood, see what else it might signify. Or see whether it might be an exception to the rest of the dream: a glimpse of sunlight in a stormy sky, or a possible hidden danger in something that is otherwise running smoothly and successfully.

Most significant dreams will tell you something about yourself, your hopes, fears, ambitions and anxieties, rather than predicting what will happen next week. If you have predictive dreams, they are less likely to tell you what will happen to you in the future, than to indicate what is likely to happen, considering the person you are and the path that you are treading. Your subconscious knows you a lot better than your conscious mind does – it is more brutally realistic – and its analysis of your behaviour patterns will be more accurate.

Things to look out for

As well as individual symbols, look for the ways in which things fit together, and how they relate to each other. Having considered the emotional content – the mood of the dream – take careful note also of the following general aspects:

Colours – often highly symbolic
Numbers – esoterically symbolic
Names – might contain meanings in themselves
Puns – dreams delight in word play
People – who you know, or not; are they aspects of yourself?
Places – familiar or strange; especially the house, and landscape
Animals – are they friendly or threatening?
Movement – up or down, forwards or backwards, fullness or emptiness, open or closed

Opposites and alternatives

These last are important. If something can be in two opposite states, it can have two opposite meanings. Climbing a ladder implies success; going down a ladder failure. In sexual terms for a male dreamer, ascending a ladder can symbolize sexual confidence; descending may imply fear of sexual failure or impotence. Similarly, a full wine cup symbolizes fulfilment, richness of emotions; an empty wine cup symbolizes the opposite: emotional loss, emptiness. An open door can mean opportunity, reaching out to new career fields or social circles; a closed door that (as in everyday speech) the door has been slammed in your face, cutting off the opportunity. But in a different dream a closed door or window could mean safety, security, with any dangers locked outside. An open door could mean an open heart, a welcome; an open window could signify allowing a fresh breeze to blow through your life; but they could also symbolize carelessness, laying yourself open to dangers creeping in.

Just like Tarot cards, for example, dream images can contain their own opposites or negatives; some of these are given here. A dog's loyalty, faithfulness, friendship and devotion can become a cloying burden, unwanted responsibility, the mindless following of a cause. In interpretation, context is all.

The construction of the A-Z

The A-Z in this book is drawn from a number of very different sources from various periods of history, as well as being based on the author's own experience and understanding of religious and cultural symbols and mythic archetypes. It is by

no means exhaustive, but for the purposes of comprehensiveness it takes in an exceptionally wide variety of references – even those with which everyone may not personally agree. In using it to help interpret their dreams, readers should always take great note of context, and take into account in their analysis what special meanings and significance different symbols and images might have for them. Symbols may mean different things to different people.

The longer definitions reflect the more sensitive interpretations now prevalent, using a great deal of twentieth-century psychoanalytical material, with more emphasis on motivation, feelings, and the deeper areas of the human mind. The shorter definitions, primarily from earlier sources – traditional interpretations, Victorian references, and folklore – come from eras when analysts perceived dreams to be more definitively predictive of specific events. These are included for their interest and charm, and because for hundreds of years they were accepted as fact. Readers must judge for themselves how much credence to give these pieces.

An A-Z of Dream Symbols

ABYSS Traditionally, to fall into one means that there is immediate danger. To see one close by is a timely warning which should be gratefully heeded.

ACCIDENT A dream of ill omen: it denotes danger – particularly concerning transportation and travel.

ACTOR/ACTRESS Someone you know is behaving falsely. Also a general warning of deceit.

ADULTERY Dreaming of committing adultery almost certainly indicates that there is a problem in your relationship – whether consciously acknowledged or not. If, on the other hand, you resist temptation in your dream, this is an enormously satisfying and positive sign, showing that you are content, strong-willed, and that your real relationship is secure. Fidelity dreams do not always simply apply to a relationship with another: they can symbolize that your own strength of purpose and self-honesty is being tested. Resisting temptation will indicate that you have the resolve to abide by your principles: giving way may be a warning that you lack moral strength.

ALLIGATOR/CROCODILE The appearance of one of these animals in a dream is ominous. It means that you are unconsciously aware that someone is secretly conspiring against you. That person, or group of people, have it in their power to act suddenly and do

you harm. Be cautious, keep your own confidence, and be very careful whom you trust.

AMPUTATION There is a risk of loss – possibly a demotion at work or a change for the worse in a relationship.

ANCHOR The interpretation depends on context. For seafarers, the anchor symbolizes safety and a trouble-free homecoming. Consequently it can also indicate that hard work, or a difficult time, will be favourably rewarded and comfortably resolved. It can also, however, indicate forthcoming separation and distance from a loved one.

ANGELS Angels are messengers, and the interpretation should be based on their attitude and demeanour. Traditional Christian angels are a propitious sign, indicating that you have good self-esteem which is reflected in the feelings of others towards you. Such a dream should bring a change of confidence and an acknowledgement of a higher status. Angels of

this type also imply spiritual well-being. Angels from other sources (remembering that Lucifer himself is a fallen angel) must be treated at face value, and their actions and warnings heeded.

ANTS Scurrying about as ants do, they denote industry, hard work and, consequently, success.

BABIES Dreaming of babies usually means acknowledging new responsibilities in your life; it can also mean a rebirth, a fresh start.

BEES Bees show richness and prosperity; they are renowned in mythology for their knowledge, and in a dream might denote

wisdom. Stings by bees can indicate a quarrel, the break-up of a friendship, or a new rival or enemy. The Victorians believed that to dream of a bee foretold a speedy marriage.

BELLS Generally these mean joy and good tidings: however, if they are tolling, it could be bad news.

BIRDS Generally birds show the freedom to fly, especially in one's imagination; they can also be messengers.
see also Eagle, Owl, Swan, Dove, Raven, Peacock

BLACK Indifference; gloom; death; darkness; obscurity; secrecy.

BLUE Heavenly; spiritual energy; purity; sincerity; truth; peace.

BOOKS (especially notebooks) These dreams concern memories, and consequently knowledge, and records of the past.

BREAD Bread is seen as the 'staff of life', and is a metaphor for 'goodness' in many cultures around the world, reflecting its place as the primary source of nourishment for most races.

This symbolic meaning is exactly the same in dreams – an image of fresh, wholesome bread is extremely positive, and indicates good fortune and prosperity. A dream of making bread implies industry, and hard work that will be properly rewarded. If others are involved in making the bread, it is a powerful representation of collective harmony towards a worthy goal – good things are in store for the family or people with whom you are interacting.

Stale bread is an equally strong indicator of hard times ahead – struggle, fatigue, and wasted effort.

BROWN Introverted; concealing (identity); sensation; material things.

BUILDINGS/SHAFTS/STAIRWELLS etc. Given Freud's pre-eminence amongst twentieth-century dream interpreters, and the special nature of his theories on phallic imagery, the definition of the meaning of buildings in dreams is given over to one of his case studies, as both an explanation, and an example of his methodology:

THE DREAM OF A YOUNG MAN INHIBITED BY HIS FATHER-COMPLEX (1911):
"He was walking with his father in a place which must have been the Prater, since he saw

Angels are regarded as magical as well as religious figures; in dreams, as in early literary references, they bring messages which should be heeded. (opposite)

Buildings and stairs imply a strong compulsion towards investigation and exploration, as shown in some of Freud's dream interpretation. (left)

Books in dreams denote knowledge, an association that has continued from early times when only the learned were literate and gained scholarly status. (below)

the Rotunda, with a small annexe in front of it to which a captive balloon was attached, though it looked rather limp. His father asked him what all this was for; he was surprised at being asked, but explained it to him. Then they came into a courtyard which had a large sheet of tin lying in it. His father wanted to pull off a large piece of it, but first looked about him to see if anyone was observing them. He said that as long as they told the foreman they would get permission. A staircase went down from the courtyard into a shaft, the walls of which were covered in some sort of soft material, like the leather covering an armchair. At the end of the shaft was a lengthy platform, after which yet another shaft commenced . . .

THE ANALYSIS:

This dreamer was of a type whose therapeutic prospects are not favourable: up to a certain point they offer no resistance at all to analysis, but from then onwards prove to be almost inaccessible. He interpreted this dream virtually unaided. 'The Rotunda', he said, 'was my genitals, and the captive balloon in front was my penis, whose limpness I have reason to complain of'. Going into more detail, then, the Rotunda may be translated as the bottom (habitually regarded by children as part of the genitals) and the small annexe in front of it as the scrotum. His father asked him in the dream what all this was: that is, what was the purpose and function of the genitals. It seemed legitimate to reverse the situation and turn the dreamer into the questioner . . .

He promptly interpreted the shaft as a vagina, bearing in mind the soft covering of its walls. I added, from my own experience, that climbing down, like climbing up in other instances, described sexual intercourse in the vagina.

The dreamer personally gave a biographical explanation of the fact that the first shaft was followed by a lengthy platform, and then a second shaft. He had practised intercourse for a time but had then stopped because of his inhibition, and he now hoped to start again by the help of therapy."

BURIAL ALIVE Such an image usually implies memories of birth, or perhaps a feeling of being trapped. On a superficial, but nevertheless important level, it can also indicate real difficulty with breathing.

BUTTERFLY Because they come from extraordinary caterpillar origins, butterflies symbolize transformation and rebirth; they also mean beauty, and their fragility implies the ethereal. If the context is negative, look out for inconstancy and fickleness.

CAKE A sweet dream! Generally this indicates good fortune – especially in affairs of the heart. It can also be the "icing on the cake" of success: effort is being rewarded. Overly sweet or cloying cake can push this interpretation into more dubious areas – lust, promiscuity, and decadence.

CANDLE If alight, these indicate inner spiritual light, or in some contexts a birth amongst one's close associates or family: if extinguished, they mean frustrated ambitions or the death of someone dear. In Freud's dream vocabulary they are a phallic symbol.

CAT Cats symbolize elegant femininity, but they can also mean deception; the soft, warm, purring creatures can quickly change to aggressive, attacking hunters.

CAVE The deep inner self; the security of the womb, and/or hiding from reality.

Fears of entrapment are re-enacted in dreams concerned with being buried alive. An accompanying sense of claustrophobia may make the dream seem more vivid. (left)

To dream of a cat can denote a changeable companion. You should be wary of your friends after a cat dream. (below)

To see a crown in a dream is a sign of success; to see someone else wearing the crown shows that you will eventually achieve your goal. (left)

An iced cake in a dream indicates that effort is being rewarded; if the cake is too sweet the interpretation is less clear, perhaps like the motives for your actions. A chocolate cake, however, is particularly welcome in a dream as chocolate in any form is a sign of contentment. (below)

COW Cows give milk, so imply warmth and nourishment; the number of cows a farmer owned used to be a measure of his prosperity, and this is still symbolized by the cow. They also indicate domesticity and a warm mother figure.

CROSSROADS This symbol indicates that a major decision has to be made, and that it is time to confront the issue.

CROWN Wearing a crown, or even seeing a crown in your dreams is a sign of success and achievement.

CUPS AND CONTAINERS (bowls, glasses, bags, barrels)
If full, these indicate emotional fulfilment and contentment, but if empty, they represent emotional loss. An overflowing vessel of any type is a warning that you are being swept away by your feelings: this is not necessarily dangerous, but is a sign that you should proceed cautiously and obtain objective advice if possible.

To dream of an elephant will bring fortitude and power. To ride an elephant indicates wealth. (above)

Fish have numerous symbolic interpretations in dream, myth and astrology. They have occurred in literary and artistic references since Biblical times. (above right)

An eagle in a dream can be a contradictory symbol; it is associated with violence yet also with power. In a favourable context, it can be seen as protective. (right)

DEATH This is not necessarily a negative symbol; it implies change and transformation.

DOG Traditionally dogs symbolize loyalty and devotion, but perhaps indicate that there is an excess of these emotions. The meaning of a dog in a dream depends greatly on the type of dog, its behaviour, and the dreamer's own preferences.

DOVE The dove symbolizes love, the Holy Spirit, the Anima, and the idealized feminine principle. Dreaming of a dove can indicate that people are to be united in some form of partnership, perhaps during a wedding ceremony.

DROWNING Dreaming of drowning means that there is some aspect of your life that you want to hide away and bury deeply. To dream of rescuing another is very positive, indicating that you will prosper through your generosity. To see a loved one drowning without being able to save them is perhaps one of the most upsetting dreams of all: it is a very dangerous dream – though ironically the danger is not to the person drowned in the dream, but to the dreamer.

EAGLE Eagles feature much in dream-lore, and consequently have many interpretations (often, depending on the sources used, contradictory). Take your lead from the context of the dream: if the eagle is soaring and powerful, it should certainly indicate prosperity and achievement. If the eagle is dead, this means an end to prosperity – possibly ruin or bankruptcy. If the eagle is falling or wounded, it will

indicate a monetary loss or the failure of something for which you have worked hard.

EGGS These represent potential – new opportunities and a new life. However, just as eggs need to be fertilized in order to come to life, in dreams they indicate that the chances offered must be worked for, a contribution must be made, and effort invested, before the opportunity will bear fruit. But rotten eggs show wasted options and failure.

ELEPHANT This signifies strength and power – and possible associations with a person of status. There is a general feeling of radiance and good health.

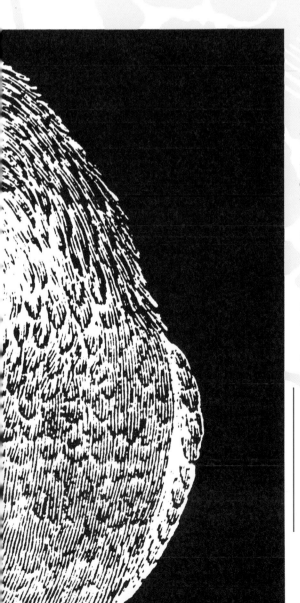

FALLING This generally indicates confusion or humility in waking life, or an accumulation of major doubts and failure. If you dream that you are falling, look to see where you are when you land: this can be very significant.

FISH Because of the depths in which they swim, fish symbolize the deep layer of the unconscious, and so also spiritual truth; but they can also show coldness and impotence. If the fish is lively this can indicate success, especially in business ventures. Other traditional interpretations are as follows:

To dream that you see a fish in clear-water streams denotes that you will be favoured by the rich and powerful.

Dead fish signify loss of power and wealth through some dire calamity.

For a young woman to dream of seeing fish portends that she will have a handsome and talented lover.

To dream of catching catfish denotes that you will be embarrassed by evil designs of enemies, but your luck and presence of mind will tide you safely over the trouble.

To wade in water, catching fish, denotes that you will possess wealth acquired by your own ability and enterprise.

To dream of fishing denotes energy and economy; but if you do not succeed in catching anything, your efforts to obtain honours and wealth will be futile.

Eating fish denotes warm and lasting attachments.

FLOWERS Generally flowers indicate vitality and freshness, and, in romantic terms, a new relationship. Receiving a bouquet from a member of the opposite sex is an exciting (or possibly disturbing) dream, as it implies that somebody is in love with you without your knowledge. At the same time, other analysts feel that giving flowers to someone you know in a dream is a sign that you wish to do them

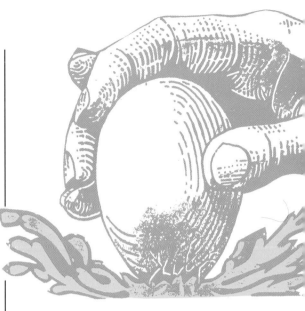

Dreams in which you see or eat an egg represent a new opportunity, brought to fruition by hard work. (above)

Flowers are often linked with romance and vitality. Their dream connotations encompass excitement as well as secret love and admiration. (below)

harm, or even harbour a death wish towards them: this is particularly so if the flowers are dead or dying. *see also* Roses

FLYING In a positive dream this can denote spiritual advancement, but in a negative dream it is more likely to show that you are feeling responsibilities. It could be the start of astral or etheric travel.

FOOD One interpretation of food in dreams implies sensuality and desire; the dreamer wants to absorb, consume and merge with their lover. Particular foodstuffs have specific meanings – *see* Bread, Cake, Meat, and so on.

FOUNTAIN A fountain symbolizes new life, rebirth and spiritual refreshment; it can also stand for womanhood, the Eternal Feminine. A broken or dry fountain is a negative symbol, indicating frustration and the loss of pleasure, and, at worst, an ending or death.

GARDEN If it is well-tended and has abundant growth, dreaming of a garden is good; it shows natural fertility. But an unkempt and overgrown garden shows disorder and disappointment in the dreamer's life.

GLOVES If you are wearing gloves in a dream, it signifies caution and care in your dealings with those around you. You may be encountering problems, but have made provision which will enable you to deal with them satisfactorily. Threadbare or badly made gloves indicate that you are vulnerable – you may be betrayed or suffer an unexpected loss.

GOD On a simple level, seeing God signifies happiness, contentment and well-being. Meeting or seeing God in a dream represents an

KNIGHT OF PENTACLES

attempt to get close to perfection, thus implying that the dreamer is aspiring to self-improvement and betterment. There may be an implication that the dreamer feels guilt over his human failings – about falling short of perfection – and is seeking enlightenment, forgiveness, or approval. More analytically, God, in the dream, probably symbolizes someone in the dreamer's life who has come to represent an ideal figure – and whom the dreamer fantasizes about emulating.

GOLD Sun; sun king; the Royal Way; God; enlightenment.

GREEN Natural life; vigour; growth; hope; health; healing; balance.

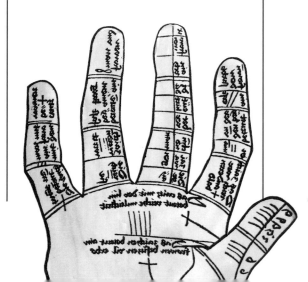

GUN This is a dream indicating distress and the likelihood of irrational behaviour. It is a dream that arises from your present worries, and your search for a quick solution. It has associations with dreams of violence (*see below*), the implication being that if you carry or use a gun in your dream it is a sign of your deep frustrations and anger in reality. The use of the gun can be cathartic, as it at least allows you to act out scenes of revenge and retribution that would be impossible outside the dream world.

HAT Dreams of losing hats mean that business affairs may go wrong, and that those with whom you are dealing could let you down, or pull out suddenly. Putting on a hat in a dream is a good sign – there will be an unexpected advantage gained.

HELL A very ominous dream image, to be taken as a serious warning. When hell appears in the dream it symbolizes a major temptation that must be avoided. If the warning is ignored monetary loss, ill-health, and unhappiness will follow. In twentieth-century analytical interpretation, hell represents the lowest parts of the dark side of the unconscious: one must visit hell to gain self-knowledge and self-awareness, returning stronger and wiser to the surface. Thus dreams of trips to hell may indicate a courageous and desperate search for the essence of the self.

HELMET To dream of seeing a helmet is a warning of threatened misery and loss: it can be avoided by wise actions on your part.

HORSE Horses have been man's ally for thousands of years. They represent controlled strength and meaningful progress; if they are seen when plodding slowly they can indicate ponderous progress.

To dream of a horse indicates reliability and strength, perhaps in the inner self, or else as demonstrated in the affection of a friend. (opposite, above)

Hands can be of varied appearance: large or small, dirty or clean, perhaps with fingers of a particular shape. Each characteristic can be defined symbolically through dreams. (opposite, below)

Dreams of hell and the devil represent a serious warning, usually of a hidden temptation that could prove very distracting. The anxiety instilled in those who dream of hell can also act as a cleansing vibrant force. (above)

If you dream of a house, note its appearance carefully. You should also pay attention to which rooms you see if you go inside. A house that appears welcoming may not always be so, as Hansel and Gretel found to their cost – do not be too trusting of your acquaintances. (below)

In a dream involving a ladder you should examine whether you are climbing up or down and where you are going. To feel fear whilst climbing indicates that you are afraid that you are trying to act beyond your capabilities. Otherwise, upward movement generally denotes freedom and exhilaration. (below, right)

HOUSE A house or parts of the house can be particularly significant in dreams; it can represent the human body and personality; the dreamer himself or herself. Specific meanings are attached to the following:

Attic: higher consciousness

Basement: the subconscious

Bathroom: cleansing the mind or spirit; ridding oneself of dross

Bedroom: rest and renewal

Doors: bodily orifices

Hearth, whether in living room or kitchen: safety, warmth, companionship, domesticity

Kitchen: sharing work together

Living room: communication, sharing

Rooms in general: the womb

Stairs: sexual excitement or activity; exploring other levels

Walls: separation, cutting off dreamer from outside reality

Windows: eyes, the windows of the soul

To kill someone you know in a dream shows that you feel intense animosity towards that person. If you are killing in self-defence this can act as a useful route towards relieving stress in your waking life. (right)

Dreaming of a real or imaginary King (this is George II of Great Britain in 1743) can mean that you have problems with your status or self-esteem, or that you are anxious about your relationship with an authority figure at work or in your family. (opposite below)

ICE This is usually a bad sign, meaning either that you are on a slippery slope in real life, or that you are "frozen" in your present position; also that someone close to you, is cold at heart.

IDOLS Should you dream of an idol, and particularly should you see yourself worshipping it, this means that you have been seduced into following the wrong course. Your efforts are being wasted because they have been channelled in the wrong direction – you should analyse all your motives, and prepare yourself for a disappointment. Dreaming of breaking an idol is very positive: it signifies self-revelation and a sudden insight. Such a dream will inspire you to clear away obstacles and find a straight path to your objectives.

INN If noisy and ill-decorated, this signifies worries and nuisances that are bothering you, and an unwanted task that you have to finish. Dreams of inns and hotels are generally most unfortunate, foretelling a great reduction in financial circumstances, and monetary loss. They can also imply infidelity and abandonment.

ISLAND This depends on the feeling of the dream and its context: it could mean welcome solitude and safety; or isolation, loneliness and separation.

KEY This is much the same as the normal metaphorical meanings of the word. It can be the key or solution to a problem, the key to happiness, or even the keys to the kingdom of heaven.

KILLING SOMEONE If it is someone the dreamer knows, then this is a magnified expression of hatred for that person; often a dream is a safety valve for a harmless and cathartic release of extreme anger. If the killing is in self-defence, or the thing killed is a violent animal or enemy, a killing dream can be very positive – indicating triumph over adversity (*see also* Violence).

KING This traditionally means the dreamer's father, but it can also mean any authority figure, or anyone who is grand and majestic.

KNIFE This represents brightness, sharpness, or a clean cut; also, more obviously, a weapon, or danger.

KNOT A knot usually implies complications in the life of the dreamer that are the cause of worry and need to be resolved. If the context is more positive, it could indicate the tying up of loose ends.

LADDER If ascending, this symbol means some form of achievement, or in sexual terms, arousal. It is a very positive image for happiness, business success, and great reward and recognition. When descending, damaged, or broken the reverse is true – you will encounter failure, unrequited love or sexual inadequacy.

If in a dream you escape from captivity by use of a ladder, you will be faced in life by a very great challenge, to which you will be equal. Should you grow dizzy or afraid while climbing a ladder, you are taking on a responsibility which is greater than your talents – a possible warning that your ambitions out-run your abilities.

The lion traditionally symbolizes pride and strength, yet it is also wild: a dream about a lion can indicate a wish to dominate. (right)

Masks appear in dreams as a disguise or as a barrier between the dangers of everyday life and the inner self. (opposite)

LAMP If you dream of a lamp that is lit, it is a clear sign of spiritual or intellectual illumination, the revealing of truth. If the lamp is extinguished it shows the opposite: dullness, the concealing of truth, spiritual aridity.

LETTER Letter dreams were particularly fascinating to the Victorians and Edwardians – in those pre-telephone days, the mail was a vital lifeline for them, and letters took on great importance. Showing the variety of interpretations offered, and also quoted as an example of the style of the period, this is from one of the foremost dream dictionaries of that period – the work of American analyst Gustavus Hindman Miller:

"To dream that you see a registered letter, foretells that some money matters will disrupt long-established relations.

For a young woman to dream that she receives such a letter, intimates that she will be offered a competency, but it will not be on strictly legal, or moral grounds; others may play towards her a dishonorable part.

To the lover, this bears heavy presentiments of disagreeable mating. His sweetheart will covet other gifts than his own.

To dream of an anonymous letter, denotes that you will receive injury from an unexpected source.

To write one, foretells that you will be jealous of a rival, whom you admit to be your superior.

To dream of getting letters bearing unpleasant news, denotes difficulties and illness. If the news is of a joyous character, you will have many things to be thankful for. If the letter is affectionate, but is written on green, or colored, paper, you will be slighted in love and business. Despondency will envelop you. Blue ink, denotes constancy and affection, also bright fortune.

Red colours in a letter, imply estrangements through suspicion and jealousy, but this may be overcome by wise maneuvering of the suspected party.

If a young woman dreams that she receives a letter from her lover and places it near her heart, she will be worried very much be a good-looking rival. Truthfulness is often rewarded by jealousy.

If you fail to read the letter, you will lose something either in a business or social way.

Letters nearly always bring worry.

To have your letter intercepted, rival enemies are working to defame you.

To dream of trying to conceal a letter from your sweetheart or wife, intimates that you are interested in unworthy occupations.

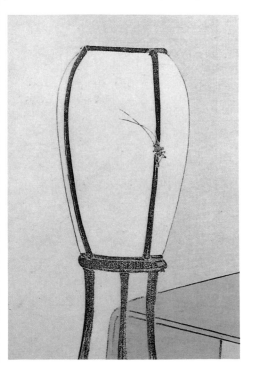

Seeing a lamp alight in a dream is a positive image: it indicates a search for knowledge and enlightenment – probably of a spiritual nature. (right)

To dream of a letter with a black border, signifies distress and the death of some relative."

And so on. It can be seen that the style is much more pedantic and prescriptive – so symbol X *always* equals meaning Y – and there is little or no emphasis placed on context or personal interpretation. In a more modern interpretation, a letter simply means news, a message or, more broadly, communication. Any further meaning must be gauged by the context.

LION The King of the Beasts symbolizes strength, force, desire, pride and mastery; but the lion is wild and can be dangerous, devouring its prey.

MASK If the dreamer is wearing a mask it can reveal a conflict between the inner self and the outward appearance. If it is someone else beneath the mask, it can reveal a fear of deception and hidden dangers.

MEAT As with bread, meat dreams, concerning as they do a substance traditionally central to man's health and welfare, are important. The usual interpretation of a meat dream would be an indication of comfort, profit, and prosperity. If the meat is actually being eaten in the dream, the world of the senses has been entered, and this is an image concerning desire and sensuality – if the consumption is extreme, beware the sins of the flesh! Some modern analysts have attributed dreams of meat to ancient echoes within the unconscious of cannibalism – the triumph of the self over the enemy, and a celebration of the survival of the fittest in the most basic of ways. In this interpretation the positive aspects of the meat dream may be confused – the personal gain and success is or will be at the expense of others.

MEDAL A symbol of glory and the respect of others. In a negative context, vanity and pomposity. Losing a medal indicates that you will come to misfortune by the treachery of others.

MILK This is a dream representing spiritual or bodily nourishment, with strong implications of warmth and tranquility resonant of the comfort of early feeding at the mother's breast. However, if spilt, milk in a dream means lost opportunity, waste, or the spoiling of something worthwhile.

MIRROR Mirror dreams are generally not good luck. To dream of seeing yourself can denote sickness and disappointment ahead. It can imply vanity and narcissism. A mirror image is a deception; it is most unlikely to imply self-examination leading to improvement. If in your dream you see friends in a mirror, question your trust of them.

MOON These dreams are mystical: the Moon represents a dreamer or visionary, for good or for bad. The Moon can also be a goddess, or a representation of esoteric spirituality. When the Moon appears in your dreams, it shows that you are close to the world of your emotions, sometimes without being aware of it. You are perhaps being misled by your conscious emotions – look to these messages from your unconscious and review your feelings.

MOUNTAIN Climbing a mountain in a dream denotes achievement through hard work; it can also denote spiritual advancement.

NAMES This is a complex area and requires personal – not general – interpretation. The unconscious mind, to put it crudely, loves puns and word play: names of places and people are therefore likely to be loaded with meaning in the most extraordinary way. It is recommended that specific names you recollect from dreams should be written down immediately on waking: they can then be closely analyzed for hidden meanings. Proper names are often the key the dream offers to our deepest unconscious thoughts and feelings. Treat these clues like the clues to a crossword puzzle or anagram – break them down, rearrange the letters, and reorder them – it is amazing how many indicators and echoes you will find.

The master dream interpreter was, as has been mentioned, Sigmund Freud. As an example of his work in this area, and an indication of the way in which a single word in a dream can lead the analysis in four or five directions, this is a short study from Freud's *The Interpretation of Dreams*:

"One of my women patients told me a short dream which ended in a meaningless verbal compound. She dreamt she was with her husband at a peasant festivity and said: 'This will end in a general "Maistollmutz".' . . . Analysis divided the word into 'Mais' [Maise], 'toll' [mad], 'mannstoll' [nymphomaniac – literally, mad for men], and "Olmutz" [the name of a town in Moravia] . . . The following words lay behind 'Mais': 'Meissen' (a porcelain figure representing a bird); 'Miss' (her relatives' English governess had just gone to Olmutz); and 'mies' (Yiddish slang term, used jokingly to mean 'disgusting'). A long chain of thoughts and associations led off from

To dream of a monster usually indicates a struggle of inner turmoil, usually depression. It is possible to emerge victorious both in the dream and in your own situation. (below, right)

If you dream of a mirror you may suffer some bad luck. Try to see who is reflected in the mirror if you do not merely see yourself. (below)

each syllable of this verbal hotch-potch."

Look out for clues in names to your innermost feelings. If you are reading a book, or have just seen a film in which the wife of a man called Jones is having an affair with a man named Brown, and these names occur in your dream, you may be harbouring worries or fears about jealousy and fidelity. If you come from a small town called Pleasant, but in your dreams Pleasant is the name of a dirty, dangerous urban centre, it may mean that you yearn for the lost innocence, comfort and security of your early years. The clues and associations are endless and fascinating.

NECKLACE Seeing someone else putting on or wearing a necklace, or viewing a necklace through a window or in some other inaccessible place is a strong dream of envy

The Moon can appear in a dream in a bodily, enchanting guise as a woman, calm and harmonious. It can also be seen in its more common astrological or planetary form. (left)

and jealousy: whether you are aware of it or not, in reality somebody has possession of something you desire, and you are having trouble reconciling your emotions. If in the dream you are wearing or putting on the necklace, this is very positive, and indicates probable success in something in which you have been investing time and effort.

NETTLES These represent niggling problems, probably not of too serious a nature, but aggravating nevertheless. Seeing nettles growing wildly in your garden indicates that you unconsciously feel beset on all sides by nuisances – a succession of small things that you cannot control, and which are combining to deeply worry and frustrate you. Cutting down the nettles is a strongly positive image: it indicates that you have the resolve to fight the problems and beat them. Similarly, walking through a field of nettles without being stung implies that, whereas you cannot immediately see how to solve your problems, you have the strength of character to get on with your life and focus on the important things without being distracted – you will be prosperous.

NOISE This means you will have worries, or that a quarrel will take place.

NUDITY The very common dream in which you see yourself as naked in a public place can be extremely vivid and upsetting. It is almost certainly an indication that you are vulnerable. It can imply that you are no longer willing to maintain the role (persona) previously adopted or thrust upon you: but the act of throwing off the role leaves you weak and isolated – naked until the uniform or clothing of your new role is established.

NUMBERS 0: circle of life, returning, continuation, the female sex
1: oneness, God, unity, the male sex, will, inspiration
2: duality, balance between masculine and feminine, partnership
3: the Trinity, the family, communication
4: foursquare, solidity, strength, authority, law

5: nature, the human body, versatility

6: sex, marriage, emotion, balanced relationships

7: sacred number: God, the mystic, the seeker after truth

8: power, infinity

9: pregnancy, success in overcoming challenges

10: completion, wholeness, marriage

NUTS Symbolic of an enterprise, in which hard work will gain its just rewards: also difficulties ahead which you will have the strength to survive.

OBSTACLES Encountering an obstacle in a dream – of a physical type, such as a locked door, fence, wall, barbed wire: or of another type, such as a lost invitation preventing entry, or fog preventing a journey – indicates inhibitions in your life that are stopping you from carrying out plans or fulfilling ideals. This need not be negative (in moral terms): one of the commonest inhibitions is conscience, and it may well be that the dream symbolizes a battle between your conscience (or super-ego) and your desire (or id), with the conscience quite properly throwing up a barrier to stop you pursuing some wild fantasy that will ruin your life. These dreams are clear warnings of danger ahead if no action is taken: the two sides of your psyche are locked in conflict, and no good can come of this.

OLD MAN An old man appearing in a dream foretells happiness in the family.

OLIVES Peace and reconciliation. Favourable business announcements, and happy surprises. Eating olives signifies contentment and conviviality.

ORANGE The colour orange implies occult power, and also passion. The fruit is generally interpreted as a symbol of achievement, health and goodness coming after hard work.

OWL Traditionally the owl shows wisdom, but the other side of wisdom is cunning; it can also mean the departed soul of the dead. Owls can be ominous – a warning of sacrifices or shortages to come. Victorian interpretation had it that you should never sign a contract or initiate a project on the day following a dream of owls.

OX Dreams of well-fed oxen peacefully grazing are universally interpreted as highly fortuitous – times of plenty, success, and good fortune are ahead. Lean beasts may token a more difficult future, and beasts with horns can indicate quarrels and disagreements.

OYSTERS Traditionally this means "a sure thing" – good luck for gamblers.

A well-fed contented ox signifies security and plenty. Oxen have symbolic importance in dreams and visions in the Old Testament and they have come to have fortuitous associations. (above)

Nudity in public implies a deep-seated fear of exposure and humiliation. It can also indicate emancipation from an undesired role in order to take on a new way of life. (opposite)

An owl represents a complicated combination of cunning, wisdom and ill omen. The traditional wise owl may not always foretell of pleasant things. (below, left)

PEACOCK The beauty and glory of the peacock shows wealth, wholeness and rebirth, in its medieval association with the phoenix and alchemy; it represents specifically male beauty, and can mean vanity.

PHOENIX Rising from the flames of its death, the phoenix symbolizes rebirth, reincarnation, resurrection and transformation.

PIT Dreaming of being in a deep pit reveals despondency; you are caught in severe problems.

POOL If it is clear, a pool is usually interpreted as representing the personal unconscious; but reflections in water can represent deception.

The peacock symbolizes both beauty and rebirth; it is connected in imagery with the phoenix. The peacock is an important image in medieval alchemy. (right)

If you dream of gazing into a pool, assess the appearance of the water. Try also to remember whether you are gazing into its depths or at your own reflection, and what you see as you look. (below)

PRISON A sign of oppression. Something is making you feel trapped, or you may simply be over-tired.

PROCESSION This is an ominous indicator that a funeral will take place soon. Even a marriage procession in your dream means a funeral.

PUNISHMENT If the dreamer is being punished it usually reveals a guilty conscience, a feeling that one deserves to be punished for some act, however small, in real life.

PURPLE Spiritual power; inspiration

PURSE In the Victorian system of interpretation, a full purse meant financial loss, and an empty purse, a sudden wind-fall from an unexpected source. Other analysts predict new friendships if you dream of a purse being filled with precious stones and banknotes.

QUAIL If you recognize a quail in your dream, and it is alive, this is most fortuitous and will bring great good luck. If it is dead, expect bad luck and serious difficulties.

QUARREL Dreaming of an argument implies some frustration in your life that you are unable to face up to and resolve – perhaps a difficulty with a superior at work, or with a family member: through your dream you are acting out the confrontational role you feel you ought to be taking in reality. At another level it can also indicate that you have serious conflicts and contradictions deep within your unconscious – possibly some aspect of your earliest conditioning that is now disrupting your adult life. These dreams are common among people who have moved to other countries, or who have had some radical change in their class or social status.

QUEEN Traditionally this means the dreamer's mother, but it can also mean a strong, perhaps domineering female figure in the dreamer's waking life.

QUICKSAND/QUAGMIRE/BOG

Dreaming that you are being sucked into any form of mud or sand and cannot get out is one of the most frightening images of all. One interpretation is that the dreamer is so terrified by the prospect of life that this is an attempt to crawl back into the womb. At the same time, there are associations with the death-wish, and the dream may also have sexual resonances. On a simpler level, the dream obviously bodes ill: the swamp is misfortune, and unless you can struggle and escape – or unless someone comes to rescue you – the dream signifies problems ahead.

To dream of a queen usually indicates a mother figure, yet can represent any strong, forceful woman. (below)

A procession is not in fact a happy sight: it usually implies sad news. (above)

To dream of passing along a road is a good omen and true intentions will be rewarded. It is important to note whether you are alone or with others and what type of road you see: the meaning of the symbol varies with its appearance. If you become lost while on a road, you should examine reasons for your actions. (below, right)

Rain can bring several omens – if it falls from heavy clouds, you will need strength to approach the task in hand; if the rain is bright and welcome, you will feel refreshed and rejuvenated. Rain can be associated with cleansing, or with the power of judgement. (below)

RAIN Generally, rejuvenation, freshness and vitality. A sweeping away of staleness, which could indicate that you should be making changes in your life.

Rain is the giver of life in nature; this applies especially to emotional life in dream imagery.

RAINBOW Since Old Testament times the rainbow has been a sign of an agreement, a promise or a solemn and worthwhile covenant; it always signifies a brighter future.

RAT A rat in your dreams means powerful enemies; it can also show disloyalty. The connotations of rats and disease come through strongly to represent something that may be unpleasant.

RAVEN This is the bird of ill tidings; it can denote the Devil, the dark side of our personality, or confusion. The raven can also represent the darker, more sinister side of the father and fatherhood – punishment, stern authority and lack of sympathy.

RED Vitality; energy; action; anger; blood; fire; wine; powerful sexuality.

ROAD These dreams indicate the journey through life or progress being made on some current project – the specific interpretation depending on the context. Simply walking along a road will indicate that your aims are good and will be rewarded. If the track is bumpy or broken, or twists and turns uncomfortably, you will find your intentions harder to realize. If the surroundings are barren, bleak or wasted, then you should look again at your plans – something may be amiss; if they are colourful and verdant, then all is well. If you are accompanied on your journey, it implies that collective effort is working well, and will bear fruit. Losing your way implies that you

are unsure about your own motives, and that you are unconsciously reluctant to fulfil your objectives (*see* Obstacles).

ROCKS A large rock or boulder by itself can show solidity and stability, or, in a different context, an obstacle. A lot of smaller rocks could mean danger and difficulties.

ROSES A powerfully romantic and potentially sexual dream image. Roses are always a positive symbol as long as they are healthy. They represent friendship, good-nature, freshness and vitality.

Rosebud: virginity, innocence, purity; potential.

Unfolding red rose amongst thorns: female sex (the rose is also a powerful alchemical symbol).

Ten of Wands

SAILING To sail on calm waters implies a bright and cheerful outlook, financial success and optimism.

SAND In dreams, sand has its traditional symbolic meaning of insecurity and uncertainty: shifting, unpredictable movement, and plans based on inadequate foundations.

The interpretation of sailing dreams depends very much on the context. If the ship is becalmed, it may indicate a period of frustration or stagnation; if it is safely anchored, it represents comfort and safety. (left)

Roses symbolize romance, friendship and natural freshness. As with all flowers, note whether you are being given the roses and the motives behind the gift. (below)

Dreams of the sea and of marine life have multiple meanings and are an indication of our deepest feelings. If you experience a dream associated with the sea or the tides, take careful note of the state of the water and the general shoreline – if there is one in sight. (below)

SCHOOL We often dream of school, a familiar and (for adults) safely past time and environment which, however happy or unhappy, was firmly ordered. This can show a desire to solve the problems and uncertainties of adult life by fitting them into a structured framework. Look for the problem in the dream to find the underlying message.

SCISSORS A quarrel or the death of a friend. A very unlucky dream: wives will be jealous of their husbands, sweethearts will argue, and business affairs will suffer or fail.

SEA These dreams are riddled with significance. Humankind emerged from the sea, and it remains a powerful influence – part of the collective unconscious of all. However far we have ranged in the search for meaning and purpose in life, the sea remains in the psyche as an emotional birthing ground, a source and starting point for the spiritual and intellectual quest. Consequently sea dreams are a very important indication of our deepest and truest feelings.

An obvious interpretation of these dreams is that if calm, the sea represents enormous peace and happiness; if stormy, anger and troubles lie ahead. However, look to the context: are you in the sea, and part of its motion and meaning, or on the shore, only looking on, and not part of the process? Is the ocean deep, representing profundity and real meaning; or is it shallow, indicating that the image,

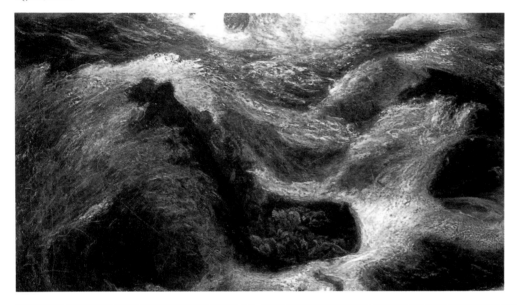

Scissors in a dream are a very unlucky omen: they symbolize severance and parting – perhaps a quarrel with a loved one or, at worst, a death. (above)

and probably your concerns, are more superficial than you realize? Waves crashing on the beach, for example, in a fountain of foam, may have sexual significance, but the violence of the desire they indicate is undermined by the shallowness of the water – this could be a realm of wasted passion.

Dreaming of hearing the sea at a distance indicates deep sadness and loneliness: you are cut off from a vital force, and disconnected from your true emotions.

SEASONS Spring: new beginnings, new hopes, new life; naïvety; childhood

Summer: satisfaction, fulfilment, completion; energy; summer of youth

Autumn: resting, re-evaluation; fruitfulness; fading power; maturity

Winter: end of cycle, death leading to life; serenity; coldness; death; old age

Oddly, shooting or fighting in a dream can be a positive image. You are probably frustrated deep down about some element of your life, and the shooting represents a method of releasing this negative energy. (above)

If you see smoke in a dream it may be of several different types. Thick or grey smoke holds a different meaning from that represented by white fumes – each type should be examined in context, particularly with regard to the source of the smoke. (right)

The season that appears in your dream can be a sign of optimism, except that winter is usually a time of less activity, symbolizing old age, slow movement and contemplation. Certain activities, such as harvesting or traditional celebrations, embody particular times of the year. (left)

SHARK Dreaming of a shark reveals a fear of a predatory enemy, possibly within a business environment or even in a personal situation.

SHOOTING *see* Gun

SMOKE Traditionally, a disastrous business affair. If going straight up, difficulties overcome. If white, small worries; if grey, painful worries; if dark or black; great sorrow.

Swan dreams are almost always fortuitous, indicating happiness, success and prosperity. In this picture Zeus visits his earthly lover in the form of a swan. (right)

SNAKE This is an ancient and powerful symbol with many meanings. It can mean the power of sexuality, but it can also convey healing and wisdom; in its negative aspect it can imply cunning and deceit; remember that many snakes are poisonous.

SPIDER This shows a fear of being entrapped in another's power, especially a predatory, devouring female. It can also denote a stifling atmosphere particularly within the family.

SUN The Sun is a symbol of joy, success and fulfilment; it can also symbolize God.

SWAN Swans indicate happiness if white, and if they are swimming, then great happiness and prosperity. If the swans are black, the reverse is true.

SWORD Commonly, a symbol of justice, and of authority and responsibility well used. For Jung, it represented a weapon that the adolescent would use in the fight against the dark forces of the unconscious in a critical period of development; Freudians would probably see it more as a phallic weapon with which the male child could wage his battle against the father in order to possess the mother. For men, if the sword is lost or broken, this symbolizes sexual failure or loss of authority – possibly a business crisis. A sword broken in a fight with a rival has obvious implications of being bested in love. Dreaming of others armed with swords while you yourself are unarmed is a strong warning that you are in a weak position in some important aspect of your life: beware – those you are dealing with have more resources than you imagined. A rusty, stained, or chipped sword could indicate an unacknowledged weakness in the dreamer.

Spiders signify a fear of entrapment, particularly by women. They are also associated with the sensation of claustrophobia, often in a domestic context. (right)

TABLE To dream of a table laden with a meal – or better still to dream of actually preparing the table yourself – denotes that good things are on the horizon: new friends, the strengthening of family ties, and general prosperity. An empty table, the remnants of a meal, or a table in the process of being cleared, signify the reverse: broken friendships, and lean times to come. Gustavus Hindman Miller offers some further early interpretations:

"To eat from a table without a cloth, foretells that you will be possessed of an independent disposition, and the prosperity or conduct of others will give you no concern.

To see a table walking or moving in some mysterious way, foretells that dissatisfactions will soon enter your life and you will seek relief in change.

To dream of a soiled cloth on a table, denotes disobedience from servants or children, and quarreling will invariably follow pleasure.

To see a broken table, is ominous of decaying fortune.

To see one standing or sitting on a table, foretells that to obtain their desires they will be guilty of indiscretion.

To see or hear table-rapping or writing, denotes that you will undergo change of feelings towards your friends and your fortune will be threatened. A loss from the depreciation of relatives or friends is indicated."

If you dream of a table, take care to remember the function the table has in the context. You may be using it as a support, for a book for instance, the centrepiece of a social gathering or in connection with certain everyday events. (below)

The snake is a powerful image within a dream: it can be both positive – representing wisdom and good – and negative, when it is the embodiment of deceit. Its appearance is largely related to the dreamer's own view of snakes and reptiles. (above)

Toads have long been associated
with ugliness and represent evil
and deceit. You should beware of
someone with a fickle nature
after a dream about a toad.
(above)

TAILOR Traditionally, dreaming about a tailor implies bad faith in business, and disappointment concerning a scheme in hand. If the tailor is measuring you, look out for a quarrel.

THIEF The traditional interpretation of this symbol is that one of your friends is false. If you are the thief in the dream, and you are caught, your business affairs are due for a fall. It is a very lucky dream to pursue and catch a thief.

TOAD Dreaming of a toad is always bad; it denotes evil, ugliness and hidden danger. It can represent the presence of someone who is unreliable or deceitful.

TRAVEL If you dream that you are travelling alone, you are experiencing some stress in your life. If the journey is long, you will become more relaxed and better able to deal with your problems after a short break.

If you dream of a tree your
emotions are closely related with
the cycle of the natural year. The
different stages of a tree's growth
are indicative of change or
stability. Certain types of tree
have very particular meanings.
It should be remembered that
trees can also appear mysterious,
with a character of their own,
and in some cases can be hostile
and frightening. (right)

TREES In the basic vocabulary of symbols, healthy green trees represent happiness, fulfilment, and contentment. Dead trees, or dying or diseased foliage, are warnings of change for the worse. Dreams of tree-felling represent a sudden loss or the breaking of a close tie or friendship. Climbing a healthy tree is a positive indication of achievement – such a dream may have a sexual orientation.

Elm: A sign of disruption and loss – possible money problems.

Fir: A positive symbol – commercial gain.

Oak: This is a traditional symbol for strength and power, a combination of both mental and physical fortitude.

Willow: These are associated with sadness.

Yew: Often interpreted in terms of disappointment and illness.

TWINS This has all the meanings of duality, good and bad, depending on the context of the dream. It can be a warning to consider both sides of a question, or it can mean that someone is being two-faced. It can also mean the beginnings of a very close friendship, one which will bring much support and comfort in times of difficulty.

TUNNEL Depending on the context, a tunnel can have several meanings. It can show that in waking life the dreamer is on a difficult path requiring much effort; it can denote an exploration of the unconscious layers of the personality.

You may dream that you are a thief or that one of your friends is stealing from you. If, on the other hand, you are involved in the apprehension of a thief you can expect good fortune. (below, left)

Twins provide a double image, either that of symmetry meaning close friendship and trust, or else the negative, two-faced aspects of their duality. (below)

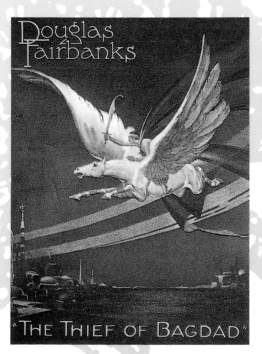

UMBRELLA An umbrella, open in a shower, represents support, protection, friendship, and consequently great happiness and prosperity. Blown inside out, it indicates change, transformation, and the chance that you will be falsely accused or misrepresented. Losing an umbrella implies abandonment, and falling out with a trusted friend.

UNICORN This mythical creature is the essence of grace, purity and virginity. A unicorn in your dreams symbolizes something you should treasure and protect. The single horn represents resolution of conflict (the more usual two-horned creatures signify conflict).

UNIFORMS These can indicate doubts about the "persona" – the outward appearance one displays to the world, and which often disguises or hides the true self. There can be an implication that the dreamer fears conformity, or that there is a feeling that too much is being sacrificed in order to keep up appearances. Uniforms on a woman may denote gender confusion, or sexual fantasy. Torn or dirty uniforms denote concerns about image, and possibly a fear of increased responsibility. At the same time figures of authority in uniform can, in context, indicate order, continuity, good relationships and good organization.

UP/DOWN, ABOVE/BELOW Height and upward movement in dreams represent the intellect and the higher spiritual concerns of man (in purely religious terms, that which is heavenly). A dream set in a high location must be interpreted in the context of high ideals – even if the subject matter is negative, the overall motivational context and concern is worthy. Anything below, underneath, or moving downwards is symbolic of the lower, baser impulses – the sensual, sexual, and selfish desires. To be truly whole, Jung taught, it is

The magical, mythical figure of a unicorn is a sign of something precious that you will protect and cherish. (above)

To dream of an open umbrella signifies support and eventual happiness. It represents a protective influence or friendship, but is not fixed, so can be seen as changeable. (right)

necessary to know both sides of the character – the light side and the dark side: so do not be ashamed or embarrassed about base concerns in dreams, as these can actually denote the continuing search for knowledge and self-improvement (*see* Hell). Dreams involving journeys between high and low places, levitation, falls, flying, and so on, can be most revealing.

VALLEY If this is an archetypal image of a valley between rounded hills, and a stream running through it, this is a strong symbol of female sexuality. A valley can also signify "the valley of the shadow of death" or "a vale of tears". Valley dreams indicate tranquility – they are a sign that the dreamer is contented. If your dream takes you on a journey into or through the valley, this implies that you are independent of thought and adventurous. A very deep valley is a good sign that a project on which you are working will be successful, resulting, if it is a commercial venture, in prosperity.

Figures in uniform usually symbolize order, regularity and conformity. They can represent a comforting security, or, in context, worries about your relationship with authority. (right)

A softly undulating, verdant valley is an image of sensuousness and plenty. A dry, arid valley, such as the one illustrated, may indicate a dangerous venture, or depression. (below)

VAMPIRE To dream of being attacked by a vampire is a common nightmarish scenario; you are probably suffering from stress and are feeling hemmed in at work.

VINEGAR An ominous substance: difficult times, quarrels, bitterness and jealousy. You may be forced into agreeing to plans that fill you with worry.

VIOLENCE Not a propitious dream, as can be imagined. If the violence is committed against you, it indicates that you are concerned or fearful that others are conspiring to do you harm. If you are perpetrating the violence, this is a sign that you are harbouring feelings of anger against others, or that a relationship that means a lot to you is failing. This can also indicate, for a man, a loss of sexual confidence, and a desire to prove manhood.

VOLCANO To see a volcano that is erupting signifies that you are about to enter into a violent dispute with a friend or business associate. If you dream of lava running down the sides of the volcano, the disagreement will become more heated before an amicable conclusion is reached – the friendship will be restored, however. A dormant volcano acts as a warning against sloth; even if you seem content to let problems sort themselves out you will benefit from taking a more active part in their solution.

Dreams involving violence usually auger bad luck. When you wake try to assess whether you were the perpetrator, witness or merely the victim of the violent act. (above, right)

Vampires are frightening when they appear in your dream. Their presence does not always herald aggression or attack, however, and is more likely to indicate problems in waking life. (right)

WATER Water is the substance of life and is obviously very important if it appears in dreams, whether as a vast lake or as a glass of water. If the water is clear it denotes well-being and prosperity, and purity of intent and emotions. If it is murky, it can sometimes show danger or guilt, or simply a lack of clarity in the dreamer's waking mind.

WEB Being caught in a web shows a fear of being trapped or ensnared by something in real life. A web can also signify the countless possible future paths ahead of you in the Web of Life – a message to pause and consider the options.

Water, the essence of life, features often in dreams. Being a natural substance it is widespread and of the utmost importance to the well-being of most lifeforms; thus it follows that its appearance is propitious. Examine, however, the type of water, its surface and, most importantly, its function. (left)

A volcano in a dream represents energy – probably, but not necessarily, of a sexual nature. If the volcano is active, it means that your energy is being healthily channeled; if it is dormant, it is likely to indicate frustration or unfulfilled desires. (below)

WHEEL A symbol of change, probably for the better, and potential. If the wheel is turning quickly, it can represent dynamic movement, and business success. If the wheel is turning too quickly it can show fear that one's life is out of control. If it is broken, or needs repair, it can indicate a lack of energy or application. A missing wheel signifies that something important is being denied to you – or that a friend or family member may be about to leave your life for a time.

WHITE Light; innocence; purity; perfection; illumination; wisdom; male sexuality.

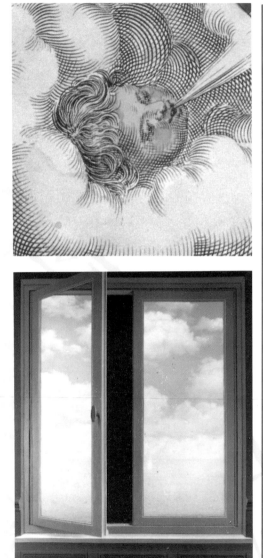

WIND A healthy fresh wind is the breath of life – a sign of normal cyclical change and development which is blowing away the past and presenting many interesting options for the future. However, gales and very strong winds can mean upheaval – transformation coming too soon or happening too quickly. If the wind is blowing you along against your will, an element of your life is out of control and may be pushing you towards great disappointment.

WINDOW An open window usually means safety, with no need to fear danger. A closed window can indicate that, although danger is nearby, you are safe from it. If in the dream you are looking through the window from the inside, this represents the dreamer's view of the world.

WINE A well-favoured dream: generosity, pleasure, plenty, and a happy old age. Spilt, sour, or wasted wine are dreams of sadness and missed or spoilt opportunities.

YELLOW Extrovert personality; mental power; determination; cowardice.

YOUTH/YOUNG In Jung's school of interpretation, the youth represents potential and innocence: the chance for a new start. He is a seeker (the female equivalent in Jung's vocabulary of archetypes is the Princess), full of purpose and ideals. To dream of a youth, or youth in general, denotes hope. A dream of the self when young, however, indicates problems with guilt and the conscience; as though the dreamer desperately desires an opportunity to live life over, or correct some tragic mistake. Such a fantasy is doomed to failure. General dreams of young people are positive, hopeful, and favourable.

Dreams of a wheel, like those involving circles, provide an atmosphere of dynamism, and the opposites of continuity and change. Wheels of fortune are a popular and traditional symbol of the unpredictability of life – both its bad and potentially good elements. (far left, below)

Dreams of young people or children often portray hope and optimism. The context should be examined, particularly if you are reminded in the dream of your own childhood. (far left, above)

Wind brings change, both refreshing and welcome as well as that which represents upheaval and disturbance. You may have to fight against the wind to retain control of your situation. (left, above)

To dream of a window in a house means that you will have extra insight into a problem or into someone's life. The house containing the window represents the human body; the windows therefore provide visions of a physical or spiritual type. (left, below)

Destiny &
Divination

*D*ealing cards, casting little blocks of wood or stone, or throwing sticks – to the outsider or the uninitiated these look like party games or childrens' pastimes. In fact Tarot cards, runes and the I Ching (*the* Book of Changes) are three of the world's most ancient and revered systems of divination: they have been used successfully for hundreds of years to reveal the secret self and predict the future with astonishing subtlety and accuracy.

These are not chance methods, dependent on simple fate. They operate as a medium which attunes itself to the deep psychic reverberations of the participant. By showing respect, and by showing faith, the subject enables the cards, runes or sticks to become aware of hidden feelings and preoccupations, and then to apply this knowledge to specific future events. When the results are interpreted, personal destiny is unveiled.

Opposite: *The images on Tarot cards were based on late medieval symbolism. The Moon card, right, of the Charles VI set depicts astrologers at work plotting the course of the planet.*

Tarot Reading

Tarot must be the most mysterious of all the systems used in prediction and divination. A Tarot pack contains seventy-eight cards: four suits of fourteen cards each, which make up the Minor Arcana, and twenty-two other cards which form the Major Arcana. Each card has a distinctive design incorporating symbols and, in some cases, numbers. The symbols are interpreted to provide an indication of future events or for analysis of an individual's characteristics.

In spite of the many attempts to prove its origins, and theories that are as colourful and intricate as the designs on the cards, the origins of Tarot remain shrouded in mystery. With the great fascination for Egyptology in the eighteenth and nineteenth centuries it was inevitable that Tarot should be said to have come from Egypt, a belief given added weight by the title of Aleister Crowley's own Tarot pack, *The Book of Thoth* (1944), Thoth being the Egyptian god of science.

A b o v e : From the same pack as the card on the far left, this one shows the constellations forming Pegasus and Little Horse.

A b o v e : One of a set of astronomical playing cards made in Nürenburg in 1719: this one depicts the star clusters Canis Minor and the Unicorn.

B e l o w : People have been trying to find the future in the cards for centuries, as in the typical "reading" scene shown in this French engraving. As well as using Tarot cards, systems of reading and divination have been developed which use the conventional playing card deck and various other non-Tarot forms of pack.

Right: *This is a modern reproduction of the Chariot card from the famous Cary-Yale Visconti Tarocchi pack. The word "Tarot" itself originates from the name of a card game – called in Italy "Tarocco" (plural, "Tarocchi") and in France, "Tarot" – for which the cards were used.*

Trismegistus, the Greek pseudo-historical founder of alchemy and teacher of magic, is supposed to have set down his hermetic teachings in this "book". Sadly the main symbolism of the cards does not bear this out, although many of today's Tarot packs do include some elements of Egyptian symbolism.

Similarly there is the belief that the Knights Templar, shortly before their dissolution and the execution of their Grand Master Jacques du Molay in 1314, found time to set the entire body of their "heretical" beliefs in the twenty-two cards of the Major Arcana. Although this itself is unlikely, the dating is closer, and there are many Christian elements in the cards, as well as some which could be called Gnostic, from "gnosis", or knowledge. Gnosticism was an early religious movement one of whose principal beliefs was that man should experience personal knowledge rather than accepting imposed beliefs of the church. (The Knights Templar also shared some of the elements of Gnosticism.)

China and India have also been given as sources of Tarot, for assorted reasons.

But of course, say others, pointing to one Gypsy Rose Lee after another in a fairground booth, Tarot must have come from the gypsies. Again, no: Tarot was already known in Europe before the Romanies arrived. It is true that they quickly picked it up and made it their own, but they did not originate it.

Whatever its roots, Tarot as we know it has its origins in the early Renaissance period. The earliest surviving cards were painted for the Visconti family in Milan in northern Italy, around 1450. Two beautiful, gold-painted packs are reproduced by US Games Inc as the Cary-Yale Visconti Tarocchi Deck and the Pierpont-Morgan Bergamo Visconti-Sforza Tarocchi Pack, named after the universities where the originals, with a few cards missing, are now held. They are also sometimes known as the Bembo cards, after the artist to whom they are usually ascribed, Bonifacio Bembo, although some authorities believe them to have been painted by Francesco Zavattari.

Many of the packs often thought of today as "early", "historical", "original" or "genuine" in their design are French; the standard eighteenth century Tarot de Marseilles is very widely known. But the French, rather than Italian, connection

stems mainly from the fact that in the seventeenth century card manufacture almost ceased in the northern Italian region of Lombardy, so cards had to be imported to Italy from France.

The "purists" who object to the various changes in the vast range of modern packs on the grounds that they represent a departure from the "original" Tarot are misguided as there is no such thing. Tarot has altered and developed in many directions over the centuries; the very popular Rider-Waite pack is different from the Tarot de Marseilles, which is different from the Visconti packs. Some of the very earliest packs had more than seventy-eight cards; some, to avoid the Roman Catholic associations, replaced the Pope and Papess with le Grandprêtre and la Grandprêtresse, the High Priest and High Priestess; others, especially in the French "Age of Reason", replaced these same two with the gods Jupiter and Juno.

evidence that Tarot was used for divination before the late eighteenth century; before that it seems to have been simply a card game, called 'tarot' in France and 'tarocco' (*plural*: 'tarocchi') in Italy, probably similar to an earlier game called 'triumphs', from which we get the word 'trumps'. In France today one can buy 'le jeu de tarot' in supermarkets, alongside more standard packs of playing cards.

In 1781 Antoine Court de Gebelin, a theologist and keen mythology scholar, published the eighth volume of his massive *le Monde Primitif Analysé et Comparé avec le Monde Moderne*, which contained a section on Tarot origins:

> *"If one let it be known that an ancient Egyptian work survived to this day, having escaped the flames which devoured their superb libraries, and which contained the pure doctrines of their interesting teaching, everyone would be keen to study such a precious and extraordinary book."*

The "book", Gebelin continued, contained seventy-seven or seventy-eight leaves, and was known today as the game of Tarot. He went on to explain the allegorical or symbolic nature of the images in terms of Egyptian gods and mythology.

Similarly, the order of the cards has changed several times; today we normally put the Fool at the beginning, before Number 1, the Magician, but the card has often been placed either at the end, or between 20, Judgement, and 21, the World. The cards Justice and Fortitude have also been swapped around; they can be Numbers 8 and 11, or 11 and 8, in different packs. Some modern packs replace the King, Queen, Knight and Page with King, Queen, Prince and Princess, or even with Knight, Queen, Prince and Princess. Most of these changes were made to fit Tarot in with other esoteric systems, particularly the cabbala, a Jewish, and later Christian, mystical and magical philosophy which was widely developed during the Renaissance.

None of these changes can be described as "wrong". Just as with translations of the Bible, such as the King James Authorised Version, the Revised Standard Version, the New International Version or any of dozens more, the preferred version is not "right" and all the others "wrong".

Recent developments

Even the "genuine", "historical", "original" (almost sacred) esoteric divinatory meanings of the cards are relatively recent. There is little

Papus

This was the pen name of Gerard Encausse, whose *Tarot des Bohémiens* (1889) extended Lévi's cabbalistic and numerological teachings, as shown in the Oswald Wirth pack. The four Tarot suits link with the four Hebrew letters for JHVH spelling the divine name Yahveh, or Jehovah. Papus was a member of the Cabbalistic Order of the Rose-Cross, forging a link between Tarot and the Rosicrucians and Freemasons which others were to develop, and which is still strong today.

Order of the Golden Dawn

Also in the late nineteenth century three members of the *Societas Rosicruciana in Anglia* in Britain formed the Hermetic Order of the Golden Dawn (OGD), which was to be of crucial importance to the development of Tarot. Samuel Liddell "Mac-Gregor" Mathers, a Scottish Freemason, developed most of the OGD's ritual, including its correlation of Tarot and the cabbala, which is quite different from Lévi's, simply because the OGD put the Fool before card Number 1 rather than after card Number 20. The OGD also greatly extended the correlations between Tarot and the astrological elements, zodiacal signs and planets,

Etteilla

One of Gebelin's followers was a Paris barber and wig-maker called Alliette, who reversed his name to Etteilla, wrote several esoteric books in the 1780s, and became well known as a teacher and diviner of people's fortunes. He extended Gebelin's ideas on the Egyptian symbolism of Tarot; one of his packs, the beautiful Grand Etteilla, is still available today – and it has several major differences from most "standard" Tarot packs.

Eliphas Lévi

This was the Hebrew name taken by Alphonse Louis Constant, who published two books of great significance to the development of Tarot in 1855 and 1856, *Dogma de la Haute Magie* and *Rituel de la Haute Magie*. Lévi was probably the first to link Tarot with the Tree of Life of the cabbala, with its twenty-two paths between the ten Sephiroth, or Intelligences, used in cabbalistic interpretation of the relationship between man and the divine, and the twenty-two letters of the Hebrew alphabet. This correlation, which many Tarot users today assume to be as ancient as Tarot itself, is less than one hundred and fifty years old.

and it was also responsible for switching the cards 8 and 11.

There are numerous packs based on the teachings of the OGD, including those by Robert Wang (the Golden Dawn Tarot) and Paul Foster Case, but the best known was by AE Waite (1910). Waite's pack was illustrated by Pamela Colman-Smith and originally published by Rider, hence its usual names of Rider-Waite or Waite-Smith.

It should be pointed out that the divinatory meanings of the Minor Arcana in the vast majority of Tarot packs today are based on those in the Rider-Waite pack. The OGD may well have had excellent esoteric reasons for ascribing the meanings to each card, but the fact remains that these "traditional" meanings, learnt so carefully and reverently by countless thousands of Tarot users, are only about a hundred years old.

Aleister Crowley

Crowley, who earned an unpleasant reputation for some of his more extreme magical practices, joined the OGD in 1898, but fell out with them and with Mathers, forming his own order, the *Argenteum Astrum* (Silver Star) in 1905. His teachings on Tarot, extending those of the OGD, are incredibly detailed and complex, and relate (in the old alchemical tradition) everything to everything. His strange and disturbing Tarot pack,

illustrated for him by Lady Freida Harris, continues the doctrine of Gebelin and Etteilla even in its title, the Book of Thoth.

The approach to Tarot

It should by now be apparent that much of the reverence shown by users of Tarot is misplaced. This does *not* mean that Tarot should be approached in an irreverent or slapdash manner. Tarot is an extremely powerful symbolic system, whichever pack you use and whichever set of beliefs you follow, but how you approach it must be up to you.

Many people keep their Tarot pack wrapped in black silk, in a handmade wooden box. Some burn incense when they use it, and perhaps say a prayer, or play new age music; they sit on the north side of the table facing south, with the client on the south side facing north; if they are alone they face the east.

Some, however, believe one should never read Tarot for one's self. Others, taking it further, say a Tarot pack should never be bought for oneself but that it must always be a gift.

Most Tarot users are uncomfortable if someone else (except for the client) handles their cards. They believe that they have

established a mystical relationship with the cards, that the physical cards become "tuned in" to their personal vibrations. Some will "break in" a new pack by sleeping with it under their pillow for a week or so; if they acquire a second-hand pack they ritually cleanse it and then tune it in, card by card, to their existing pack by laying one on top of the other.

Each person must work out their own approach to Tarot. If you feel that every reading should be a ceremony, then that is how you should do it. But do not be horrified at someone else pulling a pack out of a jeans pocket, removing the rubber band, and doing a spread by the side of a road. Similarly, if you have a fairly free and easy approach to Tarot, try not to offend someone who is, to your mind, ridiculously reverent and ritualistic.

Never dictate to someone else how Tarot should be approached. By the same count, do not allow yourself to be dictated to; find your own way.

Which pack?

Assuming you buy your own pack, take a look at what is available; these days there is a very wide range. Most esoteric shops (even some large general bookstores) have a folder with several sample cards from each of the packs they stock, or even sample packs they will allow you to look through (in which case they will probably have removed a few cards – though anyone who thinks of stealing a Tarot pack has the wrong attitude to start with).

Choose the pack that "speaks" to you; one or two cards in particular may appeal, or it may be a feeling for the whole pack. Do not buy a pack just because it is the one friends use, unless it has a special attraction. Do not buy a pack that seems to cause discomfort or unease; if a pack does not say "Buy me", try another shop; Tarot cards do not have to be bought immediately.

Many people are quite happy with just one pack; they get to know it intimately, and it is all they need. Others will have two or three quite different packs, and use them for different purposes. If for some reason you end up with a dozen packs, it is impractical (and expensive) to keep each in a square of black silk in a wooden box in a

Below: *A handsome fan of Tarot cards designed by Aleister Crowley, and named the Thoth deck. Crowley was notorious in the late-nineteenth century and early twentieth century. After early association with the Golden Dawn magical group, he broke away to become infamous as an experimenter in his own forms of black magic. His card designs are full of erotic symbolism, and lean very much towards the dark side of human nature.*

special drawer; perhaps (if the packs are kept like this at all) only the pack used for divination need be stored in this way.

The type of pack chosen obviously depends a great deal on the type of person the purchaser is, and on personal background, knowledge and interests. For someone interested in Celtic mythology then Courtney Davis's Celtic Tarot or John and Caitlín Matthews's beautiful Arthurian Tarot could be a good choice; if the area is Greek mythology, the Mythic Tarot; if Norse, the Norse Tarot. If a more traditional pack seems more suitable, the Rider-Waite Tarot has an excellent track record. If you have a deep interest in the esoteric then the Servants of Light Tarot might lead to deeper studies. The Masonic Tarot was designed as a teaching aid for Freemasons or Rosicrucians. For those who prefer to use only the Major Arcana in their readings, there are some excellent twenty-two-card packs available. The

Top left: One of the Tarot cards – the Pope – from a pack which some claim to have been painted for Charles VI of France, c.1392. This provenance is disputed, and evidence for the origin of the pack is thin.

Bottom left: The Valet of Cups, from a Tarot series painted in Bologna in 1664. Today's Tarot reader has more variations of Tarot pack to choose from than ever before: beautiful and rare decks such as this may be available in reproduction form, but there are also hundreds of modern packs, designed to suit all tastes – from Masonic to Celtic, from Mythological to Occult.

stunningly beautiful cards of the Kashmir Tarot, for example, are individually silk-screened by hand, up to a dozen times per card, to make up the two hundred colour tones of the designs.

Uses of Tarot

The type of pack, and your approach, also depend on what you use Tarot for. The popular belief is that Tarot means divination. This is only one aspect of Tarot, and in fact many people use Tarot for divination very rarely if at all.

As the cards, especially the Major Arcana, are based on mythical archetypes, they are an extremely good focus for meditation. Again, how this is done is entirely dependent on personal choice; some people take the phone off the hook, dim the lights, light incense, and say a prayer or ritual invocation before looking closely at an individual card; they then close their eyes, summon up the image in their mind, visualize it in three dimensions, watch it move, come to life almost, feel the wind, grass or sand, hear a dog barking or a bird singing, smell the trees or flowers, taste the salt sea spray. Others, not as talented at visualization, meditate on the meaning

Left: An early French printed sheet containing the instructions for interpreting the fall of the cards, presented as a system which is essentially in the form of a game.

Below left: Three cards – the Emperor, the Devil, and the Tower – from the Court de Gebelin pack. Designed around 1780, this is claimed to be the first pack to be created specifically for the purposes of divination.

of the card. Some use ritual; others will prop a card up on their desk and look at it from time to time during the day.

Instead of one card, two or three, or even a dozen might be used, arranged in a line or in various spreads, either deliberately or randomly selected. Meditating on these is more like creating the scenario of a story, either for the single user just for that moment, or for telling to others then or later, or for writing down as a short story or poem. Some writers use Tarot for inspiration in their work. A pictorial Minor Arcana is excellent for story-telling, without the "heavy" weight of meaning you may sometimes feel from the Major Arcana.

To concentrate on a particular person, for example for distant healing, one card might be selected to represent that person, and used to focus the directed thoughts.

The use of the cards again is down to personal preference, and no one and nothing else. They do not have to be used solely for a reading. There is no reason not to simply take them out and look at them for their beauty alone.

A b o v e : *The rich and famous down the years have been just as fascinated by Tarot as ordinary mortals. In this reading in progress, the French cartomancer, Lenormand, is telling the future of the Empress Josephine at Malmaison in 1827 with much drama and aplomb.*

The ritual in divination

A lot of Tarot teachers and books say the cards should be handled as much as possible, to build up the rapport between the pack and its owner. A good deal of time should certainly be spent examining the cards, each one of the seventy-eight individually, absorbing the symbolism in the designs, reading and thinking about and learning the divinatory meanings. This is easier with a pack that has a pictorial Minor Arcana, rather than just designs of 6 Cups or 8 Wands; the pictures will indicate the meanings.

If some form of ritual is used when doing a reading, do not become dependent on the ritual itself. It is only a prop, stage scenery which might well be very useful for reaching the right frame of mind (and retaining concentration despite outside distractions) – but it is not a necessity.

If you find yourself one day panicking because you are about to do a reading and you have mislaid your sandalwood incense, you are leaning on the prop too hard. You have become hooked on the trimmings; you need to stand back and re-evaluate what you are doing.

To take a Christian analogy, a priest can celebrate the Eucharist just as well wearing a cassock and stole as in the full High Mass regalia. In a Baptist or Brethren service the pastor will probably wear a lounge suit for the Breaking of the Bread; it is no less respectful or efficacious, but in some cases people prefer all the trimmings.

B e l o w : *Two cards from the Major Arcana – the World, and Death – of a privately designed pack inspired by medieval influences and imagery.*

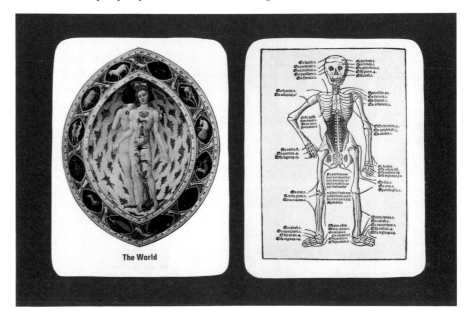

The World

Above: *Four examples from a series of lithographic Persian playing cards related to the Tarot tradition. Purists often complain that there is too much confusion between genuine Tarot and other types of elaborately designed cards. In fact this is quite understandable, and very healthy. All types of cards are part of the same tradition: Tarot, whatever the derivation you choose to believe, started out as humble playing cards; and ordinary playing cards can just as readily be used for divination and prediction.*

How does it work?

There is no doubt that Tarot does work. We react to the symbolism of the cards on many different levels, consciously and unconsciously. But how does Tarot "give an answer" when we ask a question?

Some believe that there is a guiding force or spirit which directs the shuffling and selection of the cards, so that the "right" cards appear in the "right" order in the spread.

Others, following Carl Jung, suggest the principle of synchronicity: everything in the universe is connected, including, for instance, the client's question and the selection of the cards and the time and date of birth. Certain events happen, without one causing the other; they just *happen* to happen at the same time: you could loosely call it "meaningful coincidence".

Some people think that the selection of cards is completely random, entirely unconnected to the question or to the position of the stars and that everything hangs on the interpretation – and on the abilities of the interpreter. The best professional Tarot readers, like the best palmists, not only know the tools and rules of their trade inside out, they are probably also highly sensitive to others and are reading the client as much as the cards.

There is a very strong case to be made for saying that every means of prediction or divination covered in this book is actually a means of extrapolation from character analysis. The element of prediction comes in when these considerations are taken into account:

★ this is the person I am, with all my virtues and faults, quirks and hang-ups and inconsistencies;

★ this, from my question and from our discussion, is the path I am following in this particular matter;

★ being the person I am, if I continue to follow such a path in this way, then *this* is likely to be the result – but have I also considered *these* possibilities?

Tarot can be remarkably accurate and perceptive. Whether this is because it somehow selects the exact cards which give the answer to a problem, or whether the fall of the cards is entirely random, its power is in the symbolism it contains.

Below: *A group of images from Crowley's Thoth pack.*

Symbolism

*I*t may seem strange for some readers to see analogies with Christianity in a discussion of "the Devil's picture book". Tarot is part of the Western Mystery Tradition, and for nearly two thousand years that tradition has included Christianity.

So we have, in the Major Arcana, the Pope and Papess in some packs, the symbols of the four evangelists in the corners of Number 21, the World, and three of the four great Christian virtues: Fortitude, Justice and Temperance; some say that the entire Tarot comes under Prudence, the fourth virtue.

If Tarot was originally a Renaissance teaching aid, as is quite likely, then it is hardly surprising that Christian symbols are included. Other symbols are included too: the Hanged Man can be identified with the Norse god Odin, who hung for nine days and nights from the World Ash to discover the mysteries of the runes. The Sumerian god Attis was also

Above, left and top left: Tarot, like all predictive systems, draws from a rich common well of allegory and symbolism. Similar signs and symbols can be found in astrology, alchemy, and dream imagery.

Left: *These cards are not Tarot "proper", but come from a French seventeenth-century deck designed for conjuring. Even so, the influences are clear, and it is quite evident that the Tarot symbolism is being heavily borrowed for the pastiches. In truth, there was little to choose in this period between genuine Tarot design and the design of ordinary playing cards, which were then much more elaborate and decorative.*

hung from a pine tree in an annual ritual.

The Devil, as shown in Tarot, is largely a medieval rather than a Biblical invention, based, as was so much in Christianity, on earlier gods – in this case the Celtic god Cernunnos and the Greek god Pan, amongst others.

The Wheel of Fortune shows that all things come round again: the perfection of the circle, as found in much Eastern religious philosophy, and which ultimately includes reincarnation.

The four suits of the Minor Arcana are often said to show four divisions of society: Cups (clergy), Swords (nobility), Coins (merchants) and Staves (peasants), but this is most likely a later rationalization. The four symbols are to be found in many mythologies around the world, including Ardhanari, a composite Hindu god; the left half is Shiva, holding a cup and a wand; the right half is Devi, holding a sword and a ring. The Greek god Mercury is sometimes pictured with chalice, money, caduceus (or wand) and sword. For those interested in Celtic mythology the clearest identification is shown in the Arthurian Tarot, in which Celtic scholars Caitlín and John Matthews rename the suits as the four Grail Hallows, Sword, Spear, Grail and Stone, which have both Christian and pre-Christian origins. The equivalent four Treasures of Ireland are the Sword of Nuada, the Spear of Lug, the Cauldron of the Dagda, and the Stone of Fál.

Different packs approach the symbolism of Tarot from different standpoints. The pictorial imagery they use may well be completely diffe-

rent, depending on the mythological or esoteric basis of the pack. The meanings of the cards will usually be broadly similar, but they will not be identical; this does not make one pack "better" or "worse", more or less "accurate", or more or less "authentic" – though it might make it more unusual.

The assignment and interpretation of symbolism is both universal and personal. For example, one man's strong, no-nonsense leader is another man's dictator; stability can mean stagnation, or the image of someone inside a fortified stockade can mean security and safety despite enemies all around, alternatively, it can mean that you are encircled, trapped and confined. Different packs (and different writers) will emphasize different aspects of the meanings, and this should be kept in mind when examining the cards, studying the

Below: *Judgement, the Devil, and Death, from a seventeenth-century French Tarot deck.*

accompanying booklets, or reading any book on Tarot.

Ultimately the meaning of a card is what an individual decides it to be, within the general framework of Tarot. Over a period of time your interpretation of a card's meaning might develop and change its emphasis. It could be that if you become familiar with two different packs they will develop in different directions. Learning Tarot is living Tarot – and living is never static.

The Path and Patterns of the Major Arcana

Almost every interpreter, it seems, finds a new way of setting out the path of the Major Arcana. The simplest explanation is that the Fool (i.e. the Querent, the Seeker) sets out through life, and the cards show personalities he will meet (or find within himself), the virtues he will need, and situations he will encounter, much as in Bunyan's *Pilgrim's Progress*, or many modern role-playing games.

The first nine numbered cards can be said to show a person's encounters with others, and with the external world; the last eleven numbered cards show his exploration of his own inner self; the Wheel of Fortune lies between the two.

The numbered cards can also be divided into three sets of seven:

1–7: consciousness, self
8–14: changes, others
15–21: liberation, the spirit

These same groups can be known as the Realms of Man, the Soul, and Eternity.

Alfred Douglas gives a pattern in the form of the infinity symbol ∞, with the World crossing the Wheel of Fortune at the centre and each card "mirroring" one in the opposite loop, so that the Fool and Judgement are paired, as are the Magician and the Sun, the Papess and the Moon, and so on.

The esotericist Gareth Knight identifies four quite distinct groups of four, each falling under one of the virtues (with the World representing Prudence), and the Fool and the Magician standing together as Freedom and Order:

Fortitude: High Priestess, Empress, Emperor, Pope

Temperance: Lovers, Chariot, Hermit, Wheel of Fortune
Justice: Hanged Man, Death, Devil, Tower
World: Star, Moon, Sun, Last Judgement

Cabbalists, as we have seen, ascribe each of the cards to one of the twenty-two paths between the ten Sephiroth of the Tree of Life; it was the difficulty of matching them all up sensibly which led to the switching around of some cards.

Each of these Paths has something to recommend it; but most of them require a little "tweaking" to fit every card into the desired slot. What they show is that humans delight in making patterns, and that Tarot, containing so many powerful archetypes, is ideal (and flexible enough) for illustrating the Pattern of Life in whichever way we wish to see it.

Many packs and books draw correlations between Tarot and the cabbala, astrology, runes, or the I Ching, or other esoteric systems. Because of the very nature of mythological and symbolic archetypes there are bound to be resemblances. But these systems are not the same as each other. It must be remembered that the fitting of one esoteric system on to another is *ex post facto*: Tarot was not originally developed by someone with the cabbalistic Tree of Life or a bag of runes on the desk in front of them. None of these correspondences has to be accepted as a "given truth" of Tarot.

Reversed cards
....

The idea of having an upright and a reversed meaning for each card is relatively new. It might make divination simpler to perform, because the meaning is less ambiguous, but it loses the idea, also seen in astrology, that everything contains both positive and negative aspects, and that inherent in everything is its own opposite. Cleancut, polarized values and decisions are rare in real life, and it is a mistake to impose them through Tarot.

When reading Tarot far more meaning can be teased out if all the cards are kept upright, and both the light and the dark aspects of interpretation of each card are accepted. It also means that each image is seen as the artist intended it to be, and the symbolism within it can be used more directly. If reversed cards are used the images themselves are less likely to be examined, and users are more likely to turn to books for instant interpretations.

The meanings given here for the Major Arcana

contain shades of meaning, even contradictions. Each individual should decide which aspects of each card are most relevant in the context of the rest of the reading. Always see how the cards work together; one card on its own is useless in divination.

In the case of the Minor Arcana, nearly half the cards are "negative" in any case, making reversed cards quite unnecessary. Also, no one claims that reversed "negative" cards become "positive", so why should reversed "positive" cards become "negative"?

If reversed cards must be used the meanings of the cards in question should not simply be "reversed", especially with the Major Arcana; this is naïve, simplistic, and not in the true spirit of Tarot. Reversed cards can be said to show the more problematic aspects of meaning in a card. With the briefer meanings of the Minor Arcana, look for the drawbacks that may exist even in the greatest success, for example self-satisfaction, smugness or over-confidence.

A b o v e : *Superb Persian designs on a lithographic production of playing cards strongly influenced by the Tarot. All the cards on these pages, from France, Germany (with Oriental inspiration) and Persia, clearly illustrate the changing and evolving design tradition of Tarot around the world. This is one of the delights of Tarot: nothing is "right" in absolute terms. The basic symbolism can be taken and adapted to many different cultural needs and schools of thought.*

The Major Arcana

The meanings of the twenty-two cards of the Major Arcana are both archetypal and divinatory. The Fool represents the Seeker, the Querent of either sex, most of all; but aspects of any card can be the Querent of a particular moment. A "female" card such as the High Priestess may represent a significant woman in the male Querent's life, but it may also represent the *anima*, or female side of a man's personality. The "male" cards such as the Emperor may have a similar meaning for female Querents: they may represent a significant male influence, or the Querent's *animus*. Alternatively, in each case they may not represent a person at all, but the meaning of the card.

Opposite; Top left: *The Magician from the Angel pack with the tools of his trade spread before him.* Centre left: *The High Priestess from the evocative Kashmir pack; she sits between the light and dark pillars of duality.* Bottom left: *The Empress from an early French pack; she holds a shield and a sceptre and is the embodiment of both beauty and strength.*

This page: Below: *The High Priestess, left, and a very traditional Fool from the Angel pack. The Fool here is shown as a true seeker and traveller, his bundle on his back.*

THE HIGH PRIESTESS

The Fool Not so much foolish as an innocent abroad, a young traveller setting out on life's path, unworried, inexperienced, impulsive, fresh, naïve, carefree and careless, seeking after truth and enlightenment. There can be wisdom in foolishness: the medieval fool was

THE FOOL

the only person allowed to criticize his master. Few possessions mean few responsibilities, and perhaps a lack of responsibility. A *tabula rasa*, a fresh start, potential. The beginning of the journey. The Querent.

1: The Magician The Magician shows experience, skill, discipline, self-confidence, wisdom, organizing ability, mastery and control of the four elements and the four suit symbols. He is a prophet and seer, but also the master of illusion. He is the controller and manipulator of events, and can be a cunning trickster. He shows active, creative, original thought, and implies movement and transformation.

2: The High Priestess, Papess or Female Pope The High Priestess is often shown holding a book of knowledge, and sitting between light and dark pillars, showing duality. She contains mystery, occult awareness, hidden knowledge, initiation and she has magical sexual power. She is the Guardian of the Inner Temple of the subconscious, the Otherworld, and has spiritual wisdom, intuition and insight. There can be deliberate deception, emotional instability, a lack of logical thought and planning. She is associated with all that is both positive and negative about the Moon and water. The Female Pope comes from the legend of Pope Joan in the ninth century AD.

3: The Empress As the Earth Mother goddess, the Empress encompasses the abundance of nature, fruitfulness, growth, fertility and desire. She shows both passion and sensuality, as well as warm domesticity, the home-making of the hearth. She implies beauty, creativity, the arts. She is also the strong female ruler, for good or for bad; this card can mean female domination.

4: The Emperor The Emperor displays power, majesty, strength, the four-square stability and solidity of firm rule. He suggests law, order, control and self-control, and responsibility. He is the father, the ruler, sometimes implying patriarchal and centrally imposed authority. He shows logic and reason, confidence and self-confidence, discipline and self-discipline. He represents the material rather than the spiritual world. Stability can mean stagnation.

Far right, clockwise:
This unusual Pope, "Il Papa", is from an Italian Tarot pack inspired by marine life; it was conceived as a response to the growing interest in Tarot in recent years. In an early and decorative French pack, Cupid draws his bow to unite the Lovers. The Emperor from the same pack is an imposing figure: he represents logic, power and discipline.

5: The High Priest, Hierophant or Pope Often still shown with the triple Papal crown, the High Priest is the initiatory priest, the intermediary between earth and heaven, the material and the spiritual. He can depict orthodox, traditional, and establishment religious power, and thus indoctrination, distortion of the truth and deception. But he is the guardian of tradition, the disseminator of spiritual knowledge and the revealer of wisdom. As a teacher he is usually shown with his disciples. There is also an indication of the formal solemnity of the marriage vows.

6: The Lovers or Lover Although usually shown as the Lovers, male and female, with Cupid or an Angel drawing them together, and signifying love and closeness, there is a deeper alternative meaning to this card. This is the Lover, having to choose between two loves, the spiritual and the sensual, day and night, light and dark, reason and intuition. The decision is never simple or straightforward; either choice means losing as well as gaining, and the lover can be wracked by indecision, wanting both. The implication is that the spiritual is usually the "better" choice – but perhaps not always. Whichever set of meanings is followed, this card implies change.

7: The Chariot This card shows the reconcilliation of opposites: keeping two powers which are pulling in different directions (such as the conscious and the unconscious, positive and negative, or activity and contemplation) under control and in balance, so that movement may occur under the direction of will. The conflict must be faced, and power drawn from both sides equally for progress to be stable and balanced. If there is any weakness or imbalance there will be loss of control, and the chariot will be overturned. Continual movement counters stagnation.

8: (or 11): Justice Again the idea of Justice is balance and many cards show the typical scales of justice and the sword which cleaves through ignorance and imposes a solution. Justice again represents a difficult and complex choice, but the ultimate decision, however painful, must be balanced, fair and just. There may be arbitration, but it should not be arbitrary. The choice in the Lover is personal; in Justice it lies in society, and affects others, hence the need for fairness and perhaps sternness. Justice also implies adjustment to the situation after the decision. This decision is both morally and legally binding, even if it seems to be unfavourable.

9: The Hermit Usually facing the left (inwards), the Hermit holds the Staff of Wisdom, often faith and strength, in his left hand and a lantern in his right to show the way along the difficult and stony Path of Life. His wisdom has been attained through introspection and solitary study, but he will dispense it wisely to the true Seeker after Truth and Light. Sometimes the Fool, the Seeker, must withdraw from active life and create a quiet space for solitary contemplation; this will involve sacrifice and reassessment, but must not be taken to the selfish extreme of excluding others.

10: The Wheel of Fortune ROTA, the Wheel, can be re-formed as the anagram TORA, Torah being the Hebrew book of the Law, and TARO itself. It contains the ideas of cyclic evolution, change, destiny, fate, fortune, liberation, eternity and reincarnation. The end is the beginning. The future comes from the past, through the present. The Dark Moon, the Crescent Moon and the Full Moon are a continuing cycle. This card, like the

The Hermit

The Wheel of Fortune

This page: Top left; *The Chariot from the Oswald Wirth pack.* Top right; *The Justice from a reproduction of the Cary-Yale Visconti-Sforza pack.* Middle left; *Temperance, from the Angel deck.* Middle right and bottom; *The Hermit and the Wheel of Fortune from the Dutch Haindl pack.*

World, sometimes shows the four Evangelists, illustrating the four Great Teachers, the four overlapping cycles of life. The Wheel must never be held back; circular movement means having to go down in order to come back up.

11 (or 8): Fortitude or Strength This card represents spiritual and mental strength as well as physical power. The old name of Fortitude suggests determination, and knowledge of when action is required. This is not aggressive implementation of power, but peaceful, calm, gentle use of controlled strength. Moral strength is the measured control of human passions, lusts and desires, and produces self-discipline which in turn leads to the essential spiritual attributes of health, wholeness and holiness.

12: The Hanged Man The Querent has reached a turning point. This card signifies deliberate reversal, self-sacrifice in order to achieve transformation and purification. He relinquishes material gain in favour of the spiritual. Less drastically, it suggests looking at a problem from a different direction, turning it on its head. To others, such an act might look like the behaviour of a Fool, but it is tapping the subconscious.

13: Death (sometimes untitled) As with the Wheel of Fortune, the end is the beginning. Many religions teach that death is the entrance to the new life, to a higher and greater consciousness. In many early religions the god or king was symbolically killed each year to ensure the new life of spring. This card represents challenge, transition and transformation, self-renewal and the opening up of tremendous new opportunities – but the old life must die for the new life to begin, and this takes courage.

14: Temperance Temperance is one of the four Christian virtues, and also represents balance, economy and good management. The Angel in most versions of this card is a healer, of body, mind and spirit, yet the Seeker must admit the need for healing regeneration. This is a card of moderation, not excess, with a strong element of helping others or accepting others' help. Pride must not stand in the way of healing; there must be a willingness to adapt and accept change.

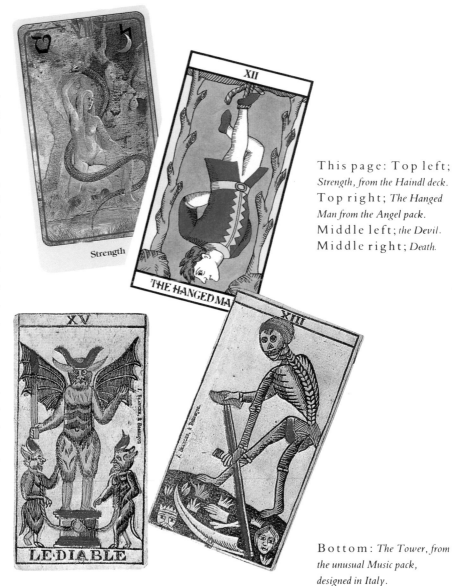

This page: Top left; *Strength, from the Haindl deck.* Top right; *The Hanged Man from the Angel pack.* Middle left; *the Devil.* Middle right; *Death.*

Bottom: *The Tower, from the unusual Music pack, designed in Italy.*

15: The Devil The man and woman bound to the Devil by chains in most versions of this card are there by their own free will – or because of weakness. There is no use blaming the Devil (or anyone else) for your own greed, lust or hatred; they are your own choice. Your pride, arrogance and selfishness are caused by ignorance and wilful immaturity. The challenge is to realize this, and break free. If not, the negative forces in you will fester and grow, hurting others who become innocent victims of your own personal weakness.

16: The Tower The Tower symbolizes sudden unexpected change which can be catastrophic, but need not be. The destruction of the Tower can be seen to represent a disaster: the loss of a job, the end of a relationship, public humiliation – but if self-destruction is avoided it can mark the beginning of a new opportunity, or a drastic change to

Right: The Moon, from the Cary-Yale Tarot pack. The Moon is a fascinating symbol, representing, as in astrology, intuition and energy, and, on the dark side, intrigue and deception.

Far right: The Star from the modern pack designed by Osvaldo Menegazzi, who draws his sources of inspiration from a wide range of images; Tarot does not have to remain within the traditional symbolic framework – each set has particular appeal to different readers.

the old order. The Tower can represent overweening pride in personal achievements, position or knowledge; it can be a good thing for this "crown" (as sometimes depicted on the top of the Tower) to be brought down.

17: The Star The Star is an inspiration, a blessing, a brightness when all else is dark, providing hope for renewal. It can signify a new age, or a rebirth, new help in the midst of adversity. There is often a similarity to the image of Temperance: a naked woman is pouring life-giving water from two pitchers, replenishing the water (the unconscious), refreshing the earth (the conscious). The peace, rest, tranquility and hope promised by the Star are healing in themselves.

18: The Moon The Moon is very much a double-sided image: intuition and inspiration with deception and danger. The Moon is cyclical, and its cycles affect us on Earth in the tides, in the visions of prophets and lunatics. But the Moon shines with reflected light, and its appearance – and the dreams and visions it engenders – can be deceptive. It can draw one into a mysterious world of fantasy and illusion.

19: The Sun The Sun is the giver of life, providing light, warmth, joy and hope. It is the essence of optimism. It has been worshipped through the ages. It signifies the start of a bright new day. It casts out darkness and deception and restores clear thinking. It signifies achievement, success and prosperity. The Sun is associated with the miracle of procreation and represents family and fatherhood. Two lovers, a child or two children are often shown on this card signifying the bright hope of the future.

XX

Judgment

Left: *Judgement, from the Kashmir Tarot. This card does not, as the name might imply to a modern reader, signify criticism, or something to be feared.*

XXI

The Universe

Far right: *The Universe, or the World, is a symbol of oneness and completion. This design is from the Kashmir Tarot.*

Below: *This is the Sun card from the Marseilles pack. The Sun represents fertility and new life – also prosperity and bounty.*

20: Judgement or The Angel In many cards an Angel calls one or more men, women and children from their graves to face Judgement – yet without any of the medieval fear of Judgement Day. Instead they are being called out of a mundane existence into a higher, greater glory. The Angel is encouraging us towards resurrection, rejuvenation and a new life. We should, however, be prepared for review and re-evaluation of our old ways, for a new life means casting off the old. We must also be prepared to accept forgiveness – which also means being able to forgive ourselves.

21: The World In the World card a figure – a transformed Fool, perhaps, or an hermaphrodite (representing balance in life) – stands or dances inside a circle of completion, which is sometimes a laurel wreath of victory, with the symbols of the four Evangelists, or the four Elements, or the four

suits of the Minor Arcana, surrounding it. It symbolizes spiritual attainment, achievement, equilibrium, completion, fulfilment. There are no restrictions any more; the testings and trials of the journey have been met, and the Fool – the Querent – has been rewarded or blessed with healing, fruitfulness, glory, joy, a new life.

The Minor Arcana

Knight of Coins

The fifty-six cards of the Minor Arcana are divided into four suits of Swords, Wands, Cups and Pentacles. Each suit contains fourteen cards.

The Suits

The Cups represent a variety of situations and emotions including: love, happiness, joy, pleasure, comfort, passions, personal relationships and deep feelings; also natural creation, the arts, and religious or spiritual tendencies. They are associated with the element of water.

The Wands or Batons represent enterprise, energy, enthusiasm, endeavour, hard work, invention, growth, progress, advancement and ambition. Their associated element is fire (in some packs, air).

The Coins, Discs or Pentacles signify material and financial matters, money, business and the qualities of reliability, resourcefulness and practicality. Their particular element is Earth.

The Swords are

Above: Although it is the Major Arcana cards which tend to steal the most attention, in design terms the Minor cards can be just as beautifully detailed and crafted. This Knight of Coins is from the Scapini Tarot.

Right: A card from each of the suits, again illustrating that charm and artistry in design are carried right through into the Minor Arcana. The 3 of Swords and 10 of Coins are from the Oswald Wirth pack, and the 10 of Wands and Knight of Cups are from the Scapini deck.

Knight of Cups

Right: *In the Angel Tarot, the suit of Coins is called the Pentacle suit. It is quite common for the names of cards or suits to change from pack to pack: this does not affect the "legitimacy" of your reading. There is no right or wrong in Tarot: find a pack that feels comfortable to you, and one that has symbolism you can easily relate to.*

associated with the mind and the intellect, with ideas, activity, force, courage, aggression, strife, difficulties, and movement for good or ill. The Swords' element is air (or, in some packs, fire).

Court cards

These usually, but not always, represent people. The King signifies man, a male principle, the authority in the suit of cards. He is connected with builders, dominators and force. He can be thought of as fire, with aspects of air.

The Queen represents woman, a female principle and the authority in the suit, with aspects of fertility and wisdom. She can be thought of as associated with water.

The Knight signifies youth, being active, mobile, a doer and seeker. He can be thought of as connected with air, with aspects of fire.

The Page represents a child (of either sex). He is associated with passivity and awakening; something new and undeveloped. His element can be thought of as earth.

In packs using different names, particularly Prince and Princess for Knight and Page, follow the meanings given for that pack. A few packs change King, Queen, Knight and Page to Knight, Queen, Prince, Princess (or, in the Servants of the Light Tarot, Maker, Giver, User and Keeper).

Although the elements are not of over-riding importance in the court cards, it is worth looking at the combination of the court element and the suit element; the Queen of Cups, for instance, will exemplify most aspects of water.

Number cards

1: The essence and creative power of the element; beginnings.

2: Duality, opposites; balance or conflict.

3: Growth, expansion, fruition, initial completion, action.

4: Four-square stability, reality, logic, reason, organization.

5: Uncertainty, changeability.

6: Equilibrium, harmony, balance.

7: Completion of a phase, success, triumph, progression.

8: Regeneration, balancing of opposing forces, harmony.

9: The ultimate force of the element.

10: Perfection through completion; the end of the road.

Cups

King: A kind, warm, friendly man, possibly religious. Perhaps not strong enough.

Queen: An "earth-mother" type of woman, sensuous, loving, caring and sympathetic. Perhaps too emotional, a dreamer.

Knight: A friendly, romantic young person representing new friends; great vision; yet can be untrustworthy.

Page: A gentle, artistic child with a reflective, contemplative nature; he can represent a new situation yet can be selfish.

1: The essence of water. The beginning of a new friendship; love, emotion, great joy and contentment. A gentle, caring person. Psychic powers.

2: A good partnership in love or business; a good balance of male and female characteristics.

3: Joy, celebration, family matters, marriage,

healing, good fortune.

4: Dissatisfaction; compromise may be necessary; boredom.

5: Loss, separation, sadness, bitterness, loneliness, disappointment in love.

6: Harmony, balance, re-evaluation, reflection on and use of past talents, ideas and friends.

7: Muddle, confusion; a bad time for decision-making.

8: Turning away from a bad situation, giving up on it as more trouble than it is worth.

9: Satisfaction, pleasure, success, achievement; possible self-satisfaction.

10: Joy, happiness, prosperity, healing, good family life, solutions to personal problems.

Wands

. . . .

King: A good communicator, negotiator and mediator; fatherly and generous. He can be auto-cratic.

Queen: A good businesswoman, appearing warm and attractive. She can be proud and temperamental.

Knight: A cheerful, alert young person involved with travelling, business and great change. He can be wilful.

Page: A lively, enthusiastic and impulsive child; the purveyor of good news. He can be unreliable.

1: The essence of fire, representing inspiration, excitement, enthusiasm, ambition, a new initiative, the birth of a new enterprise or of a child; news.

2: Partnerships which may be causing delays; bold ventures yet with restrictions.

3: A new project or job; progress and a sense of achievement, but of a hectic nature.

4: A job well done, satisfaction; a new house.

5: A challenge successfully met; clearing obstacles; courage.

6: Victory, achievement, public acclaim, celebration; good news.

7: Opposition; health problems; courage in adversity.

8: Travel, new experiences; communication; an unexpected but satisfactory solution.

9: Great opposition, some setbacks, an eventually satisfactory outcome should arise if the situation is not exacerbated.

10: Burdens and responsibilities; a lot of work for

Right, above: Some beautiful Tarot cards were produced during the French Revolution, including this Queen of Cups and King of Coins.

Below: The magnificent golden 9 of Batons from the Visconti-Sforza pack.

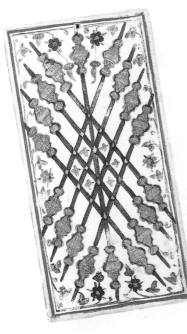

little pleasure or sense of achievement, whatever the success.

Coins

. . . .

King: A good businessman, reliable, conscientious, cautious and methodical, but not creative or artistic. He can be dull and materialistic.

Queen: A tough businesswoman, determined, practical, capable, sensible and ambitious. She can love comfort and extravagance.

Knight: A sensible, dependable, practical young person, being steadfast, reliable and meditative. He can be complacent.

Page: A practical child, student or scholar, purveyor of improvements, pleasing messages or examination results. He can be too proud of his own achievements.

1: The essence of Earth. Material, physical, practical success and security; financial improvement; new beginnings.

2: Spreading resources thinly, could be gain or loss, with natural fluctuations.

3: Laying good foundations; financial opportunity; employment or influence.

4: Security, solidly-based power or wealth.

5: Loss; the need for support or a break; financial problems leading to marriage problems.

6: Repayment of loans; generosity, charity, success through hard work.

7: Slow growth despite hard work, and disappointing results.

8: A new job, promotion; a strong, secure, well-prepared base for the future.

9: Improvement; impressive and probably unexpected success, perhaps leading to jealousy from others.

10: Achievement, security, success, maturity, power and a strong position.

Swords

King: A clever, serious, intellectual man; a good judge, who lives by the rules. He can be too calculating.

Queen: A clever, cool, confident, inventive woman. She can be devious and cunning.

Knight: A clever, ambitious, aggressive young person; an opponent to be avoided. He can be headstrong.

Page: A clever and serious child, representing strength of mind. He can be an untrustworthy spy.

1: The essence of air. New idea, thinking clearly, reason, justice, sense of power, great force, the need for great control.

2: Stalemate, delay, compromise settlement of a dispute.

3: Loss, separation, heartache, illness; broken promises.

4: Rest and recuperation, peace, serenity, relief from anxiety.

5: Arguments, fights, ruined plans, frenzy, violence, grief.

6: An important journey, a move away from problems.

7: An adjustment, or careful move after sacrifice or theft, or other external intervention.

8: A difficult situation that continues for a while, with excessive detail.

9: Worry, misery, tension, utter despair, suffering, martyrdom.

10: Treachery, a trap; ultimate failure of plans; absolute downfall.

Below left: A lovely 3 of Swords from the Oswald Wirth Tarot.

Below right: The "Valet d'Epée", or Page of Swords, also from the Oswald Wirth pack.

Doing a Reading

It is quite possible to select any number of cards, lay them out at random, and see what is in them. Most people prefer the more structured framework of a formal layout, and there are many to choose from. Some spreads use twenty or thirty cards and take a very long time (and a good memory) to interpret. Others use just a few, and seem to give equally good results, while being manageable. Many people use different layouts for different types of question, or devise their own spreads, or adapt existing ones. For example, the positions of cards signifying past or future influences and events are quite often different in different books; choose what feels right for you and stick to it. It seems more sensible for past to be to the left or below, and future to be to the right or above, but any variation can be adopted.

Similarly, whatever ritual you use is up to you; the only vital requirement is that there be enough peace and quiet for full concentration, and immersion in the cards. If incense, a candle, soft music and a black table-cloth help the reading use them; if not, ignore

The sumptuous Visconti-Sforza Tarot deck was originally used by the nobility of northern Italy in the fifteenth century. The designs of the cards and the costumes of the characters featured on them reflect the status of their users. Above left: The King of Batons; below, right: The Knight of Batons and, below, left , one of the trump cards, the Mountebank.

Far left: *A card from a fifteenth-century Florentine Tarot deck; this pack, like those of other "minchiate" cards, is unusual in that it contains many more cards than the standard number.*

Left: *A spread of cards from a traditional Marseilles-type pack.*

them. You may feel that the card themselves are magical or sacred, or they may be merely pictures on cardboard to you; whichever, have respect for what you are doing. Whatever one's beliefs on Tarot, the reading is an interpretation of another's future or characteristics, and that is not something to be done carelessly. It can be helpful to the reader to have a sketch of the layout with the meaning of each position, and the order in which the cards should be laid down.

Normally the reader sits opposite the Querent, who concentrates on the problem or question while cutting and shuffling the cards. The reader may or may not be told what the question is; obviously it makes it easier if the reader does know, because the reading can be related directly to the problem, but it can be astonishing how clear and relevant a "blind" reading can be. Also, a reading should not be a monologue; the Querent should respond to what the reader sees in the cards. This is not just for the benefit of the reader; it is vital that the Querent should be involved in the reading.

The cards are laid out, usually face down, in the order specified in the layout, then turned over one by one. If the reader and Querent are seated opposite each other, the cards should appear up-right to the reader.

In passing the pack from Querent to reader, or in turning the cards over, it is very easy to reverse either the whole pack, or individual cards, by accident. This is another argument for not using reversed cards. If reversed cards are used, it is important that both the reader and the Querent know which is the top edge of the pack, and that the cards are turned over sideways, not top to bottom. Some books advise that if the first card turned over, or a majority of all the cards, is reversed, the whole spread should be turned around "the right way up" – which seems to make a foolishness of the whole idea of reversed cards.

Some Tarot readers like to select one card, the Significator, to represent the Querent; this is usually the Court card closest to them in appearance or astrological or character attributes. This can be extremely useful in meditation, but in divination it is imposing a card on the spread, and removing that card from the rest of the spread.

Some layouts are good for general questions, such as an overview of either the Querent's position in life or a broad problem; others work well with specific questions. Avoid questions which ask Tarot to give a yes/no answer, or to say when something will happen – such as, "Will I get the job?", "How many days/weeks/months will it be until x, y, z?" Instead, ask "How can I best . . . ", "Should I . . . ", "What are the problems surrounding . . . ", "How do I overcome these problems?"

Tarot is a way of looking into yourself, analysing strengths and weaknesses, exploring probabilities, learning how to step along the Path of Life; it does not foretell a fixed future. Tarot should not be trifled with; Tarot is a library of

Below: *The goddess Juno, who is featured in an early Marseilles-type pack.*

powerful archetypes, not a quiz game for trivial questions.

These three sample layouts show how different spreads are suitable for different types of reading. Normally the full pack should be used, certainly for questions about everyday life; but sometimes for a deep question or problem you can get a deeper answer through accessing the concentrated power of the archetypal symbols of the Major Arcana by itself.

It should be stressed again that the whole spread must be examined to see how the cards relate to each other. The general tone of the reading should be ascertained with a quick preliminary look to cover such questions as:

~ When using a full pack, are there a lot of Major Arcana cards in the spread?
~ Are one or two suits predominant?
~ Are there a lot of Court cards?
~ Is there a general feeling of joy, or danger, or disappointment?

Next the cards should be examined in more detail, letting instinct or intuition draw out the aspects of each card most relevant to the reading. Finally, in the light of all that has been said during the reading, try to draw an overall conclusion. It is not unusual for the final conclusion to differ from the initial impressions; after fifteen or twenty minutes, maybe more, of teasing out a meaning, a card that originally gave one impression may now quite clearly fit into the overall pattern in a completely different way.

After the reading, the reader and the Querent should relax for a while, perhaps by having a coffee, going for a walk, kicking a ball around, or playing some music. Producing a reading is hard work, at a much higher pitch of concentration than normal and you need to quite deliberately wind down the tension.

Three Sample Layouts

The Celtic Cross

This layout is very good for general situations. It can of course be used with the full pack, but for this reading the Major Arcana by itself is more suitable. The pack is the Kashmir Tarot (Major Arcana only).

"*I seem to have hit a low point in my life, and need guidance,*" is a typical question to which a Tarot reading can be applied.

At first sight this seems a very dark spread, and also very confusing: how can the Sun be an obstacle? But follow it through. The Querent is judging himself, which shows a realization of the need for re-evaluation (Judgement), but it seems he is finding himself inadequate. The Sun, repre-

Below: The Lovers, from two unusual Major Arcanas of Italian packs called "le Mani Divinatorie" and "le Conchiglie Divinatorie."

JUDGMENT

THE WHEEL OF FORTUNE

senting brightness, hope, joy and blessing, is seen as the obstacle. Perhaps he feels that he can never attain this state; everything looks so dark, the very idea of the glory of the Sun mocks him.

But he has had strength in the past, and although this may seem lacking, it needs to be drawn on now. The Wheel of Fortune is continually turning; the Querent feels he is caught on a downturn. For the Wheel to start moving up again he must accept a drastic change in his life (the Tower), discarding his self-pity, self-mortification and lack of self-esteem. He must open himself up to achieve insight, spiritual awareness and power (High Priestess).

At present he is being pulled in many different directions, but he must take a firm grip of the reins of his life and pull everything together (the Chariot). This means the Death of his old self, which will be a change in him very visible to others. This is a major challenge, and he is frightened of facing up to it and facing up to himself, breaking the chains of self-doubt and self-hatred.

But there is a positive outcome with healing washing through him (Temperance). Once he has broken the chains all those negative aspects will be washed away and he will be refreshed and renewed.

L e f t : *Judgement and the Wheel of Fortune from the Angel Tarot.*

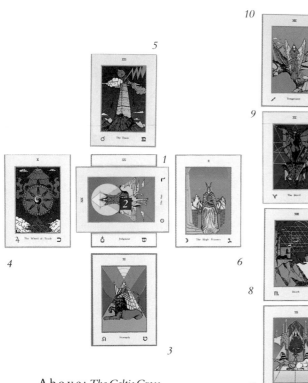

A b o v e : *The Celtic Cross layout illustrated. In this format each card deals with a particular area of concern, as follows: 1 = your present situation; 2 = obstacles; 3 = past influences; 4 = past events; 5 = future influences; 6 = future events; 7 = self (i.e. how you view yourself and/or effect others); 8 = others (how they view and effect you); 9 = hopes and fears; 10 = outcome.*

B e l o w : *The Chariot from the Angel pack.*

The Horseshoe Spread

This is good for clear questions on difficult issues such as "*Should I move in with my boyfriend?*" The pack used her is the Angel Tarot (the full pack). Tarot rarely gives a definite yes or no answer, but it can give a pretty strong idea. The tenor of the cards makes it very clear that if the Querent does move in with her boyfriend there will be many difficulties – caused, as much as anything else, by his personality. If she is prepared to struggle through there will (eventually) be a successful outcome, but it will not be easy; she should certainly think it through very carefully rather than rushing into it.

The 2 of Coins card in the past shows that resources are spread thinly, which is often the case when two people in a relationship are living separately. Things are going better at the moment (Page of Coins), because of some success in her boyfriend's life – a good exam result, perhaps, that he is very proud of; he is made confident by his success, which may be why he has asked her to move in with him. If she decides to (2 of Wands), there will be problems, delays, setbacks, restrictions; it is a bold move, and will not be easy.

Her best course right now, quite frankly, is to take a long hard look at him (Knight of Swords). He is clever and ambitious, and perhaps these are qualities she likes in him. But he is headstrong; is he bullying her into the move? How will he behave once she has moved in with him? He would be a great ally, no doubt, but there is a strong undercurrent that he might not always be supportive, and he would make a dangerous opponent; is this what she wants?

What do her friends and family think? They are against it (9 of Wands); she can always go against what they think, but she should at least listen to what they have to say.

It looks (4 of Cups) as if the move would be unsatisfactory, bringing disappointment and dissatisfaction; she would have to make a lot of compromises, and would acquire the weary state of someone who becomes accustomed to giving way all the time.

But Tarot does not dictate a fixed future; the Querent is free to follow its advice and heed its warnings or not, to make her own path in life. The 5 of Wands indicates that if she does move in with her boyfriend it will be challenging, but all the obstacles will eventually be overcome, though

1

2

3

4

5

6

7

A b o v e: *The Horseshoe spread illustrated. In this format each card position represents a particular concern, as follows: 1 = the past; 2 = the present; 3 = the future; 4 = the best course to follow; 5 = other people – their influence and attitudes; 6 = obstacles; 7 = outcome.*

it will take great courage on her part. It will take courage to say no as well (it might surprise her boyfriend, if he is not used to people challenging him); this certainly looks like the most satisfactory outcome.

The Alternatives Layout

This is particularly useful when there is a choice between two alternatives: one more probable, or more conservative, or the *status quo*, the other perhaps a little more unusual. The pack used here is the Angel Tarot (the full pack).

"Should I accept this exciting, well-paid but risky new job, or stay in my current boring, moderately-paid but secure job?"

There are no easy answers in this spread, but there is something to give pause for thought. The top three cards show the probable or orthodox choice and they seem to be indicating that the current job is not as much of a dead end as the Querent feels. The Sun, in pole position, can hardly be a more positive card. It suggests a bright new day as if the job is going to improve; if the Querent takes a different attitude towards it, he may suddenly see it in a very different light. The Sun's relationship to the family should also be considered; if the Querent is the breadwinner, he has a responsibility to his family.

The flanking cards are also positive: the Empress indicates growth and fruitfulness and again the home, while the 2 of Cups shows a good partnership. Perhaps there are major new opportunities in the current job.

The pole card of the alternative choice (the 8 of Wands) shows why the Querent is so interested: travel or new experiences, bringing a very satisfactory outcome. It may not be quite as rosy as the Querent thinks, however. The Hierophant represents a revelation of new knowledge but it might be more orthodox and hidebound than the Querent expects, possibly with an element of indoctrination and deception. He knows it is risky; perhaps it is also slightly suspect. The 9 of Coins card indicates great success, even better than expected, but this may well bring envy and jealousy from others.

The centre card can show the outcome or, as

in this case, the problem: which way should the Querent turn? His desire to take the exciting new job is obvious, but he feels a strong sense of responsibility as well. The 2 of Swords card also has an element of compromise. Perhaps he can get some interest and excitement in his current job; the cards certainly indicate the possibility of this.

A b o v e : *The Alternatives layout illustrated. In this format each group of cards represents an area of choice and indicates possible consequences. The upper cards – 1, 3, and 5 – deal with the probable or orthodox choice, or with the implications of maintaining the status quo.*

The lower three cards – 4, 2, and 6 – explore the consequences of change – these are the alternative choice. The centre card – 7 – can represent either the outcome, or a problem, depending on the nature of the decision and the way the cards fall.

I Ching

The *I Ching*, or *Book of Changes*, is one of the oldest books in the world. It is the distillation of thought of a number of Chinese sages, incorporating the philosophies of Taoism and Confucianism. Everything is seen in terms of the balance between Yin and Yang, terms used to represent the opposite and complementary rather than opposing qualities of the universe.

Above: *The lone fisherman in his boat. Chinese thought and philosophy is greatly influenced by the* I Ching, *which in turn draws its advice from the cultural beliefs of the time.*

Yang is positive, masculine, active, penetrating and light; Yin is negative, feminine, passive, receptive and dark. Neither is "better" than the other; both are necessary, in greater or lesser proportions, in balance each with the other.

Below: *Chinese coins traditionally have a hole in the centre. This one shows the eight trigrams of the* I Ching.

The Yin-Yang basis of the *I Ching* can be thought of in terms of binary mathematics. The simplest oracle gives a yes/no answer to questions: on/off, up/down, white/black, hollow circle/ solid dot (also represented by ——/– –):

Yang ○ bright, sun-like, strong, hard, vigorous, authoritative, commanding

Yin ● dark, moon-like, weak, soft, feeble, sub-missive, obedient.

The symbolic representations of these opposites produced the trigram, three lines, each either solid (Yang) or broken (Yin). In all, there are eight trigrams which represent eight natural forces, eight characteristics, or eight members of the family.

Ch'ien ☰ *heaven*	creative, male, active	father
K'un ☷ *earth*	receptive, female, passive	mother
Chen ☳ *thunder*	movement, perilousness	1st son
K'an ☵ *water*	a pit, danger	2nd son
Ken ☶ *mountain*	arresting progress	3rd son
Sun ☴ *wood, wind*	gentle, penetration	1st daughter
Li ☲ *fire*	brightness, beauty	2nd daughter
Tui ☱ *marsh, lake*	pleased satisfaction	3rd daughter

In 1143 BC the feudal lord Wên was imprisoned by the last Shang Emperor Chou Hsin; in his year in prison he studied the eight trigrams, drew out their meanings still further, and paired them to produce the hexagrams we know today. His son Duke Chou defeated the Emperor, wrote commentaries and developed the idea of the moving lines (and also posthumously promoted his father to king).

Confucius (who lived in the fifth century BC) is believed to have written more of the commentaries, and to have said in his old age that if further years could be added to his life he would spend fifty of them studying the *I Ching*. In 213 BC the *I Ching* was considered to have sufficient practical merit (along with texts on medicine and farming) that it escaped Ch'in Shih Huang Ti's great burning of books.

For the modern Western user, the phraseology of the *I Ching* often presents problems. This is hardly surprising; the oracle goes back almost five thousand years in its development, and in its present form around two thousand years, in a culture that is quite different. The Chinese laid great emphasis on order and responsibility, on

Chart of corresponding numbers and trigrams

UPPER TRIGRAM	Ch'ien ☰	Chen ☳	K'an ☵	Ken ☶	K'un ☷	Sun ☴	Li ☲	Tui ☱
LOWER TRIGRAM								
Ch'ien ☰	1	34	5	26	11	9	14	43
Chen ☳	25	51	3	27	24	42	21	17
K'an ☵	6	40	29	4	7	59	64	47
Ken ☶	33	62	39	52	15	53	56	31
K'un ☷	12	16	8	23	2	20	35	45
Sun ☴	44	32	48	18	46	57	50	28
Li ☲	13	55	63	22	36	37	30	49
Tui ☱	10	54	60	41	19	61	38	58

wise decisions and actions not just for the individual but for the good of the family, the community or the kingdom. The "wise man" or "superior man" of the *I Ching* is a leader, whether a king or general or sage; his decisions affect others. There is a lot of talk of overcoming enemies, of crossing a great river, of ancestral temples, of hunting foxes, for example – all of which is unfamiliar to the Western beginner, but which begins to fall into place as one grows more familiar with the oracle.

Using the I Ching

Like all forms of divination, the *I Ching* should be approached with some respect – not necessarily because the book itself has any powers, but because it is a book of wisdom. As the questioner, you are asking a question which is important to you; you are looking for wisdom, guidance and advice. You should then approach it with a serious mind, open to what you may be told.

Many users believe that there is a guiding spirit behind the *I Ching*, a real personality. Certainly if you treat it flippantly or carelessly, the *I Ching* has a habit of putting you firmly in your place. Perhaps the best approach is to treat the *I Ching* as you would an aged and very respected great-uncle from whom you want serious advice.

Other users rationalize their use of the *I Ching* by saying that the answers it gives are so difficult to understand that in order to find a connection between the answer and the question they are forced into thinking about their problem from

Above: *Within this beautiful painting of a Chinese dragon we also see the perfectly-matched complementary opposites of the Yin-Yang symbol, which is the basis of the* I Ching.

different angles, and so often find an unexpected solution.

The phrasing of the question is important. The *I Ching* does not foretell the future; it does not say that something will or will not happen. What it does say is what is likely to happen regarding a specific matter if a plan of action continues unchanged; it warns of dangers ahead; it gives guidance on actions and attitudes. It is also very good at saying whether the time is right for a proposed action, or whether it is better to wait for a while.

Specific questions such as "Will I pass my exam?" or "Will I become rich tomorrow?" should be avoided and phrases like "How may I best achieve . . . ?" or "Should I . . . ?" or "Would it be wise for me to . . . ?" used instead.

Keep the question clearly in your mind while casting the oracle. It is a good idea to write it down, then draw the hexagram, and write the main points of the answer; if you keep a notebook specially for this purpose you will build up a record of your relationship with the *I Ching*.

Methods of casting the oracle

The oldest method of consulting the *I Ching*, or "casting the oracle" uses fifty narrow wooden sticks. Three coins can also be used yet the stick "casting" is the most traditional.

The sticks are traditionally made from the dried stalks of the yarrow plant. In China the yarrow is commonly found on uncultivated land where sacrifices were once held. It has come to be regarded as being endowed with magical properties. The stalks are now quite widely available in specialist shops; in their place, however, pieces of bamboo or thin wooden rods may also be used.

Traditionally the book and yarrow stalks are kept wrapped in black silk on a shelf above shoulder level. Before a reading a cloth is spread on the table and the book and yarrow stalks are laid on the cloth, and incense is burnt. The questioner sits (or, more properly, kneels) facing north to consult the oracle; a Chinese sage or ruler always faces south when granting an audience.

Yarrow stalks

In order to gain fully from consulting the *I Ching* follow this method calmly and slowly:

1) Take the fifty yarrow stalks, and put one aside.

This is used to make a total of fifty sticks, fifty being a number thought to have magical meaning.
2) Divide the remaining stalks into two roughly equal piles.
3) Using the right hand, take one stalk from the right-hand pile and place it between the little finger and the ring finger of the left hand.
4) Now separate out four stalks at a time from the left-hand pile and put them aside. Four or fewer stalks should remain in the pile. Place these remaining stalks between the ring and middle fingers of the left hand.
5) Repeat with the right-hand pile, putting the four or fewer remaining stalks between the index and middle fingers.
6) You should now have either five or nine sticks between the fingers of your left hand. Note down the number of stalks between your fingers and put these stalks to one side.
7) Now turn to the pile of stalks you discarded four by four. Divide it into two roughly equal piles.
8) Repeat steps 3–5, taking first a stalk from the right-hand pile and placing it between the little finger and the ring finger; continue until you have a total of either four or eight stalks in your left hand.
9) As before, note down the number of stalks in your left hand and again put those stalks to one side.
10) Take the pile of discarded stalks and repeat the process. This time you should again have either four or eight stalks in your left hand.
11) Finally, add up the numbers you noted down at the end of each division of the stalks.
(5 or 9) + (4 or 8) + (4 or 8) = ?

The possible combinations are:

5 + 4 + 4 = 13	*(9)*	—o—	Old Yang
5 + 4 + 8 = 17	*(8)*	— —	Young Yin
5 + 8 + 4 = 17	*(8)*	— —	Young Yin
9 + 4 + 4 = 17	*(8)*	— —	Young Yin
5 + 8 + 8 = 21	*(7)*	——	Young Yang
9 + 8 + 4 = 21	*(7)*	——	Young Yang
9 + 4 + 8 = 21	*(7)*	——	Young Yang
9 + 8 + 8 = 25	*(6)*	—x—	Old Yin

(The numbers in brackets are the "ritual numbers" of each type of line.)

Having established which type of line it is, draw this as the *bottom* line of the hexagram. Go through the entire procedure with the forty-nine yarrow stalks again, from beginning to end, to find the second line from the bottom, and four more times for the remaining four lines of the hexagram, always building up from bottom to top.

Casting with coins

This is a simpler and quicker method. If you use the traditional brass Chinese coins with a hole in the middle, then the inscribed side counts as 2, and the blank side as 3. If you use ordinary currency, then tails (showing the values of the coin) is 2 and heads is 3.

Keeping the question you wish to ask clearly in your mind, toss the three coins in your cupped hands then carefully let them fall to the table. Total them as follows:

3 heads	9	—o—	Old Yang
2 heads, 1 tail	8	— —	Young Yin
1 head, 2 tails	7	—	Young Yang
3 tails	6	—x—	Old Yin

Draw the bottom line of the hexagram. Repeat five times, building the hexagram up from bottom to top.

The Hexagram, Trigrams and Moving Lines

Each of the six lines of the hexagram will be either Yang — or —o—, or Yin — — or —x—. Remember that the hexagram is made up of two trigrams; refer to the chart; the upper trigram is along the top and the lower down the side; the hexagram number is given at the point of intersection.

The meaning of the hexagram comes from the interaction of the upper and lower trigrams, with additional input from the two inner or "nuclear" trigrams, consisting of lines 2, 3 and 4, and 3, 4 and 5 (always counting up from the bottom). Some lines, especially 2 and 5, in the centre of each

trigram, are said to be strongly or weakly situated, which also affects the overall meaning.

Having read the meaning, go back to your hexagram and see if you have any "moving lines." These are the 9s and 6s created by a throw of 3 heads or 3 tails, or by totals of 13 or 25 yarrow stalks. Their names, Old Yang —o— and Old Yin —x—, refer to the concept of change which is central to the philosophy of the *I Ching*. Death gives life; the old seed dies and a new plant springs from it; old becomes young, and in doing so changes into its polar opposite. So Old Yang —o— changes to Young Yin — —, and Old Yin —x— changes to Young Yang —. If you have any 9s or 6s, draw a second hexagram, changing each one to its opposite; look this one up in the chart and read its meaning.

If you have moving lines, giving two hexagrams, the first one describes your situation now, and the second refers to later developments. In a full edition of the *I Ching*, each moving line (eg 6 in the first place, 9 in the fourth place, 6 at the top) also has its own meaning, and this should be studied carefully when reading the meaning of the first (but *not* the second) hexagram.

Meanings of the Hexagrams

Here we can only give a brief meaning for each of the sixty-four hexagrams, and unfortunately do not have the space to list the meanings of the four thousand and ninety-six possible moving lines. If you want to look further into the *I Ching*, you should buy a full edition. There are many versions on the market, but the two most widely available are the translations by Richard Wilhem and Cary Baynes, and James Legge. Each is an excellent translation, but each has its own problems.

Legge was a Victorian scholar who wrote meticulous translations of many oriental classics; however, he was not a believer in the use of divination, and this comes through from time to time in his text. There is a very good edition of Legge edited by Raymond van Over.

The Wilhelm-Baines translation is often thought of as the principle work of its kind being considered the classic, authoritative edition; however, its layout can make consulting it a cumbersome task, with the reader having to flip

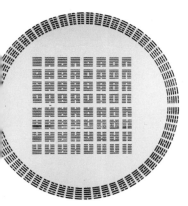

B e l o w : *The 64 hexagrams of the* I Ching *arranged in both a circle and a square.*

backwards and forwards through the book.

There are also simplified translations by John Blofeld, Alfred Douglas and RL Wing. Most other editions, including this one, are simply renderings of one or more of these translations into modern English.

We have, where suitable, kept some of the original imagery. A recurrent phrase, "crossing the great water", means an important undertaking, sometimes including a journey, or a spiritual progress, or taking a step with significant consequence.

Usually only one meaning of each trigram is given here, but any or all are involved in the symbolism and its interpretation. Thus ☰ (Sun) means wind, gentle, wood, penetration, first daughter.

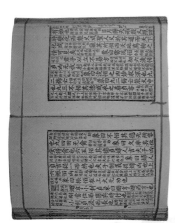

Above: *A page from a blockbook edition of the* I *Ching.*

1 CH'IEN ~ Creative

| ☰ | *heaven* |
| ☰ | *heaven* |

Understand the connections between the end and the beginning; there will be change and transformation, with everything gaining its proper advantageous nature. Be steadfast and persistent, showing firm and correct leadership. Strength, completion, success, harmony, peace.

2 K'UN ~ Receptive

| ☷ | *earth* |
| ☷ | *earth* |

It is better to follow than to lead. Be supporting; serve others. Do not take the initiative; be firm and strong, but docile, like a mare. Avoid stubbornness. Good fortune comes from sensible compliance. Gain suitable friends and lose unsuitable ones. Work with others rather than retreating into yourself. Passive success.

3 CHUN ~ Initial Difficulty

| ☵ | *water* |
| ☳ | *thunder* |

There will be many problems and obstacles, but these can be overcome through firmness and correctness. Do not undertake new initiatives;

consolidate your present position with the help of others. Patience and perseverance will guide you through the confusion and help you to weather the storm. There will be success.

4 MENG ~ Youthful Inexperience

| ☶ | *mountain* |
| ☵ | *water, a pit* |

Seek guidance and teaching from one who is wise, and he will teach you – but he will not come looking for you. Be sincere and sensibly persistent, not frivolous and rude. Pestering the sage is troublesome, and he will not teach the annoying, foolish child. Accept the greater maturity of your teacher.

5 HSÜ ~ Waiting

| ☵ | *water, a pit* |
| ☰ | *heaven* |

Wait patiently for the right moment to cross the great stream, and you will avoid the danger there. Do not rush into a new situation; choose your moment carefully and decisively, and you will succeed. Enjoy and make good use of your time waiting by using it for sensible preparation, rather than being impatient and fretful.

6 SUNG ~ Conflict

| ☰ | *heaven* |
| ☵ | *water, a pit* |

There will be conflict, danger and peril; proceed cautiously and carefully, taking advice from a wise one, and you will succeed. Do not rush into things; do not push too hard, however sincerely; do not rely on your belief that you are right; do not cross the great water, or there will be disaster.

7 SHIH ~ The Army

| ☷ | *earth* |
| ☵ | *water, a pit* |

A powerful force should be led strongly by a strong and experienced leader, who uses discipline wisely. To achieve success in a time of confusion and conflict, you must be organized and sensible, rightly earning the trust and confidence of those both senior and junior to you.

8 **PI** ~ Union

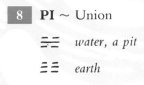

    ☵   *water, a pit*

    ☷   *earth*

There will be success and good fortune if you re-examine yourself, perhaps through the oracle, for rightness of thought and action. Others will come to you for help with their problems, and co-operation, trust and goodwill under your co-ordination will bring good results, a group consciousness from which latecomers will not benefit.

9 **HSIAO CH'U** ~ Small Restraint

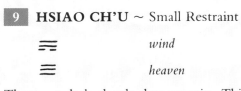

    ☴   *wind*

    ☰   *heaven*

There are dark clouds, but no rain. Things look discouraging; there may be delays caused by disproportionately small things, but there will be success in the end. Restraint works both ways: be patient and gentle, exerting only a small influence. Do not make any major decisions or actions. Use the time to develop your skills and wisdom.

10 **LÜ** ~ Treading Carefully

    ☰   *heaven*

    ☱   *a marsh*

One treads on the tail of a tiger, but is not bitten. If you are the one treading, you are fortunate, and should tread more carefully. If you are the tiger, you show admirable restraint. The strong person shows mercy and restraint; the weak has been allowed to overstep the mark because of his gentle manner. There is progress and success; despite the inherent danger, both parties maintain their composure, with love or friendliness.

11 **T'AI** ~ Peace

    ☷   *earth*

    ☰   *heaven*

The high and low, the superior and inferior, the strong and docile, work peacefully and harmo-niously together; there is good fortune and success, peace, prosperity and growth. The influence of the mean-minded fades, while that of the superior man grows. You are in a position to help others; do so.

12 **P'I** ~ Stagnation

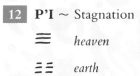

    ☰   *heaven*

    ☷   *earth*

Heaven and Earth are not in communication with each other; there is a lack of understanding between the high and low, the superior man and the inferior; the inferior may get the upper hand. Delay, decay, stagnation, disharmony, destruction.

13 **T'UNG JEN** ~ Companionship

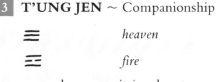

    ☰   *heaven*

    ☲   *fire*

Progress and success; it is advantageous to cross the great stream. The superior man, with intelligence, strength and elegance, shows perseverance, leadership and wisdom; he can understand all minds under heaven. There will be friendship, fellowship, companionship, harmony under his guidance. A good hexagram for unselfish lovers.

14 **TA YU** ~ Abundance

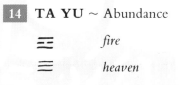

    ☲   *fire*

    ☰   *heaven*

Great progress and success, with strength, creativity, inspiration, brightness and fruitfulness, perhaps in cultural or artistic areas. Beware pride and complacency; this success has been achieved through humility. Uphold what is good; suppress what is not.

15 **CH'IEN** ~ Modesty

    ☷   *earth*

    ☶   *mountain*

Modesty and humility, even in greatness, brings progress, success and good fortune with honour and respect. The great should display moderation, not excess and pride.

Below: *The sage and emperor Fu Hsi, said to have devised the eight trigrams around 2,852 BC.*

16 **YÜ** ~ Harmony, Calm Confidence

☳ *thunder*

☷ *earth*

Feudal princes may be set up, and the hosts set in motion. A good time for well-organized, well-structured endeavours, with delegated responsibility. Thunder clears the air like inspiring music clears and concentrates the mind. The spiritual and the material elements should be in balance.

17 **SUI** ~ Following

☱ *marsh*

☳ *thunder*

Great progress and success as a result of being firm and correct, but also flexible and adaptable to changing conditions. The strong and serious must sometimes defer to the weaker and light-hearted. Others will follow your lead as long as they retain confidence in you; it is up to you to maintain this.

18 **KU** ~ Arresting Decay

☶ *mountain*

☴ *wind*

There will be progress and success, and advantage in crossing the great water. By carefully thinking through the situation before acting, and evaluating it afterwards (three days for each stage is suggested), you will halt the decay and confusion which currently besets you. If you act on it, this is an auspicious hexagram.

19 **LIN** ~ Approach, Advance

☷ *earth*

☱ *marsh*

Progress and success for some time (a period of eight months is suggested in the original), then there will be decay and decline. This is natural, as the growth of Spring gives way eventually to the decay of Autumn. Show a good example to those under you, through your concern and responsibility for them.

20 **KUAN** ~ Contemplation

☴ *wind*

☷ *earth*

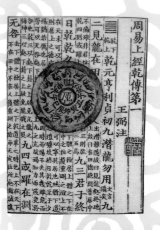

The worshipper has washed his hands but not yet presented his offerings; you are seen to show sincerity, seriousness and dignity as you contemplate the natural cycle of the seasons. Keep in touch with your kingdom and your people; watch them, take in their concerns and ideas, and give them your help. Remember that while you are contemplating them, they are also watching you.

21 **SHIH HO** ~ Biting Through

☲ *fire*

☳ *thunder*

By biting through an obstruction you unite your jaws. So "bite through" obstacles and problems, administer the sword of judgement and justice, perhaps by exercising the law, to bring unity, success and harmony to and with others.

22 **PI** ~ Adornment

☶ *mountain*

☲ *fire*

Adornment and ornamentation are part of society, and have their rightful place, but we should not confuse them with things of genuine importance. Here we see form – public image – raised over content; small things of little importance but which look good may be done, but avoid major decisions.

23 **PO** ~ Falling Apart

☶ *mountain*

☷ *earth*

It is not advantageous to make any move in any direction. Strengthen your current position, and wait; the small men currently in favour will not be there for ever. Stay where you are; do not try to put anything right. Remain calm; you can do nothing to help yourself right now, so help others instead.

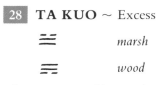

Left: *A page from a tenth-century edition of the ancient Chinese divinatory text, the I Ching.*

Below: *The trigrams of the I Ching and the twelve Chinese zodiacal animals are seen in this image of the spiritual world of the all-encompassing Tao.*

24 FU ~ Returning

☷   *earth*

☳   *thunder*

You may move freely; there is advantage in all directions. No one will oppose you; friends will come to you. Everything becomes harmonious and successful; good fortune is returning. Keep a firm goal in mind; this is a cycle of new growth, so let things grow.

25 WU WANG ~ Innocence, Integrity

☰   *heaven*

☳   *thunder*

There will be great progress and success if you are firm and correct, but if you and your actions and motivations are not correct and pure there will be error, and no advantage in any direction. Integrity is the key to success. Insincerity will bring failure. You must be in touch with the simple flow of nature, the will of heaven.

26 TA CH'U ~ Restraining Force

☶   *mountain*

☰   *heaven*

Good fortune and powerful force and energy if you can give yourself to the service of others without trying to keep honours and advantages for yourself and close family and friends. It is advantageous to cross the great water. Keep in mind the words and wisdom of great ones of the past, so strengthening your character.

27 I ~ Nourishment

☶   *mountain*

☳   *thunder*

With firm correctness there will be good fortune if you look to the nourishment of others, their bodies, minds and spirits, as well as nourishing yourself. What goes in and comes out of the mouth – food and words – should be moderate.

28 TA KUO ~ Excess

☱   *marsh*

☴   *wood*

The main roof-beam is overloaded and could collapse at any time, bringing everything down on top of you. You can avoid disaster by fast action and movement, and bring success. This is a critical moment; gentle behaviour is indicated.

29 K'AN ~ The Pit

☵   *water, a pit*

☵   *water, a pit*

Water pours unceasingly, maintaining its flow; so should our sincerity and virtue. There is great material danger, which sharpens the mind; the danger will not harm if you maintain confidence in your ability to succeed and learn from it, teaching others virtue.

30 LI ~ Brightness

☲   *fire, brightness, beauty*

☲   *fire, brightness, beauty*

Everything in nature fits in place: the Sun and Moon in the heavens, plants drawing their life from the Earth, the docile cow depending on its owner. Your brightness and clarity of mind depends on righteousness and virtue, which provide natural nourishment for enlightenment. Your brightness will then spread to the four corners of the Earth, bringing good fortune.

31 HSIEN ~ Attraction

☱   *marsh*

☶   *mountain*

As heaven and Earth attract each other, bringing creation, so do a man and a woman, bringing good fortune; sages influence and attract the minds of men, bringing harmony and peace. The stronger man freely lies under the weaker woman, bringing joy to both; so should the superior man submit to the heavens. The marriage of opposites, the firm and the yielding, involves submission of the one to the other, bringing strength and joy.

32 HENG ~ Continuity

☳ *thunder*

☴ *wind*

Successful progress and no error come from being firm and correct; movement in any direction is advantageous because of perseverance and continuance. Stand firm, be constant, have endurance and determination, and perpetuate your way with your goal in mind.

33 TUN ~ Retreat

☰ *heaven*

☶ *mountain*

Retreat or withdrawal from a harmful position will be successful, but it is important that your timing be right, neither too soon, before you are ready, nor too late, when you are trapped. Do not show fear or anger in retreat, but remain dignified. Only small actions will be successful.

34 TA CHUANG ~ The Power of the Great

☳ *thunder*

☰ *heaven*

It will be advantageous for the superior man to be firm and correct, displaying the character of heaven and Earth. Be careful in your strength to do only what is right; avoid anything that is improper, which would be an abuse of your power.

35 CHIN ~ Progress

☲ *fire*

☷ *earth*

The prince is rewarded for his service in securing the peace, showing loyalty to his king; the king presents him with numerous horses and receives him three times in one day. The superior man shines with his virtue.

36 MING I ~ Darkening of the Light

☷ *earth*

☲ *fire*

Brightness enters into the midst of the Earth and is obscured. Realize the difficulty of your position, and keep the brightness of your intelligence, character and feelings hidden, meanwhile constantly improving your virtue.

37 CHIA JEN ~ The Family

☴ *wind*

☲ *fire*

Let each in the family behave as befits their position: the father and the son, the elder and younger brother, the husband and the wife; this is an image of society. It is most advantageous that the wife be firm and correct. Co-operation between the husband and wife in their different roles maintains the strength and stability of the family.

38 K'UEI ~ Disunion

☲ *fire*

☱ *marsh*

Fire moves upwards while the waters of the marsh move downwards. Two sisters living together will disagree. Yet the superior man accepts the need for diversity; through co-operation and appreciation of differences there can be unity, as between a man and a woman with a common will.

39 CHIEN ~ Obstacles

☵ *water*

☶ *mountain*

There are difficulties; arrest your steps to avoid the peril ahead. Going to the south and west is favourable, but not to the north and east; be responsive, not immobile, and there will be success. There will be advantage in going to a great man.

40 CHIEH ~ Removing Obstacles, Liberation

☳ *thunder*

☵ *water*

There is advantage in the south and west if there is a need for movement; and in returning home if not, to the old, normal ways, the middle course.

B e l o w : *A porcelain figure of Kuan Yin, the Chinese goddess of mercy and compassion.*

When winter ends, the rains bring the plants into bud: natural fruitfulness. The superior man forgives errors and is merciful.

41 SUN ~ Decrease

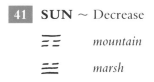

mountain

marsh

If there is sincerity there can be good fortune even in decrease. A sincere offering of just two small bowls of rice is better than a much greater but insincere offering. It is good to reduce that which is in excess, curbing anger, controlling desires, refining the character.

42 I ~ Increase

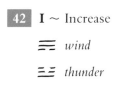

wind

thunder

In this matter there will be advantage in every movement. Now is the right moment to cross the great stream. The satisfaction of the people is unlimited because of the brilliant blessings from heaven, and the Earth is fruitful and bounteous. Those above, who are rich and generous, must show no pride; to rule is to serve. The superior man, seeing what is right, emulates it, and corrects his faults.

43 KUAI ~ Resolution

marsh

heaven

He who wishes to proceed must denounce the wrongdoer in the Royal Court, and appeal sincerely for sympathy for his own cause. This will place him in peril. He must also make his own people understand that he is unwilling to take up arms, which would be weakening. He must keep his goal firmly in mind. There will then be good fortune.

44 KOU ~ Encounter and Temptation

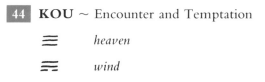

heaven

wind

An unexpected encounter and temptation. Do not marry or associate for long with a bold, strong

woman. When heaven and Earth encounter in a balanced way there is natural creation; but beware when the inferior person has too much influence, however tempting it is to give in. The sovereign should rule, and make pronouncements. What is done at this time is of vital importance.

45 TS'UI ~ Gathering Together

marsh

earth

The king goes to his temple to meet his ancestors and make offerings. It is advantageous to meet the great man. If there is firmness and correctness there will be great success. Making sacrifices will bring good fortune. Keep your goal firmly in mind. Joining with others brings understanding.

46 SHENG ~ Ascending

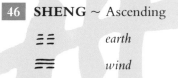

earth

wind

There will be great progress and success in upward advancement from obscurity into power. Meet with the great man without anxiety; there will be congratulation and merit. Have both flexibility and obedience. Advancing south – persistent activity – brings good fortune.

47 K'UN ~ Oppression

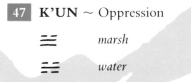

marsh

water

Restriction and exhaustion; there is a possibility of progress and success. The truly great man, prepared to sacrifice even his life for his purpose, will fall into no error and will have good fortune; but simply making speeches will do no good. If you can endure the oppression, maintain your integrity and gain self-understanding, there will eventually be regeneration.

48 CHING ~ The Well

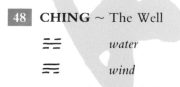

water

wind

A town may be moved, but not its well. A well does not become exhausted; however many peo-

Above: *The eight trigrams in a circular formation.*

PEACH

A b o v e : *Chinese fortune-telling cards can have very beautiful illustrations. A variety of symbols is used, including people, fruit and animals.*

F a r r i g h t : *It is now possible to buy both* I Ching *cards and Mah Jong cards for use in Chinese fortune-telling.*

ple draw from its depth it provides nourishment and refreshment. But if the rope is too short or the bucket is broken there will be misfortune. Needs remain constant; the superior man gives guidance and encouragement. Beware of superficiality, carelessness and neglect.

49 KO ~ Revolution

☱   *marsh*

☲   *fire*

A time of change; it will only be believed after it has been accomplished. Like fire and water extinguishing each other, or two daughters in the same home fighting, there will be upset and disruption. But the seasons supplant one another in their advance; once the benefits can be seen there will be approval and no regret. Gradual, regulated, well-timed change brings transformation.

50 TING ~ The Cauldron

☲   *fire*

☴   *wind*

The sages cook their offerings before presenting them to God, and prepare great feasts to nourish their wise and virtuous ministers. The practical is dedicated to the spiritual, with understanding, obedience and devotion, and increased perception. Great progress and success.

51 CHEN ~ Thunder

☳   *thunder, movement, perilousness*

☳   *thunder, movement, perilousness*

Ease and development, movement and success. He waits apprehensively, but outwardly cheerful. When the thunder crashes, terrifying everyone else, he is unperturbed and able to present his sacrificial wine at the temple without spilling it. By being aware of forthcoming danger you are prepared for it and overcome it through self-possession and concentration on what is pure. Good fortune and happiness.

52 KEN ~ Stillness

☶   *mountain, arresting progress*

☶   *mountain, arresting progress*

Rest when it is the time to rest, act when it is the time to act, each at its proper time, and one's progress will be brilliant. Quiet meditation, composure and inner stillness overcome outside distractions, and allow one to be ready to act at the right time.

53 CHIEN ~ Gradual Progress

☴   *wind*

☶   *mountain*

The marriage of a young lady brings good fortune. Gentleness and steadfastness together with being firm and correct in one's steady advancing, following the right path step by step in virtue, brings great advantage. A tree growing on the mountain symbolizes gradual progress and growth.

54 KUEI MEI ~ The Marrying Maiden

☳   *thunder*

☱   *marsh*

The marriage of the younger daughter to an older man means the end of her maidenhood and the beginning of her motherhood. There is misfortune and no advantage; the balance is wrong; she is becoming the junior wife, the concubine, and must remain subordinate and passive.

55 FENG ~ Abundance

☳   *thunder*

☲   *fire*

Greatness comes from movement directed by intelligence. The king has reached the zenith, but must not have any anxiety for what must follow, for naturally the Sun declines once it has climbed the sky, and the Moon wanes once it is full. This is the way of nature, and must also be so with man. Abundance and brilliance do not last forever; use them to sustain you through the period of decline.

56 LÜ ~ The Travelling Stranger

☲   *fire*

☶   *mountain*

There will be some progress and success, in small

matters; a traveller cannot hope to achieve great things. If the traveller is firm and correct, displaying humility and integrity, there will be good fortune.

57 **SUN** ~ Gentle Penetration

≡≡ *wind, gentle*

≡≡ *wind, gentle*

There will be achievement and progress in small things. There is advantage in movement in any direction. It is also advantageous to see the great man. Do not aim for revolution, but for improvement and delicate correction, as a gently penetrating wind slowly bends the trees; suggest rather than dictate.

58 **TUI** ~ Joy

≡≡ *marsh, lake*

≡≡ *marsh, lake*

Pleased satisfaction. Progress and attainment will come from being firm and correct. When the feelings of men are in line with the will of heaven, pleasure makes them forget their toils, and even the risk of death when they are surmounting dangerous difficulties. The superior man enjoys stimulating conversation and joint activities with friends.

59 **HUAN** ~ Dispersion

≡≡ *wind*

≡≡ *water*

Progress and success. The king goes to his ancestral temple without being distracted; it is advantageous to be firm and correct. It is advantageous to cross the great stream. The wind blows on the water, dispersing the waves. Egotism and divisiveness are dispersed by integrity, persistence and continuity, allowing the release of co-operative, creative energy.

60 **CHIEH** ~ Restraint

≡≡ *water*

≡≡ *marsh*

Understanding of limitations brings progress and

success, but if the regulation or restraint is too severe it will lead to exhaustion. Gentle restraint, like the cycle of the seasons, allows the natural governing of the country, and no one suffers for it.

61 **CHUNG FU** ~ Innermost Sincerity

≡≡ *wind*

≡≡ *marsh*

Sincerity reaches to and affects even pigs and fishes, and brings good fortune. With pleased satisfaction and flexible penetration, sincerity will transform a whole country, avoiding unnecessary punishments. There is advantage in crossing the great stream, and in being firm and correct. Selfless sincerity brings success in even the most difficult things.

62 **HSIAO KUO** ~ Small Things

≡≡ *thunder*

≡≡ *mountain*

Do not aim too high; the bird's song is sweeter when it is flying low. Small things may be done successfully, but not large things. Attend to the small details, especially in public endeavours.

63 **CHI CHI** ~ Completion

≡≡ *water*

≡≡ *fire*

At the point of completion there will be progress and success only in small matters, by being firm and correct. Good fortune and order at the start turn, at this point of completion and equilibrium, to disorder at the end. The superior man guards against evil before it comes.

64 **WEI CHI** ~ Before Completion

≡≡ *fire*

≡≡ *water*

Some success, but it does not follow through to the end. The little fox has almost crossed the stream, but gets its tail wet. There is still danger. The superior man carefully studies all matters and their rightful places.

Runes

Above: *One method of casting the runes is simply to shake some out of the bag, and read these. This is a modern manufactured set available in esoteric bookshops.*

The ancient Norse use of runes as an alphabet is probably around two thousand years old, although many of the symbols themselves are much older. Runes marks on stone or wood are today used as a powerful divinatory system. The word "rune" is linked with the Old Norse word for "mystery" or "secret", and with an old German word for "whisper", so runes have always had an esoteric element. It seems likely that runes were developed as a means of carving symbols and words on wood or stone, hence the characteristic straight lines.

In the same way as the word "alphabet" comes from the first two Greek letters, alpha and beta, the usual name for the runic alphabet is Futhark, taken from the first six letters, FUThARK.

Just as there are several variations of the Latin alphabet, similarly there are several versions of the runic alphabet, the most common being known as the Elder Futhark,

Below: Runes continued to be used magically, in prayers, invocations and charms, long after Christianity and the Latin alphabet spread through Scandinavia. They were outlawed in Iceland in 1639 as "witchcraft", but were still used secretly; one user was burnt at the stake in 1681.

the Younger (or German) Futhark, and the Anglo-Saxon Futhark. These, and others, have had 14, 16, 24, 28, 29 or 33 characters, the last being found in ninth century AD in Northumbria. The Elder Futhark, which is used in divination, has 24 characters.

It is important with runic divination, as with every divinatory system, to place it in the setting of mythology. In Norse mythology, Odin hung upside down from a tree for nine days and nights in a deliberate self-sacrifice, at the end of which he discovered, was given, or created the runes; the Tarot Hanged Man recalls his sacrifice.

With the tremendous reawakened interest of the last few years in all things Celtic the Norse influence is again being emphasized as a vital part of our cultural background. The English language, for example, is largely Norse Germanic in origin. Four days of the week are named after Norse-Germanic gods, rather than the more familiar Greek and Roman deities:

Tuesday – Tyr/Tiw/Zio/Ziu – the defender god
Wednesday – Odin/Woden/Wodan/Wotan – the All-Father
Thursday – Thor/Thunor/Donar/Donner – the god of thunder
Friday – Frigg/Fricg/Frigga/Fricka – the spinner of thread
(or) – Freyja/Freo/Frija/Freia – love and war, life and death

(The Old Norse, Old English, Dutch and German names are given in order.)

Anyone wanting to learn the use of runes must also become familiar with Norse mythology: they are inseparable.

Meanings of the Runes

These are the twenty-four runes of the Elder Futhark, giving each symbol, its name, the phonetic sound, and the meaning of the name, and then the divinatory meanings. If when runes are turned over their symbols are upside down, these meanings should be reversed, or seen in a more problematic light. Note that several of the runes are non-reversible, i.e. they – and their meanings – are the same either way up.

A b o v e : *There are many different magical elements in this page from "Book of Shadows," including vertically-running runes, the seven-branched tree of Judaism, a bat-winged androgyne symbolizing alchemical union, and a two-headed dragon.*

First Aett

Feoh – F – Cattle

Income, wealth, prosperity, property, status, power, control

Ur – U or W – Wild Ox

Strength, raw power, a chance to prove yourself, sudden change

Thorn – Th – A thorn

Protection (physical, mental and spiritual); raw double-edged luck

As or Ansur – A – A god

Odin, authority, divine force, wisdom, knowledge, communication

Rad – R – A wheel

Movement, a journey (including spiritual), exploration, progress

Ken – K or hard C – A bonfire

Primal fire, illumination, creativity, health, recovery, new love

Gyfu or Geofu – G – A gift

Giving (and receiving), talent, opportunity, partnership, union

Wyn – W – Joy

Joy, happiness, peace, creative work, winning, success, travel

Second Aett

Hagal – H – Hail

The completely unexpected, a disruptive sudden event

Nyd – N – Need

All needs and necessities: shelter, food, warmth, safety, security

Is – I – Ice

The freezing of movement or action, immobilization, a pause or delay

Ger – J or soft G – season

Harvest, fruits, a fitting conclusion, justice, the cycle of the year

Eoh or Yr – EO or Y – Yew tree

The longbow, protection, defence, death and rebirth, struggle

Peorth – P – A dice cup or game piece

The game of life, potency of fate, divination, disclosure, secrecy

Eolh – Z – Protection, or a hand greeting

Friendship, protection, a willing sacrifice, healing

Sigel – S – Sun

Victory, a successful resolution, brilliance, clear vision, consciousness

Third Aett

Tyr – T – The war god

Justice, courage, honourable combat (physical, emotional or spiritual)

Beorc – B – Birch tree

Purification, regeneration, fertility, the home, beginnings

Eoh or Eh – E – A horse

Travel, co-operation, trust, partnership, marriage, change, adjustment

Man – M – Man, as in human, rather than male

Human experience, co-operation, interdependence, sharing, assistance

Above: An early sixteenth-century English Shepherd's Calendar, showing the seven astrological planets and the days of the week named after them; note also the zodiacal signs ruled by each one. In English, Sunday, Monday and Saturday are named after the Sun, Moon and Saturn, but the other four days are named after Norse gods, showing the tremendous Norse influence on British and other cultures.

ᛚ **Lagu – L – Water**

Spiritual or psychic power, intuition, imagination, flowing movement, love

ᛜ **Ing – ng – The god Ing**

Protection of the home, male sexuality, energy, light, completion

ᛞ **Daeg – D – Day**

Light, divine light, increase, growth, a change of heart, a new start

ᛟ **Othel or Odal – O – Native land, possession, home**

Belonging, togetherness, the family, integrity, property, the land

Using runes

Runes can be bought from most esoteric shops, but in order to establish a close identity with them it is better for users to make their own. They should be made of a natural substance, such as stone or wood. Small flat pebbles of roughly the same size are ideal. The runes can be painted on, and the pebbles varnished. Or cut slices from a thin piece of wood, preferably a discarded tree branch, about an inch (or 2.5 cm) in diameter, and either carve or burn the runes into the wood.

It is very common to find a blank rune in modern shop-bought sets; this is not a spare, but is

a recent addition to the twenty-four runes of the Elder Futhark. It is called the Wyrd, and is supposed to represent Karma (the idea that fate or destiny holds each of us in its web) though the web of the Wyrd allows far more freedom of movement than its eastern counterpart. Those who use it say it rules all the other runes either by dominating any spread in which it appears or (with some spreads) by indicating that a particular question should not be pursued. But apart from doubts about the legitimacy of adding a new (non-)symbol to a two-thousand-year-old system, the concept of destiny is already quite adequately covered by the Peorth rune.

As with Tarot, the rituals followed with runes should be what feels right for each individual. The runes can be kept in a cloth bag (of natural material), and many people, with new runes, keep the bag next to their skin for a week or two, and sleep with it under the pillow. It helps to handle the runes as much as possible, especially when learning their meanings.

The runes can be cast on any flat surface, but again it is customary to spread a white cloth on the table or the floor. The presence of Odin or another Norse god or goddess can be invoked before starting. The user's attitude, as with all divinatory systems, should be respectful; runes are ancient symbols that can "speak" on many levels.

A basic principle of Norse philosophy is that if you receive a gift you must give something in return. If you ask the runes for advice, at the very least they should be given serious attention – and you should be careful to thank whatever power you believe lies behind them when the advice is obtained.

There are many different ways to cast the runes. The simplest is to reach into the bag, draw out a handful, and cast them on the cloth, only reading those which fall with the rune visible. Alternatively all the runes can be spread face downwards on the cloth, and then swirled around to "shuffle" them; the right number is then selected for the spread that is used. Unlike the "random" deal of Tarot cards, runes can be chosen (sight unseen); many users say that they get a clear feeling from the ones they are to pick up.

Initially it is probably wise to keep spreads simple. Again like Tarot, there is no reason why different spreads should not be devised, as long as it is understood what each position means.

And once more like Tarot, it is the combination of runes in a spread which is important. Any rune can modify – perhaps strengthen, weaken, freeze (hold) or delay – any other. This principle is even more important in rune-script and bind-runes. Pairs of runes must be interpreted as a combination, affecting each other, as in this example, which also illustrates the effects of reversed runes.

This is a useful straightforward spread, here addressing the question, *"How should I get out of debt?"*

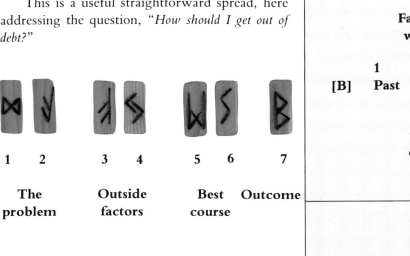

1	2		3	4		5	6		7

The problem		Outside factors		Best course	Outcome

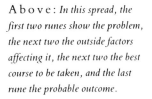

A b o v e : *In this spread, the first two runes show the problem, the next two the outside factors affecting it, the next two the best course to be taken, and the last rune the probable outcome.*

The problem, as is often the case with finance, seems to be a matter of bad advice (AS reversed) as much as anything else. DAEG in a combination is an increase-rune, so the bad advice – or lack of communication and wisdom – may seem to have been increasing. However, DAEG is a very favourable, positive rune, and when in combination with a reversed rune it often mitigates the bad effects of that rune, meaning here that the result of relying on the bad advice might not actually be quite as bad as it seems.

The hoped-for harvest (GER) is non-existent, in fact negative (though GER itself is non-reversible). The very clear lack of money and control (FEOH reversed) may be rightly deserved; one meaning of GER is justice, or just fruits. There is also a strong sense of the passing of the seasons, however; the debt might be seasonally caused – a lot of bills coming at the same time of the year, for example.

MAN reversed looks negative, but it is in fact the solution: the successful resolution (SIGEL – and it is very promising to see this rune in the Best Course position) is to stop depending on others, and sort it out for yourself through clear vision. Remember that the problem seemed to stem from accepting bad advice. You must learn to rely less on others and step out on your own.

The outcome is extremely positive (BEORC): regeneration and renewal, movement towards becoming a purer and fuller person.

Here are two different versions of another rune layout:

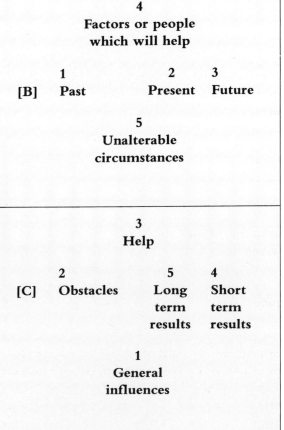

There is no reason why the popular Celtic Cross Tarot spread should not be used for runes as well.

A more complicated spread is to lay out twelve runes in a circle or clockface, starting (usually) at the nine o'clock position and proceeding clockwise, then placing a thirteenth rune in the centre. Each of the twelve represents an equivalent to one of the twelve astrological houses, as in the list below; the central rune represents both the essential characteristics of the rune caster and the overall influence of the spread.

1. Health
2. Finance
3. Family, close friends and communications
4. Home and home comforts
5. Talent and creativity
6. External influences, the outside world
7. Love and sexual relationships
8. Legacies, deaths and serious illnesses
9. Travel and spiritual progress
10. Career success
11. Social relationships
12. The inner life, desires and fears of the rune caster

Rune Magic

If a rune cast can predict what lies ahead in the Web of Life, it might be possible to bring about a desired effect by deliberately creating a group of runes in a particular order: a rune-script. Usually three or five runes are written out to draw and hold on to love, or peace, or success, or wealth, either for the writer or for the person for whom he is performing this magic. Because of the power within runes, and the ease of making a serious mistake, perhaps by putting the runes in the wrong order, rune-scripts should only be attempted by those who are used to casting runes.

Bind-runes are a similar idea, but here the runes (usually only two or three) are superimposed on each other. Bind-runes can make attractive pieces of jewellery and can be worn as charms or talismans to ward off danger, for example, or to encourage a peaceful atmosphere, or protect the wearer against ill health. There is no question of magically binding a person (this would be dark magic and an extremely dangerous practice which should be completely avoided); the runes are

Above and below:
Runes are usually made up from straight lines, which are easier to carve in stone or wood.

bound to each other.

To make a bind-rune, or buy one from an esoteric shop, it is important to know which runes are within its design, and how they react together. It is a mistake to wear any esoteric jewellery or talismans without knowing exactly where they come from symbolically – and, preferably, physically. If it is not home-made, it should be made specifically for the wearer by someone well trusted. The intent which goes into its making is at least as powerful as the symbolism in its design.

N u m e r o l o g y

*N*umerology is a special part of the art and science of numbers, which seeks to find a hidden significance in words, particularly in people's names, by changing the letters to numbers.

As children, many people devised simple codes (more correctly, ciphers) in which numbers were substituted for letters or vice versa. The Elizabethan Occultist John Dee, official astrol-oger to the court of Elizabeth I, did much the same – and in fact the most complex, and theoretically almost unbreakable govern-ment ciphers today start off from the same principle. In telecommunications it is standard practice for the top row of a typewriter keyboard to be used as digits so that Q represents 1, W=2, E=3, R=4, T=5, Y=6, U=7, I=8, O=9 and P=0.

In the history of written communication, letters were developed long before numbers (though simple tally marks probably pre-dated letters by just as long). Today in much of the world the Arabic numerals 1, 2, 3, 4, 5, 6, 7, 8, 9 are used, as well as the later addition of 0. In many early cultures, though, the same symbols

A b o v e : *The realm of numbers and words has always had great significance for divination and prediction. Numerology, codes, cyphers, secret writing, automatic writing and graphology all play their part in unveiling the mysteries of the future, and all have their particular devotees. This magic illustration depicts sigils (representative symbols) which form a secret code, based on a geomantic design which consists of four levels of stars or pairs of stars subjected to graphic analysis.*

stood for numbers as for letters; Norse runes are one example, as are the Roman numerals I, II, III, IV, V, X, L, C, and M. But we must look to Hebrew for the origins of modern numerology.

The cabbala (spelt variously with a C, K or Q, with one "b" or two, and with or without a final "h") is an ancient and complex Jewish esoteric system; it is from the cabbalists that present day numerology originates.

The basic idea is very simple: the letters of a name are reduced to numbers, which are further reduced to (usually) a single digit from 1 to 9, each of which has an esoteric meaning which can reveal the character of the person concerned. The numbers 11 and 22 are also significant.

Below: *Dr John Dee (1527–1608), one of the founding fathers of numerological study. A major figure in the world of the occult sciences, he was a magus, world-renowned scholar, and adviser to Queen Elizabeth I.*

Latin alphabet numerology

Immediately there is a problem. Hebrew has twenty-two letters, while the Latin alphabet as used in English has twenty-six; other languages use more or fewer letters. Some English-speaking numerologists ignore the problem (and the links with Hebrew) by using this simple table:

1	2	3	4	5	6	7	8	9
A	B	C	D	E	F	G	H	I
J	K	L	M	N	O	P	Q	R
S	T	U	V	W	X	Y	Z	

The name Charles Black would thus be converted to:

C H A R L E S   B L A C K

3 +8 +1 +9 +3 +5 +1   + 2 +3 +1 +3 +2

giving 30 + 11

The 3 and 0 are added, giving 3, and the 1 and 1 are added to give 2.

Charles Black is then represented by 3 and 2, totalling 5.

For a lot of people, this is all there is to numerology; Charles might say, using just his first name, that his "lucky number" was 3.

But some numerologists, still using this basic ABC=123 system, add a complication from the Greek alphabet, which has:

θ **Theta** = **TH** = **8**   χ **Chi** = **CH** = **4**

φ **Phi** = **PH** = **3**   ψ **Psi** = **PS** = **5**

Using the same example, we see a difference:

CHARLES   **BLACK**

$4 + 1 + 9 + 3 + 5 + 1$ $+ 2 + 3 + 1 + 3 + 2$

giving 23 + 11

The 2 and 3 are added, giving 5, and the 1 and 1 are added to give 2.

Charles Black is then represented by 5 and 2, totalling 7.

Which is correct? Serious numerologists would say neither: they would turn to Hebrew. The twenty-two letters of the Hebrew alphabet do not relate exactly to the Latin alphabet, so again Greek correspondences are drawn in to fill out the total:

1	2	3	4	5	6	7	8
A	B	C	D	E	U	O	F
I	K	G	M	H	V	Z	P
Q	R	L	T	N	W		
J	S			X			
Y							

The transposition, addition and reduction are done in exactly the same way as before, but with different values for many of the letters:

CHARLES   **BLACK**

$3 + 5 + 1 + 2 + 3 + 5 + 3$ $+ 2 + 3 + 1 + 3 + 2$

22 + 11

4 + 2

6

Coincidentally the surname is the same each time (BLACK = 11 = 2), but the first name comes out differently: CHARLES = 3 or 5 or 4. This makes a major difference when we come to look at the meaning ascribed to each number. As numerology is, at heart, a cabbalistic system, it makes more sense to use the Hebrew table from here on.

Vowels and consonants

The number we have derived so far, using all the letters of the given name and surname, is variously known as the vocation, key or character number. If only the vowels are used the heart number, which is supposed to be "the inner you" is obtained. Just using the consonants gives the personality number, which is how we present ourselves to the outside world – how others see us. (Y can be a vowel or a consonant, depending on its usage.)

Using the same method as above, we can find these for Charles Black:

  1   **5**   **1**   **= 7**

CHARLES   **BLACK**

3 5   2 3   3   2 3   3 2 = 26 = 8

Character number: 6
Heart number: 7
Personality number: 8

The meanings of the numbers

The personalities ascribed to each number are by no means random; the esoteric meanings of each number have developed over thousands of years, with influences from the Hebrew cabbalists, the Greek Pythagorean thinkers, and the seventeenth century Hermetic philosophers. The personality types described here are derived from very detailed and very carefully worked out meanings.

The Hebrew letters and their exoteric and esoteric meanings are very important in this form of interpretation. Each number here is followed by the word for the number, and its meanings. We also give the equivalent Latin letter in brackets. Odd numbers are regarded as masculine, even numbers as feminine, in much the same way as the Chinese Yang and Yin.

A D R I A N
1 4 9 9 1 5
5 4 9 1 6
9 4 1 7
4 5 8
9 4
4

A L I S O N
1 3 9 1 6 5
4 3 1 7 2
7 4 8 9
2 3 8
5 2
7

A N D R E W
1 5 4 9 5 5
6 9 4 5 1
6 4 9 6
1 4 6
5 1
6

B E N J A M I N
2 5 5 1 1 4 9 5
7 1 6 2 5 4 5
8 7 8 7 9 9
6 6 6 7 9
3 3 4 7
6 7 2
4 9
4

B R I A N
2 9 9 1 5
2 9 1 6
2 1 7
3 8
2

C A T H E R I N E
3 1 2 8 5 9 9 5 5
4 3 1 4 5 9 5 1
7 4 5 9 5 5 6
2 9 5 5 1 2
2 5 1 6 3
7 6 7 9
4 4 7
8 2
1

C H A R L E S
3 8 1 9 3 5 1
2 9 1 3 8 6
2 1 4 2 5
3 5 6 7
8 2 4
1 6
7

D A V I D
4 1 4 9 4
5 5 4 4
1 9 8
1 8
9

D I A N A
4 9 1 5 1
4 1 6 6
5 7 3
3 1
4

E D W A R D
5 4 5 1 9 4
9 9 6 1 4
9 6 7 5
6 4 3
1 7
8

E L I Z A B E T H
5 3 9 8 1 2 5 2 8
8 3 8 9 3 7 7 1
2 2 8 3 1 5 8
4 1 2 4 6 4
5 3 6 1 1
8 9 7 2
8 7 9
6 7
4

G E O F F R E Y
7 5 6 6 6 9 5 7
3 2 3 3 6 5 3
5 5 6 9 2 8
1 2 6 2 1
3 8 8 3
2 7 2
9 9
9

G E O R G E
7 5 6 9 7 5
3 2 6 7 3
5 8 4 1
4 3 5
7 8
6

H E N R Y
8 5 5 9 7
4 1 5 7
5 6 3
2 9
2

I R E N E
9 9 5 5 5
9 5 1 1
5 6 2
2 8
1

I S A B E L
9 1 1 2 5 3
1 2 3 7 8
3 5 1 6
8 6 7
5 4
9

J A M E S
1 1 4 5 1
2 5 9 6
7 5 6
3 2
5

J A N E
1 1 5 5
2 6 1
8 7
6

L A U R A
3 1 3 9 1
4 4 3 1
8 7 4
6 2
8

M I C H A E L
4 9 3 8 1 5 3
4 3 2 9 6 8
7 5 2 6 5
3 7 8 2
1 6 1
7 7
5

P A U L
7 1 3 3
8 4 6
3 1
4

R I C H A R D
9 9 3 8 1 9 4
9 3 2 9 1 4
3 5 2 1 5
8 7 3 6
6 1 9
7 1
8

S U S A N
1 3 1 1 5
4 4 2 6
8 6 8
5 5
1

T H O M A S
2 8 6 4 1 1
1 5 1 5 2
6 6 6 7
3 3 4
6 7
4

Names and Personal Numbers

There are a variety of ways of working out personal numbers from names, as explained in this section. One common way is to use the inverted pyramid system shown here: add up the pairs of numbers going downwards from line to line, until you reach the single figure at the bottom, which, in this system, is the personal number for that particular name. As the descending lines only allow for single-digit numbers to be used, while adding the numbers, convert double digits to a single number in the normal way, by calculating that 10 = 1 (1+0), 11 = 2 (1+1), 12 = 3 (1+2), and so on.

1

Hebrew: Aleph (A). Ox. Wealth.
Number: Achad. Unity.
This is the number of the Originator, of God the Father. In personality terms, therefore, it means a leader, a strong, assertive personality, self-reliant and determined. Negative aspects are egotism, aggressiveness and selfishness.

2

Hebrew: Beth (B). House. Family, creation.
Number: Sheni. The essence of creation.
This denotes a passive rather than an active person, a follower rather than a leader, someone who is conciliatory, tactful and diplomatic, and who makes a good subordinate being, conscientious and reliable. Negatively, there may be traits of shyness, insecurity, even deceitfulness and malice.

Below: *This atmospheric and highly romanticized nineteenth-century engraving shows a geomancer at work in his study producing a reading for a client.*

3

Hebrew: Gimel (G). Camel. Nature.
Number: Shalosh. The triad.
This signifies good fortune, whether in love or money. It represents a character which is bright, cheerful, energetic, creative, naturally talented, versatile, witty and attractive to others. Negatively, it may show superficiality, showing off and demanding to be the centre of attention. It can indicate conceit, egotism and self-indulgence.

4

Hebrew: Dalet (D). Door. Authority.
Number: Arba. Foursquare.

This depicts a person who is solid, reliable, dependable and hard-working, who plods along with steady determination. It can indicate a very conservative, and sometimes dull nature. When things go wrong the tendency is towards gloom and depression – or an excess of rage.

5

Hebrew: He (H). Window. Religion, linking.
Number: Chamesh. Armed.
The keynote of this personality is variety, change for its own sake, adaptability. It indicates an adventurous and vivacious spirit, one which is interesting, lively, full of the love of exploration

Above: *A magical seal with the Magic Square of Mars. This was originally published in Kircher's* Oedipus Aegyptiacus.

and discovery. The person may not always be dependable as there is a tendency to fall madly in love, and just as quickly out again. Irresponsibility, eccentricity to the point of extremism, fickleness and a quick temper are also likely traits.

6

Hebrew: Vau (V). Nail, doorknob, hook. Liberty.
Number: Shesh. White, bright.
This is the complete opposite of 5: quiet, dependable, reliable, well-balanced, home-loving and caring; a liking for what is familiar: situations, places, people. Complacency may set in, and might come over as an attitude of smugness or superiority; there is the tendency to be self-sacrificing, to become a martyr to others.

7

Hebrew: Zain (Z). Sword, weapon. Ownership.
Number: Shebay. At rest.
This represents a loner, a natural recluse, someone who enjoys solitude and working alone. A deep-thinking, scholarly, imaginative, but introspective character with a tendency towards being withdrawn, over-serious and pessimistic.

8

Hebrew: Cheth or Heth (CH). Fence, hurdle. Distribution.
Number: Shemonah. Fertility.
Worldly rather than other-worldly. This does not indicate brilliance, but a practical and dogged nature. Material values are held as important, but success docs not always come easily. It signifies a lack of imagination and an excess of caution; they can be tactless.

L e f t : *A thirteenth-century manuscript page from a document in the Bodleian Library showing Venus and Mercury with their corresponding geomantic symbols.*

9

Hebrew: Teth (T). Serpent. Prudence.
Number: Thshay. The gate.
In many ways this represents a combination of all that is best in all the other number. Nine is the number of completion, and people with this number are achievers. They are inspired and intelligent, and put their knowledge to good use – though sometimes their wild enthusiasms are short-lived, and their natural talents are not fully realized because they do not put in the necessary hard work. They often tend to dominate the scene, and their desire to help others can come over as interference and nosiness.

Many numerologists also pay attention to the double numbers 11 and 22, in addition to reducing them to 2 and 4. 11 is the number of revelation and idealism, but can denote impracticality. 22, being the number of letters in the Hebrew alphabet, signifies completion; even more than 9, it combines all the best of all the other numbers. People with a name number of 22 will be great – but as with all numbers, it can be negative, which would denote great evil.

Character, Heart and Personality numbers

Let's consider once again the character Charles Black. In order to know more about himself he needs to look at three numbers to see his overall character, which comprises his destiny and vocation, his hidden, inner nature, and the manner in which others see him. If there are major differences, as there are here, especially between his inner nature (7) and his outward appearance (8), then there will be inner conflicts; how he resolves these contradictions, probably through his character number (6), is what makes Charles Black the individual he is, rather than simply one of nine personality types.

At heart a deep-thinking loner, Charles Black is seen by others as very practical and materialistic; the clue to this is in (6): he extends his "self" to include his family, for whom he cares deeply, and works hard to achieve the best for them. It can sometimes be a struggle for him to do this, and he may well at times resent the demands of his family; perhaps in his gloomiest moments he

B e l o w : *A printed plate based on The Magus by Barrett which shows the geomantic figures (on either side) with associated planets (to the right) and the geomantic characters derived from the geomantic figures.*

longs to shut himself away from them for a while. The 11 of his first name could fit in well with the 7 of his heart number, though it is most usual, as we have seen, to study the more normally used full name. For this reason, the 22 of his surname is unlikely to be significant.

Criticisms and responses

There are two major criticisms of name-numerology, quite apart from common scepticism about the whole business of substituting numbers for letters and adding up the numbers to

reveal someone's character. First, our names are bestowed on us as a result of all sorts of reasons including sudden whim, insistent grandparents, and favourite film or pop stars; it is more or less pure chance what names we are given, so why should they be so significant?

The usual answer is based on synchronicity. In the same way that planets and stars "happen" to be in a certain pattern at our birth as part of the overall pattern of everything that exists, including the character of the new-born baby, so the names given to us "happen" to match our character. Everything is part of the pattern; everything affects (or more likely *reflects*) everything else.

Secondly, what happens when someone changes their name, by marriage or for any other reason? If the pattern argument is valid, should numerology only be applied to the original given name? And also, which part or form of the name should be used? What if Charles Black has a middle name, Alexander? What he is called could depend on different circumstances: he could be Charles at work and Chas in his club, and sign all letters and forms Charles A Black, or he might prefer his middle name, and be known as Alexander at work or Alex or Sandy at the club.

Here are just some of the permutations of his character number:

Charles Black	22 + 11 = 4 + 2 = 6
Charlie Black	20 + 11 = 2 + 2 = 4
Chas Black	12 + 11 = 3 + 2 = 5
Chuck Black	19 + 11 = 1 + 2 = 3
Charles A Black	22 + 1 + 11 = 4 + 1 + 2 = 7
Charles Alexander Black	22 + 32 + 11 = 2
Alexander Black	32 + 11 = 5 + 2 = 7
Alex Black	15 + 11 = 6 + 2 = 8
Alec Black	12 + 11 = 3 + 2 = 5
Sandy Black	14 + 11 = 5 + 2 = 7

Below left: *An image of Luna – the Moon – in her chariot, with the corresponding geomantic symbols for "Populus" and "Via".*

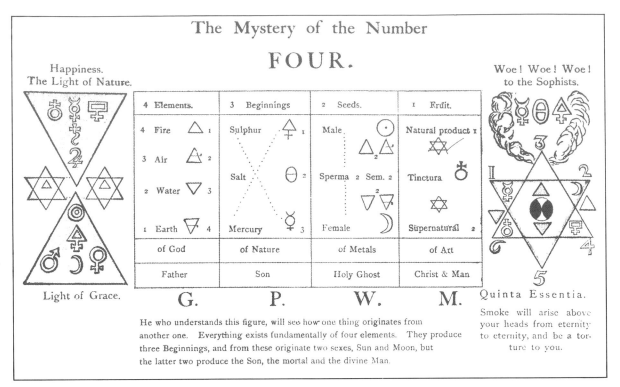

The Mystery of the Number

FOUR.

Happiness.
The Light of Nature.

Woe! Woe! Woe!
to the Sophists.

4 Elements.	3 Beginnings	2 Seeds.	1 Fruit.
4 Fire △ 1	Sulphur �※ 1	Male ☉	Natural product 1 ✡
3 Air △ 2		△₂ △	
	Salt ⊖ 2	Sperma 2 Sem. 2	Tinctura ☿
2 Water ▽ 3		▽ ▽₂	✡
1 Earth ▽ 4	Mercury ☿ 3	Female ☽	Supernatural 2
of God	of Nature	of Metals	of Art
Father	Son	Holy Ghost	Christ & Man
G.	P.	W.	M.

Light of Grace.

Quinta Essentia.

He who understands this figure, will see how one thing originates from another one. Everything exists fundamentally of four elements. They produce three Beginnings, and from these originate two sexes, Sun and Moon, but the latter two produce the Son, the mortal and the divine Man.

Smoke will arise above your heads from eternity to eternity, and be a torture to you.

Right: *An alchemical/ hermetic discourse on The Mystery of the Number Four. The hermetic movement took its name from Hermes, the Greek god of science: it flourished in the sixteenth century as a semi-secret cult of esoteric scholars and experimenters in the occult disciplines. They had many detractors and attackers, amongst whom were the Sophists, who are most delightfully and resoundingly cursed on the right hand side of the document.*

This is quite a selection to choose from, and cynics might suggest that Mr CA Black choose the character description he prefers, and then pick the variant form of his name which will give the right number.

Numerologists say – perhaps quite fairly – that the name to be used for working out a character number is the one by which we are most usually known; this is "the real you". And if someone uses the name Charles in the office but Charlie to his friends, or, similarly, Margaret in the office but Maggie to her family, then perhaps we show two quite different sides to our character in the different surroundings. This may also account for the differences between character, heart and personality numbers.

Some numerologists say that a married woman who takes her husband's surname should work out her character number with both her maiden name and her married surname; although her basic character may remain the same, her outlook on life will change as a result of being married.

As for people who change their name, many are unhappy with their given name – it has always felt wrong. They put a great deal of thought into choosing a new name which they feel is more suitable. It could be that quite deliberately (but unconsciously) they are choosing a name which numerologically reduces to their character type.

Birth numbers

You can change your name, but you cannot change your date of birth. Most numerologists work out the birth number by adding the day of the month, the month and the year together. If Charles Black was born on 19 September, 1967 his birth date would be:

$$19 + 9 + 1967 = 1995.\ 1 + 9 + 9 + 5 = 24 = 6$$

In this case it is the same as his character number, which is a good sign. If, for example, he had been born three days earlier so the total came out to 3, there would have been still more conflicts between his quiet, reclusive inner self and the bright, vibrant, witty character of the 3. Indeed, some numerologists call the birth number the lesson number, with the idea that this is the lesson Charles Black needs to learn in his life.

The idea can be taken further. By adding your day and month of birth to any year you are supposed to get an idea of how that year will be for you. For instance, if Charles Black wants to know about 1993:

$$19 + 9 + 1993 = 2021.\ 2 + 0 + 2 + 1 = 5$$

1993, then, will be a very hectic, changeable year for Charles Black, the sort of year, perhaps, to which you could apply the famous Chinese curse: "May you live in interesting times".

Every nine years, of course, the number will coincide with your own birth number, and this gives special opportunities for you to work out your "life lesson".

However, birth numbers break a cardinal rule of logic by adding to each other numbers not just of different things (day, month, year) but of things which are progressively parts of each other. It may also seem strange to use a year system based on the birth of Christ to work out an esoteric system which is Hebrew and pre-Christian Greek in origin. The fact that Christ was almost certainly *not* born in 0 BC/AD strips away any sacred value of the year number. Also, the lengths of some of the months were arbitrarily altered by Julius and Augustus Caesar; there is a vast difference between, for example, 31 July

(31 + 7 = 2) and 1 August (1 + 8 = 9); in fact, every date after the end of February will be "out" by one or two. The calendar has also been adjusted over the centuries (such as the famous "eleven lost days" in 1752 in Britain and America), so the dates we now use are quite different from what they would have been even five hundred years ago. Even so, calendraic numerology can often be used as a form of prediction, combined with intuitive interpretation, to examine the possibility of the unknown.

Whatever the verdict on numerology, whatever your name and number, whatever you were dealt at birth, remember that you are in charge of the course of your own life. Whichever form of prediction or divination you explore and whatever basic character you have, you can mould yourself for good or bad. Dipping into the realm of the unconscious, the unknown, may well provide possible answers to otherwise inexplicable mysteries of character, events and the future.

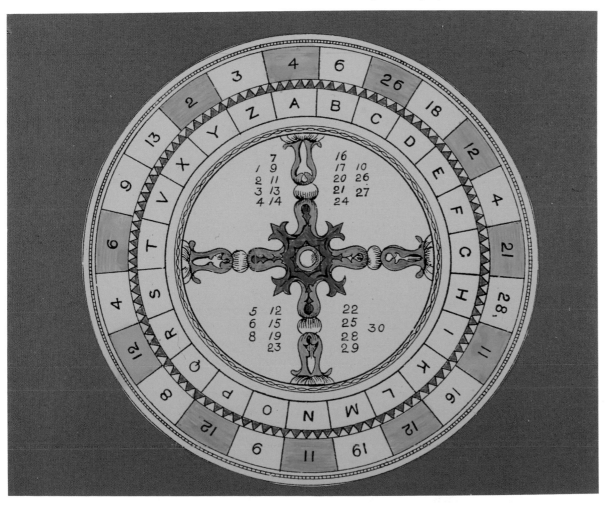

L e f t : *The numbers and letters on the Wheel of Pythagoras were used in a system of fortune telling. This coloured plate was first published in Rosa Baughan's 1891 book* The Influence of the Stars: A Book of Old World Lore.

Astrology: Orbits of Divination

*E*verybody knows their star sign – whether or not they believe in astrology, or, indeed know anything about it at all: and nobody, however cynical, can resist turning to the 'stars' page in the newspapers or magazines to see what it says about them. It is one of the commonest collective themes in life, and a day seldom passes without astrology, the zodiac, or the stars catching the attention – either as a design motif, in advertising, on TV, or in conversation. Why would there be all this interest if there were nothing in it? Yet can we really take it seriously?

The reason that astrology permeates our lives is that it is an ancient divination system that has been with us for centuries – so much so that it has become part of our cultural furniture. The future is in the stars, and there is an enormous and proven significance in astrology and the zodiac, but these ancient truths have been buried in the devalued system popularized today.

Right: *The personifications of Mars, Mercury and Venus, and the lunar and solar symbols, from a plate in the seventeenth-century alchemical work,* Philosophia Reformata.

Introduction

Below: *An ancient map of the heavenly spheres: the figure in the centre is macrocosmic man, and the presiding woman is Astronomia. The plate is from the Shotus edition of* Margarita Philosophia.

Can the stars really foretell the future? Millions turn to their star-sign horoscope in magazines and newspapers to see what is predicted for them: this is great fun yet in reality these horoscopes are too vague and generalized to provide real guidance. Remember that you share your sign with roughly one twelfth of the population, so it is difficult to see how these nuggets of racy advice and comment can be accurate for everybody. But there does seem to be a real truth in astrology: something that goes much deeper than a simple star sign and its generalized attributes. As in all matters of the mind, the unconscious, and hidden knowledge, the system applied will offer guidance in relation to effort invested in it. The practical guidance in this section is designed for those who wish to delve deeper than their daily newspaper predictions, to discover the secrets of their destiny by working on their own personal horoscope.

Astrology has a long and at times

Above: *A very early carved stone tablet showing all the signs of the zodiac. The individual signs are called sigils, and this name is also sometimes applied to the item on which single sigil images appear.*

Below: *Much of the earliest recorded scholarship was inspired by the search for astrological and esoteric wisdom.*

Right: A seventeenth-century engraving showing an early astrologer/astronomer at work with his telescope. At the beginning, astrology and astronomy were essentially one and the same thing, and even the most scientific of the observers believed that the heavens were populated by all manner of gods, beasts, and monsters.

distinguished history which – as with both dream analysis and Tarot cards, for example – is inextricably interwoven with the many religious, mythological and magical beliefs held through the ages.

The stars have always been a source of wonder to man: those familiar pinprick lights in the sky which fall so readily into familiar patterns. There is a reliable constancy about them as well, so that they have been used for navigation from earliest times.

The more man looked at the stars, the more he saw in them. And if someone is looking for signs and portents, where better to look for them? The awe and excitement that an eclipse brings even today, when we know exactly how it is caused, must have been much more powerful thousands of years ago.

The Babylonians and the Chinese especially studied the heavens, as far back as two or even three thousand years before Christ. The origins of our present astrology can be traced back to the Babylonians, although it is uncertain exactly when the division of the sky into the signs of the zodiac occurred. At one time, it is thought, there were only ten signs; at another, perhaps eighteen. At that time astrology, however it was then worked, was concerned not with the fate of individuals, but rather with the fate of the nation, or the king,

which came to the same thing.

There is evidence of astrology in Egypt from the sixth century BC, and from there it was picked up by the Greeks, who did the most to codify it in a form which would be recognizable to us today.

The Greek philosophers were in advance of their time in many respects. In around 550 BC Pythagorus claimed the Earth was a sphere rather than a disc, as was then believed; and in the third century BC Aristarchus worked out that it circled the Sun, not the other way around.

However, the Greeks were not right about everything; Pythagorus (who related almost everything to music) believed the planets were attached to concentric spheres or wheels that revolved around the Earth, humming as they went. We still speak of the "music of the spheres" today, and scientists now measure the different electromagnetic vibrations of the planets. It was probably Pythagorus who worked out the idea of the octave, as well as much of the geometry still taught in schools.

Everything was interrelated: music, mathematics, the gods, the planets and stars, our individual lives. When EM Forster wrote "Only connect!" in *Howards End*, he was saying nothing new. After a couple of centuries of "rationalist" science, physicists are now saying that everything

Above: One of the most compelling elements of astrology – both for believers and cynics – is the incredibly rich vein of its symbolism and the beauty of its iconography. From the earliest woodcuts onwards, astrology, the zodiac and the personifications of the zodiacal signs have inspired some of the greatest artists who ever lived.

has an effect on everything else; philosophers and astrologers have been saying exactly this for thousands of years.

What the Greeks had, the Romans soon acquired; some of the greatest minds of both peoples worked on the theory and practice of astrology. It was Ptolemy (second century AD) who designed the horoscope much as we have it today. His *Tetrabiblos* or *Quadripartite*, a four-volume work, became the standard astrological textbook for centuries to come. Ptolemy was one of the first to have the troublesome thought that it would make far more sense to draw a horoscope for the moment of conception rather than birth, with the attendant problem that people very rarely know when they were conceived. Serious astrologers still find this problematic, but there is little that can be done about it.

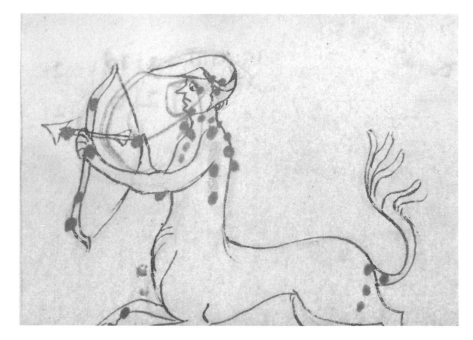

A b o v e : *A fifteenth-century constellation image of Sagittarius from a manuscript in the Bodleian Library. It shows how creative the early astrologers were in shaping such detailed figures out of a very few observable stars.*

The idea of "mundane houses" was also Ptolemy's; his "equal house" system of dividing up the horoscope is by far the simplest and most logical way of doing it; 30 degrees per sign, and no complex calculations. Over the centuries many other, more complicated ways have been developed, each claiming to be the most accurate.

The medieval Arabs were responsible for a large number of developments. One of these was Jabir ibn Hayyan, a Sufi mystic who died around AD 815, known in the West as Geber. The complexity of his many writings on magic, alchemy, astrology and medicine has almost certainly given us the words "jabber" and "gibberish".

Part of the reason for the complexity of astrology is that the deeper we reach into any metaphysical subject, the less useful everyday language becomes; everything is symbolic of something else, and everything that can conceivably be linked together is so, with ever more abstruse connections.

The other reason, of course, is secrecy. Occult comes from a root meaning "to hide"; esoteric from a root meaning "within" (i.e. excluding outsiders); while hermetic, although coming from the cult of Hermes Trismegistus, the imaginary and mysterious god-figure associated with alchemy, has now taken on the meaning of "airtight", as in an hermetic seal.

The secrecy was for two reasons. Firstly, Christian authorities have nearly always been inimical towards anything smacking of magic. Many leading thinkers through the ages have been killed by the Church on charges of heresy; Giordano Bruno was burnt to death in 1610; even Queen Elizabeth I's astrologer John Dee came under suspicion of heresy and witchcraft. Hierarchical religions have always been hostile to and distrusted anyone who thinks independently, whether mystics with what appeared to be a direct link to God, or "magicians" who tap powers not under the control of the Church. Evangelical Christians today still view anything remotely "occult" with horror, but you can now openly buy books on Christian astrology.

The second reason for secrecy was simply human nature. If someone has worked long and hard to find out certain rare truths, these are not going to be passed around on a plate; everyone likes the feeling of knowing they know something no one else knows.

Arabic thinkers, particularly the Spanish Moors, added much to the philosophy of astrology and alchemy. One of the greatest of them, the eleventh century Ibn Ezra, came up with another way of calculating the twelve houses, modified and introduced to the West as the Regiomontanus method (the name taken by the fifteenth century German mathematician Johann Müller).

The twelfth and thirteenth centuries were, compared with both earlier and later eras in Western Europe, times of learning and the love of

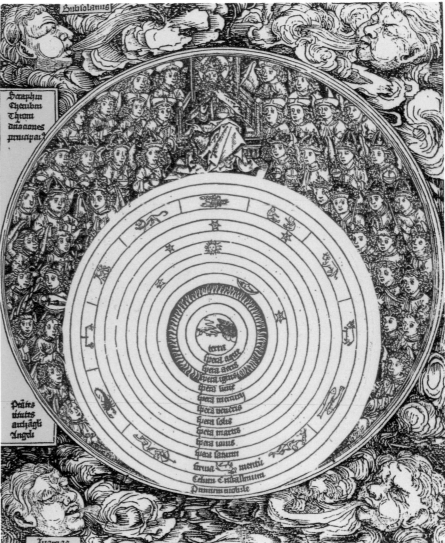

learning. Oxford University was founded in 1167, about ten years after the university at Paris. Astrology was taught as part of astronomy, and was held in high esteem by the friar-philosopher-scientist Roger Bacon, who studied in both cities. Bacon, incidentally, was a great proponent of "the scientific method" of repeatable experiments; he carried out a lot of work on optics (he invented the magnifying glass, and may have invented the telescope); he also worked out the complex system (still used today) for determining when Easter falls each year.

Bacon distinguished carefully between "natural magic" (including astrology, alchemy and medicine), which did not conflict with Christian belief, and demonic magic. Sadly, he too ended up imprisoned for heresy for fifteen years near the end of his life; he died in 1294, aged 80.

The hermetic philosophers of the seventeenth century took their name from Hermes (the Greek messenger god) Trismegistus ("the thrice-greatest"). Although an imaginary figure, he was held to be the author of more than 20,000 books. It is now thought that the books came from the hands of several writers, over several centuries, and, more than likely, several countries; but their authorship is unimportant compared to their content. It was the figure of Hermes Trismegistus who (amongst many other teachings and a variety of beliefs) codified the idea that each of the twelve zodiacal signs rules a different part of the human body.

These writings had only just surfaced in the Western world, and became source material for the alchemist-philosophers of the seventeenth century. As well as Dee and Bruno, Robert Fludd, William Lilly and the earlier Cornelius Agrippa were amongst the significant names of the period.

The hermetic philosophers, operating for the most part in secrecy, are important not just because of their discoveries and teachings, but also because they were the last people who happily mixed science and religion. A well-educated "Renaissance man" could still know just about everything that was known; the split between the sciences and the arts, and the increasing compartmentalisation of the sciences, were about to begin.

It did not matter that the Earth had now been shown to revolve around the Sun, rather than vice

Top, left: In the early years of astrology, there was no perceived conflict between astrological study and religion, as can be seen from the zodiac in the thirteenth-century nave of San Miniato al Monte, in Florence.

Above: A beautifully detailed fifteenth-century chart of the zodiac and planetary spheres, set within a crescent of the nine angelic hierarchies.

Above: *As the science of astronomy developed, and technical expertise and equipment became more sophisticated, it became increasingly obvious that many of the early beliefs on which astrology had been founded were now untenable. At this stage a schism occurred: astrology became less connected with pure science, and more associated with divination and predictive systems such as the Tarot, from which this image of the Fool derives.*

versa; this could be accepted as a fact, as one kind of truth, while for astrological purposes the Earth was still at the centre of the universe. There was no conflict; for one thing, truth was higher than fact, and for another, it was all a matter of perception anyway. The relative relationship of the Earth and Sun remained the same. (We are still perfectly happy today to speak of the Sun rising, though we know it is the Earth's rotation which has brought the Sun into view; similarly, scientists are prepared to think of light as both a wave and a particle, in different contexts.)

Astrology, alchemy, and all the magical arts very soon fell into disrepute. The eighteenth century was the "Age of Reason"; magic was superstition, and superstition was irrational; this is a view still held by many today, despite the more liberal scientific thinking of the last few decades. Popular scientific belief is always a good half century behind the forefront of scientific thought; it comes from what we were taught in school, which depends largely on what our teachers (and textbook writers) were themselves taught as students.

In 1781 Uranus was discovered, followed by Neptune in 1846 and by Pluto in 1930. Astrologers were shattered, their enemies gleeful. The old planets had developed their "personalities" over thousands of years, but what were the personalities of the new planets? Some astrologers looked at social developments in the world from around the time of each planet's discovery. Uranus thus became responsible for revolutions (America in 1776, France in 1789) and the Industrial Revolution. Neptune was held responsible for mysticism and the occult revival of the nineteenth century; and Pluto for the underworld, death, the rise of the Nazis and the atom bomb.

The names of the new planets have obviously influenced what astrologers say about them, but it has to be pointed out that the names are quite arbitrary. Uranus was originally called Herschel, after its discoverer, William Herschel, while the story about the naming of Pluto is that its discoverer asked his young daughter what name he should give the planet, and she named it after her favourite cartoon character.

However, there are some astrologers who actually believe that the names were "imposed" by the planets themselves. In any case, the idea

Below: *Ptolemy was one of the greatest early philosopher-scientists; he was an astronomer, geographer and mathematician. The Ptolemaic System, in which the planets and Sun revolve around a stationary Earth, was accepted for fourteen centuries after his death.*

A b o v e : *This diagram represents the male and female elements, set against the zodiacal band.*

B e l o w : *A representation of the sign of Cancer, from a hand-coloured print in a 1496 edition of Hyginus's* Poeticon Astronomicaon.

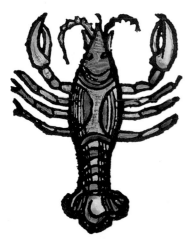

that the planets' personalities should be determined by social developments around the time of their discovery implies that they had no astrological effect before their discovery, which is a rather silly extension of solipsist belief (for example, if a tree falls in a forest and no one hears it, does it make a sound?).

Once they knew the orbits of the new planets other astrologers, perhaps more sensibly, tracked them back in history, taking their positions into consideration in their calculations. A new question arose: should the new planets be given signs of the zodiac to rule? The previous system had been quite neat: the Sun and Moon each had one sign, and the five planets two signs each, in a logical arrangement. What now?

Uranus, Neptune and Pluto have now been given zodiacal signs, but there is still some disagreement about which ones they should have, and it is noticeable that they accompany, rather than supplant, the old planets in those signs.

Some astrologers, not wanting to be caught out if yet more planets are discovered (which is quite likely), have already given names – and orbits – to them. One of these, Chiron, does exist, but is actually a comet, not a planet at all. Another, Vulcan, supposedly nearer to the Sun than Mercury, has been comprehensively disproved. Despite this, it is possible to buy ephemerides for them.

Does astrology work? And if so, how?

Does astrology have any validity? Certainly some of the greatest minds in history have used it and believed in it, but the modern rationalist wants more than that.

The main difficulty with testing the claims of astrology scientifically is that there is far more to it than simply calling someone Leo because they were born in late July or early August. An hour's difference – or much less – in birth can make a tremendous difference to a horoscope; so can a few miles' difference in birthplace.

Statistical studies have been made to both prove and disprove astrology, and the results have been ambiguous. It is always possible for critics to cast doubt on the methodology of a study, then to come up with a study of their own "proving" the opposite, which in turn is discredited.

Probably the best-known studies were carried out in the 1950s by the Frenchman Michel Gauquelin who, with very large samples, found no correlation between horoscope readings and personality, but did find significant correlations between certain factors (mainly the Moon, Mars, Jupiter or Saturn in the ascendant or descendant) and people's career choices. Many athletes and soldiers have a dominant Mars, scientists a dominant Saturn, and clergymen, actors, politicians and journalists a dominant Jupiter; the Moon appears to be responsible for writers. But the sign of the zodiac, the aspects of the planets, and the houses they lie in all appeared to be irrelevant.

Other studies, including one involving the psychologist Hans Eysenck, do appear to show correspondences, at least between the elemental

Left: *A coloured engraving showing Tycho Brahe, the Danish astrologer and so-called occultist, at work in his observatory at Uraniborg, on the island of Hveen. Brahe (1546–1601) worked at the cusp of the schism between astronomy and astrology. He is known to have cast many horoscopes and to have made predictions, while at the same time being extremely cynical about the work of other astrologers, whom he described as charlatans.*

Below: *A personal horoscope of Tycho Brahe which was cast for 13 December 1546.*

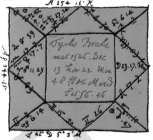

groups of signs and personality traits. Apparently neither Gauquelin nor Eysenck expected to find any "proof" that astrology works.

For those who believe in astrology, how does it work? Is it possible that the planets and stars do actually influence us at the moment of our births? It is certainly well proven that the Moon affects far more than the tides; molluscs open and shut their shells, rats become more or less active, and the behaviour of mentally disturbed people fluctuates along with the movements and phases of the Moon. Sunspot cycles have also been shown to be linked to all sorts of things on the Earth, from stock market prices to the incidence of particular diseases to, it is said, the rise and fall of hemlines.

A recent book by astronomer (not astrologer) Dr Percy Seymour, *Astrology: The Evidence of Science* (1988), argues strongly for the influence of the gravitational pull of the planets on Earth's own magnetic field, setting up resonances which affect us all our lives, but most of all in the womb.

Others prefer to accept the idea of synchronicity, a term coined by Carl Jung. Going back to the ancients, and the alchemists, "as above, so below" does not necessarily mean that "above" causes "below"; the relative positions of the planets, and the future personality of a new-born baby, may be linked because *both are aspects of the whole.*

The Signs of the Zodiac

Above: *The personification of Mercury, who rules over the symbols for Gemini and Virgo.*

Below: *This zodiacal plan of the universe shows man bound together with all the other elements of the universe – animal, vegetable, mineral, and aetherial.*

We are all familiar with our own sign, and sometimes with all twelve, but for a fuller picture it is worth examining how the signs fit to-gether in relation to each other, before going on to examine them individually.

Twelve is a very versatile number; it can be divided by two, three, four and six, as well as, of course, by one and twelve. The numbers two and four are significant in themselves: two forms the basis of the binary system, and also makes up the fundamental elements of Eastern beliefs based on the opposites of Yin and Yang; four is the number of seasons of the year and so is associated with the natural cycle of life. Numbers underlie everything to do with astrology; numerical principles were used by the Babylonians, by Pythagorus, by the medieval Arabs and by the seventeenth century hermetic philosophers, in fact by everyone who has had anything to do with formulating astrology.

In the Western world, a complex system based

Above: *A seventeenth-century representation of the twelve sigils of the zodiacal signs, together with additional planetary sigils.*

on the number twelve was devised to account for everything we experience in life, every quality, every occurrence; it was a key to a full and deep understanding of the individual, the world, the universe; twelve is also the basis of the astrological zodiac. Some authorities have shown that even the qualities ascribed to each sign and each planet have a numerical basis, rather than simply being based on detailed observation of types of people, as

A b o v e : *This stunning anatomical study by William Blake shows a mathematician from the ancient world at this work. The study of numbers, mathematical relationships and geometry lies at the heart of esoteric philosophy.*

T o p , r i g h t :
Mythological-style figures were very often used in early astrology to depict the personifications of the planets and other zodiacal entities.

many astrologers believe. It is thought that the idea of having twelve men in a jury was to have a fair balance of all types of man, and perhaps this may also have applied to Christ's twelve disciples.

Hemispheres

The zodiac always starts at 0 degrees, Aries. The first 180 degrees are the northern signs (remembering that north is at the bottom of the zodiac): Aries, Taurus, Gemini, Cancer, Leo and Virgo. From 180 degrees to 360 degrees are the southern signs: Libra, Scorpio, Sagittarius, Capricorn, Aquarius and Pisces.

Polarity

Half the signs are positive (sometimes known as masculine), the other half negative (or feminine), alternating from one sign to the next. The positive signs are Aries, Gemini, Leo, Libra, Sagittarius and Aquarius. The negative signs are Taurus, Cancer, Virgo, Scorpio, Capricorn and Pisces. Depending on your sign of the zodiac, the elements affecting you will, in turn, be either positive or negative.

The Elements

For thousands of years it was thought that everything was made up from four elements: earth, air, fire and water, not in a physical or chemical sense, but in the sense that the nature of everything depends on the precise mixture of elemental principles. Zodiacal signs, gods, spirits and "little people", Tarot suits, and much else are divided into these four elements. Objects, personalities, relationships and so on are made up from a balance of the four elements. (Sometimes in esoteric circles a fifth element, spirit, is mentioned, but it does not form part of the four elements of matter.)

Each element has its own attributes:
Earth: earthy, practical, solid, materialistic, constant, dependable, diplomatic, cautious, sometimes dull or suspicious.
Air: mental, intellectual, reasoning, analytic,

Right: *The twelve houses, with zodiacal signs and planets, as depicted in Leonard Reymann's* Nativitat Kalendar *of 1515.*

Below: *In many mythologies, man and animals are merged to form fabulous new creatures.*

idealistic, good at communication, sometimes coldly logical, sometimes "head-in-the-clouds".

Fire: fiery, warm, sunny, idealistic, artistic, creative, energetic, excitable, passionate, headstrong, hot-headed, hot-tempered.

Water: emotional, sympathetic, deep-feeling, romantic, artistic, spiritual, receptive, sometimes hypersensitive.

Many people are clearly more one type than another, but most people are a mixture of all four; anybody who is *only* one elemental type is seriously unbalanced, while someone who is completely missing one type is lacking in one personality area. (Compare the Yin and Yang of the Chinese Tao; it is the balance which is important.)

The twelve zodiacal signs are divided between the elements:
Earth: Capricorn, Taurus, Virgo
Air: Aquarius, Gemini, Libra
Fire: Aries, Leo, Sagittarius
Water: Pisces, Cancer, Scorpio

Quadruplicities

As well as four sets of three, the signs are also divided into three sets of four, known as the quadruplicities, or qualities. The cardinal signs mark the beginning of each season, and have the idea of a new start, leadership, activity, restlessness. The fixed signs are in the middle of each season, and denote stability but inflexibility, dependability but dullness. The mutable (or common) signs mark the change from one season to the next, from the old to the new, and show flexibility and adaptability, but instability; they also show selflessness and service.

The twelve signs are divided as follows:
Cardinal: Aries, Cancer, Libra, Capricorn
Fixed: Taurus, Leo, Scorpio, Aquarius
Mutable: Gemini, Virgo, Sagittarius, Pisces

Rulers

Each sign is ruled by one of the planets, which also has its part in defining the character of the sign (see the section on Planets).

The Sun rules in Leo by day, and the Moon by night next door in Cancer. Each of the other "old" planets rules two signs, one by day, one by night, determined by how far away from the Sun the planet is. Thus Mercury's two signs are the next on either side, Virgo and Gemini; Venus rules the next two, Libra and Taurus; then Mars rules Scorpio and Aries; Jupiter rules Sagittarius and Pisces; and finally Saturn, the coldest planet, furthest away from the Sun, rules the two signs opposite to those of the Sun and Moon, Capricorn and Aquarius.

The "new" planets of Uranus, Neptune and Pluto have, according to some astrologers, become "junior partners" or co-rulers on some signs, though there is some disagreement, especially over Pluto. Other astrologers seem to have made the new planets sole rulers of the signs given to them. The signs and their planetary rulers can be listed as follows:

Aries	Mars (night) (and/or Pluto, say some authorities)
Taurus	Venus (night)
Gemini	Mercury (night)
Cancer	Moon (night)
Leo	Sun (day)
Virgo	Mercury (day)
Libra	Venus (day)
Scorpio	Mars (day) (and/or Pluto, say more reliable authorities)
Sagittarius	Jupiter (day)
Capricorn	Saturn (day)
Aquarius	Saturn (night) (and/or Uranus)
Pisces	Jupiter (night) (and/or Neptune)

All of these factors work together to determine the character of each star sign. More importantly, the combinations made by the planets lying within different signs in a horoscope, and the relationships between them all, are what determine the detailed individual interpretation of each person's birth chart.

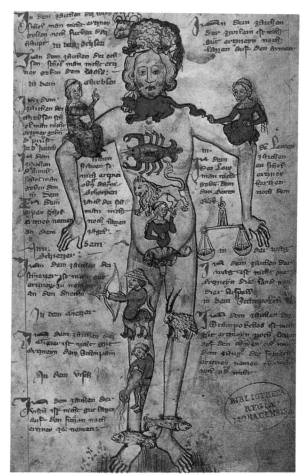

L e f t : *An early anatomical plan of the body, showing the areas thought to be governed by the different signs of the zodiac.*

The Signs and what they Signify

Everyone is aware of which sign of the zodiac they are born under, and which qualities it represents. There are often subtle differences in the attributed qualities, according to each astrologer's own interpretation of the other elements affecting the signs. The characteristics given here are of classic examples of each star sign. They are archetypes; very few people of any sign are exactly like these descriptions, although some may prove surprisingly accurate and relevant. Scientific and mathematical calculations are used in combination with a keen, observant eye and a strong intuitive sense to draw up a horoscope. There are certain pieces of information you need to bear in mind: as well as the Sun sign, determined by your date of birth, you should also take note of which sign is in the ascendant, which signs all the planets lie in, and how the planets relate to each other in position: in conjunction, opposition, trine and square.

Above: *An engraving of the Egyptian zodiac, formerly from the Temple of Osiris.*

Below: *Henry Cornelius Agrippa (1486–1534) wrote some of the seminal works on occult philosophy and greatly influenced the hermetic thinkers of the sixteenth century.*

Below: *Seventeenth-century planetary sigils from an alchemical diagram published in 1677.*

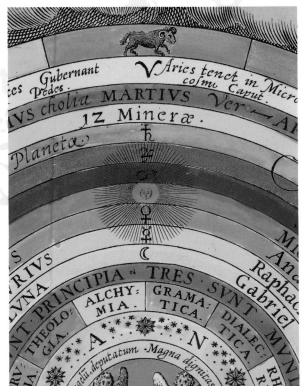

ARIES *(the Ram)*

21 March – 19 April

Northern, Positive, Cardinal, Fire, Mars (night)

The Aries person is strong, determined, forceful, a born leader. Aries people may be aggressive, domineering and irritable, perhaps even violent and destructive. They are energetic, ambitious, full of energy, full of new ideas and the drive to go out and put them into action. This drive is powered more by initial impetus than by a steady, continuing perseverance, so Aries people can be unreliable.

TAURUS *(the Bull)*

20 April – 20 May

Northern, Negative, Fixed, Earth, Venus (night)

Taurans are strong too, but in a different way. While the Ram is aggressive, the Bull has the advantage of sheer weight and solidity. They are slow, patient, and careful, but they are tenacious, and will get there in the end. They are reliable and dependable, and good family providers. They are slow to anger, but if they are provoked, stand well clear; they can have a vile and violent temper. They are extremely possessive, both in love and in their creature comforts; taken to extremes they can be gluttons and drunkards, but they can be excellent cooks.

GEMINI *(the Twins)*

21 May – 21 June

Northern, Positive, Mutable, Air, Mercury (night)

Gemini people are usually argumentative and often self-contradictory. Being both intellectual and emotional, they are likely to hold at least two different viewpoints on everything, and, being

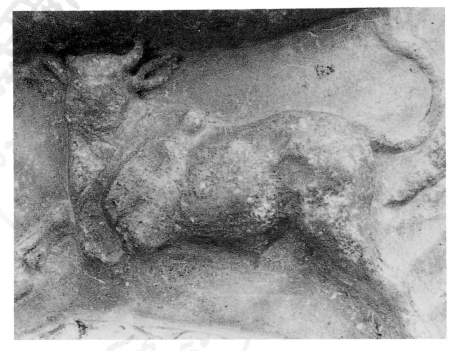

Above: *The sign of Taurus, from a second-century Roman carving.*

mercurial, to skip between them without warning. They can also be very changeable in mood, going from being happy, light and carefree, to sullen and moody in a split second. They are intelligent, adaptable, inventive and versatile, and if you can take the pace, they are great fun to be with. They are charming and ingenious, and they know it; but they can turn these virtues into vices.

CANCER *(the Crab)*

22 June – 22 July

Northern, Negative, Cardinal, Water, Moon

Cancer people are sensitive (often over-sensitive), romantic, warm, gentle, considerate, protective (often over-protective) and home-loving. They are good at listening to other people's problems, but have a tendency to become over-involved; if they do not maintain a certain distance they can become "swamped" by others' emotions and problems. They also tend to hug their own problems to themselves, which can make them introspective. They often brood over their mistakes for far too long. Cancer men may have strong shoulders, but they are very sensitive, and are easily hurt by a harsh word. They may have an exaggerated sense of fair play, and can over-react if they feel they are unjustly criticized. On the other hand, they are tenacious (sometimes stubborn) and very protective, especially of those dependent on them. They possess both the good and the bad aspects of a "maternal" nature.

Below: *A fifteenth-century manuscript depicting a stylized constellation image of Leo.*

LEO *(the Lion)*

23 July – 22 August

Northern, Positive, Fixed, Fire, Sun

Leos are strong, independent and masterful; they know they are natural leaders, which can make them seem proud, haughty and patronizing. They are courageous, honest and loyal, but they expect the same in return. They are also perfectionists; they set high standards and live up to them, but they expect others to do the same. They are methodical, clear-thinking and tidy-minded; they do not suffer fools. They are warm and friendly, generous and sincere, and enjoy a good social life, but they expect to be the leaders of the pack.

VIRGO *(the Virgin)*

23 August – 22 September

Northern, Negative, Mutable, Earth, Mercury (day)

Below: Scorpio, seen here in a painting on the wall of the Capitol building in Washington DC. The design was originally made by Constantino Brumidi in the nineteenth century, but it has been much restored since.

Virgo people have common sense and intelligence. At their best they can have a practical innocence; at their worst, they can be like a fussy old maid. They are quiet and dependable, not terribly creative and not great leaders. They are conscientious, neat, exact, and careful about detail: good people to whom to delegate the practicalities of organization. They tend to know themselves well, and are even more critical of themselves than they are of others. They are not great romantics, but their devotion (in love or caring) is unselfishly given. Their apparent coolness sometimes covers nervousness and tension. Their sharp intelligence often makes them quick-witted, shrewd and perceptive.

LIBRA *(the Scales)*

23 September – 23 October

Southern, Positive, Cardinal, Air, Venus (day)

Librans, like their symbol, are well-balanced people who weigh things up carefully instead of jumping to impetuous conclusions. In extreme cases they continually make comparisons, which can be undesirable. Normally, however, they are good peacemakers because they will look at all sides of a dispute, although this does sometimes mean that they are incapable of coming to a decision. They are generally diplomatic and tolerant, but can be very easily influenced by others. Their desire for peace and harmony around them also leads to a liking of beauty.

SCORPIO *(the Scorpion)*

24 October – 21 November

Southern, Negative, Fixed, Water, Mars (day) (and/or Pluto)

Scorpios are unusual and complex characters, and can be extremely powerful people. Perhaps more than those born under any other sign, they are egocentric in that they see the world through their own eyes and do not easily accept other people's points of view; they certainly will not take advice from anyone. They see everything as very clear-cut, and will come down firmly on one side or the other, with no hint of conciliation or compromise. They rarely open up their inner selves to others, and they tend to be secretive. Yet because they throw themselves into life with passion they can

Below: *Attempts to reconcile astrology and Christianity included this constellation image of the Three Magi by Julius Schiller in 1627: here they take Hercules's usual place in the firmament.*

Above: *Virgo as a young woman surrounded by flowers, seen in a carving on the Notre Dame Cathedral in Paris which dates from the thirteenth century.*

Top: *A copy, probably dating to the tenth century, of a zodiac from classical antiquity,*

Above: *Capricorn, as seen on the Fitzjames Arch in Merton College, Oxford.*

be compelling, almost hypnotically fascinating, to other people, and can inspire fiercely loyal friendships. There is a dark side to them: they can use their undoubted charm to their own ends. Their uncompromising attitude can be aggressive; they can be dangerous enemies to have (and they do make enemies easily), and their love life can be passionate and stormy.

SAGITTARIUS *(the Archer)*

22 November – 21 December

Southern, Positive, Mutable, Fire, Jupiter (day)

After the dark power of Scorpio, it is a relief to turn to the integrity, openness, maturity and success of the centaur-archer. Sagittarians can be just as outspoken as Scorpios, but their bluntness is without malice and rarely causes the same offence. They are full of cheerfulness, life, energy and enthusiasm, but they can show inconsistency, and impulsive anger; they often act before they think. They tend to be restless people, bounding about from one place to another (they love travel) or from one job to another. But they are honest and trustworthy, and are good teachers, if sometimes too opinionated.

CAPRICORN *(the Goat)*

22 December – 19 January

Southern, Negative, Cardinal, Earth, Saturn (day)

Capricorns make natural leaders, whether managers or politicians. They are confident, ambitious, hardworking, strong-willed and generally successful. Like the goat of their sign they will leap over obstacles or butt them out of the way, but they can also sometimes act on a capricious whim, and carelessly risk throwing everything away. However, they also remain calm and collected in difficult situations. They tend to like tradition and order, and have a "correct" way of doing things; they are deliberate, determined and practical; given these qualities, Capricorns often excel at mathematical or scientific professions. They are sometimes considered to be cold and distant because they are good at controlling their surface emotions; this can make it difficult to become close to them, but they are loyal and loving to those who are. They are also very good

Right: *A magnificent depiction of Sagittarius from a Latin manuscript in the French National Library in Paris.*

at understanding others' needs. At emotional extremes they can be overly serious, melancholic and depressive.

AQUARIUS *(the Water-Carrier)*

20 January – 18 February

Southern, Positive, Fixed, Air, Saturn (night) (and/or Uranus)

In some ways Aquarians are like a light, airy version of Scorpios, definitely without the dark side found in Scorpios, but sharing their complexity and contradictions. They attract followers because they are strong, forceful and charming, but they are quiet and well mannered. They are independent and freedom-loving, but if they sometimes shock others it is out of a sense of fun and nonconformity, or occasionally fanaticism. They are quick and bright, creative, original and artistic, sometimes wilful, sometimes conceited, arrogant and dogmatic, but also thoughtful and understanding. They enjoy company, but love their own above all. In many ways they have the archetypal virtues and flaws of the artistic genius, whether a writer, composer or painter; they also make good inventors.

Right: *Conrad Lycosthene's extraordinary sixteenth-century vision of the Moon. Lycosthene developed the theory that there were, in fact, three Moons circulating the Earth.*

PISCES *(the Fishes)*

19 February – 20 March

Southern, Negative, Mutable, Water, Jupiter (night) (and/or Neptune)

At their worst Pisces people will be aimless drifters, tossed about by the current: confused, muddled, malleable and lacking in stability. However, Pisceans are generally friendly and sympathetic. They can be keenly aware of others' emotions and feelings; if they become too receptive to these, they can be easily swayed or swamped by them. They are usually gentle, shy and retiring, but have a deep urge to help others less fortunate than themselves. They often have a strong imagination; like Aquarians they can be artistic, but they are too easily distracted.

The Planets

The patterns of the stars remain the same, but the planets wander across them; the word "planet" originally meant "wanderer". This is why, although the Sun is very clearly not a planet it can be treated as one in astrology, because it too wanders across the sky. (The Moon, although a satellite of Earth, can quite legitimately be thought of as a planet; because of the Moon's size some astronomers refer to the Earth-Moon double-planet.)

It was natural that, as man created gods, he should link them with the planets, those lights that strode across the heavens. The Sun and Moon have always been objects of worship – or, to be accurate, symbols of sets of ideals which made up the character of different gods and goddesses.

The Sun gives heat and light and life; it is obviously very powerful. The Moon is cool, mysterious, changeable, the mirror of the Sun's power at night. Mercury flits around the sky as if on urgent errands: the messenger. Venus, the morning and

Below: Man has been fascinated by the firmament since primitive times. Every culture has developed myths and explanations which attempt to explain the movements of the heavenly bodies.

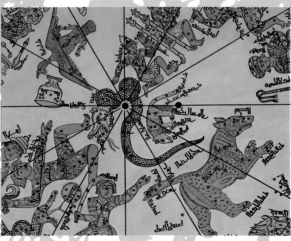

Above: *Many of the greatest of the early astrologers were from Egypt and the Middle East. This detail from an Arabian map shows the constellations according to the theories of Mulhammad ben Hilal, c 1275.*

Right: *Sol – the Sun – personified here in the form of a god, ruling over the symbol of Leo. Sol is traditionally the bringer of life, fertility, and prosperity.*

Below: *Detail from a representation of the zodiacal sigils carved on to the Salt Tower at the Tower of London. The carving is dated 30 May 1561, and signed Hugh Draper.*

evening star, became linked with love. Mars, fiery red and aggressive in its movements around the sky, was warlike. Jupiter was stately, strong, constant: authority, but big-hearted. Saturn was much paler, slower: dying and death.

Gustav Holst's suite *The Planets* is a marvellous evocation of the characters of the planets and, like the planets themselves, it is both inspiring and awe-inspiring.

The Sun

The Sun is the largest, brightest, and most powerful object in the heavens. The Aztecs and Incas of Central America built vast cities, containing temples and observatories from which to worship and observe the Sun, which they considered most holy. Solar deities have usually (though not quite

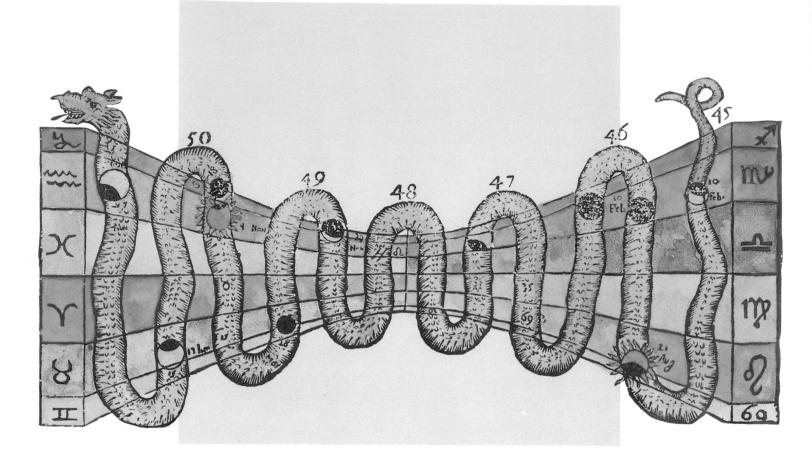

The Moon
. . . .

always) been male, and obviously connected with the seasons of the year. It is the Sun's position in the zodiac at our birth which gives us our "star sign" of Gemini, Cancer, Libra, Aries and so on. Solar eclipses, when the Sun is blotted out for a while, have always been portents of great disaster.

Astrologically there has been disagreement amongst the authorities whether the Sun rules the outside of a person and the Moon the inside, or the other way around. Generally, though, the Sun stands for the conscious mind, the real essence of the ego. We speak of people having a sunny disposition; generosity and faithfulness are Sun attributes, but the Sun also implies strength, power and dignity.

The Sun gave his name to Sunday, the first day of the week and the Christian holy day.

The Sun rules Leo.

The Moon takes around twenty-eight days to orbit the Earth.

The Moon runs close to the Sun in importance. She lights up the night; she rules the tides, and all things watery; she changes through the month, giving her an obvious link, through menstruation, to the eternal female. Moon deities are almost invariably female. She has long been associated with all things mysterious, and with the subconscious mind. She also has an effect on madness (hence the words "lunatic" and "lunacy"), as pointed out by Paracelsus in the sixteenth century (though believed long before this), and confirmed by psychiatrists today.

The Moon gave her name to Monday.

The Moon rules Cancer.

Above: This image shows the lunar dragon (combining the Caput and the Cauda associations) set against the twelve divisions of the constellational zodiac.

Opposite: Luna – the Moon – represents mystery and intrigue as well as intuition and sensitivity.

Mercury

The planet Mercury takes only eighty-eight days to orbit the Sun.

Mercury, who races around the sky, is the Roman messenger of the gods, the equivalent of the Greek Hermes. He is often depicted as having wings on his feet. He is the god of childhood. Astrologically, he denotes intelligence, memory and communication, a quick-witted nature – but "mercurial", in that he will flit from whatever (or whoever) catches his attention at one moment to the next, so he is not always dependable. He is generally described as the patron of both businessmen and thieves – profitable, but living on the speed of his wits.

Mercury gave his name to "mercredi" in French and "mercoledí" in Italian; "Wednesday" is named after the Norse-Germanic god Odin or Wotan, the All-Father, who is somewhat more important in the hierarchy of gods than Mercury, but shares his attributes of wisdom and energy, and, similarly, also represents thieves, as well as those involved in business and marriage deals.

Mercury rules the two signs closest to those of the Sun and Moon: these are Virgo by day, and Gemini by night.

Venus

The planet Venus takes two hundred and twenty-five days to orbit the Sun.

Venus is the Roman goddess equivalent to Aphrodite, the earlier Greek goddess of love, beauty, peace and harmony. She is the essence of the female (her symbol is the universal scientific symbol for female or feminine). She is also the goddess of youth or adolescence. Venus governs the emotions, and also æsthetics, the appreciation of beauty.

The word venereal, now usually only associated with sexual diseases, in fact means anything to do with sexual intercourse; venery is sexual indulgence. It should always be remembered that all the planets and gods, like all the zodiacal signs, contain both good and bad. Sensuality and passion are natural and healthy feelings, but because they are so powerful, they can be mis-directed. Over-indulgence in the gratification of pleasure can be associated with Venus – as can indolence.

Right: Here a rustic figure, inspired by the music and cosmic influence of the stars and zodiac symbols, is playing the bagpipes. This is a plate from a late fifteenth-century Shepherd's Calendar.

Venus gave her name to "vendredi" in French and "venerdí" in Italian; "Friday" is named after the Norse-Germanic goddess Freyja, or more likely Frigg, whose symbol, the distaff (or spinning-stick), has become the term for the female side of the family.

Venus, the next planet out from the Sun after Mercury, rules the next two signs out: Libra by day and Taurus by night.

Mars

The planet Mars takes six hundred and eighty-seven days to orbit the Sun.

Mars is the Roman god of war and battle, but not necessarily of aggression; here he differs from the nearest Greek equivalent, Ares, who was a lot more bloodthirsty, and not a popular god at all. Mars' strength, like any good soldier's, is disciplined, and he is likely to attack in order to defend, rather than for conquest. Mars has given us the word martial, meaning to do with warfare.

He is honourable, courageous, active and energetic – and is seen as the universal symbol for male or masculine. Modern astrologers often say that if Venus is love, Mars is sex, but this is far too

Imagine di Venere nata dalla spuma del mare, della bellezza Dea, & della libidine, madre d'Amore, simbolo della lasciuia, qual fù anco tenuta Dea delle nozze & del matrimonio, intesa per il pianetta di Venere, detta ancor Lucifero, & Hespero, che induce la virtù generatiua nelle cose.

nagini de Tritoni & delle Nereide buomini & donne mari ue secondo Alessandro Napolitano, Theodoro Gaza, & altri antichi, & moderni; con l'imagine di Galatea nereide principale, & suo carro significante la doppia virtù delle acque.

A b o v e : *Two visions of Venus, after the style of Lorenzo Pignoria Padonvo, from his book* Le Vere e Nove Imaginini de gli Dei delli Antichi, *which was produced in Padua in 1615. Venus is seen being born out of the sea spray; she is in the traditional pose on the half-shell. In astrological terms, she represents love, sensuality and desire.*

simplified. In the ages of man, Mars is the young adult.

Mars gave his name to "mardi" in French and "martedí" in Italian; "Tuesday" is named after the Norse-Germanic god Tyr, the defender-god.

Mars, the next planet out from the Sun, after Venus, rules the next two signs out: Scorpio by day and Aries by night.

Jupiter

The planet Jupiter takes nearly twelve years to orbit the Sun.

Jupiter is mature and expansive, good-hearted and merciful, majestic and magnificent. He is powerful, and he can be dangerous; his thunderbolts have been known to miss. He is the mature adult, the successful businessman; he denotes prosperity and good fortune, order and organization. He is associated with good health, and his symbol is still used to denote medicine.

The Roman god Jove, who is equated with the Greek god Jupiter, has given us the word jovial, meaning convivial or big-hearted.

Jupiter's Roman equivalent Jove gave his name to "jeudi" in French and "giovedí" in Italian; "Thursday" is named after the Norse-Germanic god Thor, the god of thunder.

Jupiter, the next planet out from the Sun, afte Mars rules the next two signs out: Sagittarius by day and Pisces by night.

Saturn

The planet Saturn takes twenty-nine and a half years to orbit the Sun.

Saturn, the furthest away of the "old" planets, is seen as dark, gloomy, melancholy and sluggish, the very essence of our word "saturnine". In contrast with Jupiter's expansiveness, Saturn is limiting. He will slow down enterprises, turning success into failure. He personifies old age, which includes wisdom and teaching as well as lameness and decrepitude.

The Roman god Saturn was originally the Roman god of agriculture, especially corn, so he wielded a sickle. So did the Greek god Cronos (or Kronos), but he used his to castrate his father

Uranus, and then ate his own children – not one of the most pleasant deities. The Romans then further confused Cronos with "chronos", the Greek word for time. So Saturn has become identified with the Grim Reaper, Old Father Time, scything down lives. The nearest equivalent of the original Roman god Saturn is actually the Greek goddess of vegetation (especially corn), Demeter, one of the children of Cronos.

Saturnalia was a Roman mid-winter festival when slaves were allowed to run free, and everyone indulged in drunkenness and orgies; the Lord of Misrule, a mock king, was allowed absolute licence. This chaotic but fun aspect of Saturn is

Below: *The planets personified, and set inside a zodiacal border.*

unfortunately often forgotten by astrologers.

Saturn gave his name to "Saturday".

Saturn, the next planet out from the Sun after Jupiter, rules the next two signs out: Capricorn by day and Aquarius by night.

The "new" planets

It should be remembered that these planets had no part in traditional astrology; their characteristics have only been developed over the last couple of centuries for Uranus, and the last few decades for Pluto. The choice of their names has also not had the blessing of time, although many astrologers work backwards from these names to ascribe astrological attributes to the planets.

How much weight should be put upon them is up to the individual. They are far away, and cannot be seen with the naked eye; whatever effects they have might be very weak. Also, because of the length of their orbits, there would be little appreciable difference from year to year, let alone from minute to minute.

On the other hand, if the planets in our solar system *do* have an effect on our lives, then so must these three, and the ancients simply did not know about them. But in deciding what effects they might have, we are denied the accumulated wisdom of millennia.

Uranus

The planet Uranus, discovered in 1781, takes eighty-four years to orbit the Sun – and seven years to pass through a single sign of the zodiac.

The god Uranus was the Greek sky-god castrated and deposed by his son Cronos. His other children included the Titans and the Cyclopes, so he can be seen as the father of disruption. He was the god of lightning, so astrologers have given him electricity to look after.

We have already seen that many astrologers believe that Uranus is responsible for political revolutions and industrial development – social changes rather than personal ones. Some equate revolutions with disruption, others with democracy and international collaboration. In individual terms, this could mean originality, unconventionality and invention.

Uranus has been given Saturn's night sign, Aquarius, to rule.

A b o v e : *An early map from late-Roman antiquity depicting the constellations, with personifications of the Sun and the Moon and the zodiacal asterims.*

Neptune

The planet Neptune, discovered in 1846, takes one hundred and sixty-five years to orbit the Sun; nearly fourteen years per zodiacal sign.

The god Neptune was the Roman god of the sea (equivalent to the Greek god Poseidon), so many astrologers ascribe watery characteristics (previously the province of the Moon) to the planet. Some say he represents "whatever dissolves", and so by inference anything vague and undefined, including alcohol and drugs. He is thought to signify, in his more negative state, deception and whatever may be illusory in a character or situation. He is also given the spiritual and mystical aspects of the Moon's personality.

Because of the idea of water, some astrologers give Neptune Jupiter's night sign, Pisces, to rule.

Pluto

The planet Pluto, discovered in 1930, takes two hundred and forty-eight years to orbit the Sun – over twenty years per sign of the zodiac. Although known as the furthest planet, Pluto's orbit is so eccentric that for the rest of this century it will be closer to the Sun than Neptune is.

Pluto is another name for Hades, the Greek god of the underworld. It was said to bring bad luck to use the name Hades, so the god had various pseudonyms, including Pluton, meaning "the rich" (hence the word plutocracy, rule by the wealthy). Most astrologers seem to be drawing the planet's astrological personality from the idea of the underworld: the dark side of mankind, death and transformation.

Some astrologers give Pluto Mars's day sign, Scorpio, to rule; others seem to prefer Pisces, which most assign to Neptune; one astrologer even says Aries, presumably on the grounds that it is the next one round after Neptune's Pisces, though Aries and Mars are so closely linked that most astrologers would find it unimaginable to separate them. It is not unusual for there to be varying opinions amongst astrologers and differences of viewpoint often occur.

Presumably if another two planets are discovered, they will each be given one of Venus's and Mercury's two signs.

Opposite: *An allegory for the perfection of humanity, with the zodiacal signs both within and around the figure: the whole illustrates the relationship between the microcosm and the macrocosm.*

A b o v e : *The seven planets shown in a schema (pattern, or plan) of roundels, from an illumination of c 1400. The original is in the British Museum. The plate is of interest, reminding us that medieval astrology comprised a complex system which functioned, of course, without the planets Neptune and Pluto. The discovery of these planets, in the nineteenth and twentieth centuries respectively, dismayed astrologers, who had to quickly revise and re-evaluate their methodology, and determine whether or not these new bodies could be legitimately incorporated into the astrological philosophy.*

The Horoscope

A horoscope is a schematic map of the heavens at a specific moment – usually, but not necessarily, the moment of someone's birth. In fact, natal astrology is a relatively late development, from around the fifth century BC.

Horoscopes can also be drawn up for countries, and even for companies; this is known as mundane astrology, and appears to pre-date natal astrology considerably.

Horary astrology uses the horoscope by taking an astrological snapshot of the moment the question is asked in order to give an answer to the question.

A progressed horoscope looks at an individual's future; in the most widely-known system the astrologer takes the birthchart and progresses it by a day for each year of the subject's life. To draw a horoscope for someone's fortieth birthday, he would, by this system, set it exactly forty days after the moment of birth; but this is only one of several ways of doing it, and many serious astrologers dismiss the idea altogether.

Electional astrology, on the other hand, has considerable support; it calculates planetary positions for given moments in the future, to find the most propitious time for a proposed important activity: a political conference, or the laying of a foundation stone, for example.

Astrology is still used medically (though rarely by "orthodox" Western doctors) to help indicate imbalances in the body. The fourth-fifth century BC Greek physician Hippocrates (after whom the medical Hippocratic oath is named) claimed it was essential for doctors to be able to interpret a horoscope.

Although we now know that the Earth, and all the other planets, orbit the Sun, for the purposes of astrology the Sun, the Moon and the planets are treated as if they orbit the Earth – which is, of course, what they appear to do. This does not automatically invalidate astrology: it is the relationship of the heavenly bodies that is important, rather than the physical position of a hunk of rock or ball of gas.

Looking up at the sky (from the northern hemisphere) we see the old familiar constellations: the Plough, Cassiopeia, Orion. If we know what to look for (and constellations are by no means obvious) we can pick out the twelve constellations which make up the zodiac. (The word zodiac comes from a Greek root meaning "circle of animals"; many of the zodiacal constellations are animals.) These all lie in one wide belt across the sky, in which the Sun and Moon also appear.

As the Earth pursues its orbit around the Sun these twelve constellations march along their path during the course of the year, which is why they made a useful calendar for the ancients. The circle of the sky, 360 degrees, divided by twelve, gives 30 degrees for each sign of the zodiac, and roughly one degree per day of the year. Each sign, though it spans two months, therefore lasts about 30 days.

Wandering among the constellations are the planets and the Moon. Although the brightness of the Sun blots out its backdrop of stars, the constellations are still behind it, and the Sun's path can be plotted across them as if it were a planet.

Because of the tilt of the Earth's axis (at an angle of 23 degrees, 27 minutes to its orbital plane), the noon Sun rises higher in the sky in summer than in winter; the summer solstice, around 21 June, is its highest point, where it

Once the basics of astrology are understood, it takes its place amongst the great systems of self-enlightenment and divination, such as those illustrated here – palm-reading, geomancy, and Tarot – and others like dream interpretation, I Ching and runes. Astrologers, such as the medieval scholar shown, bottom right, have been predicting future events for hundreds of years.

Knight of Cups

Right: *A beautiful constellation map illustrating the planetary movements according to the Copernican heliocentric (Sun-centred) system, c 1661.*

appears to pause before sliding back down the sky through autumn and into winter. The winter solstice, the Sun's low pausing point, is around 22 December. So, the Sun is in the sky for longer in the summer than in the winter; day is longer in summer, night is longer in winter. The spring and autumn equinoxes, around 20–21 March and 22–23 September, are the mid-points at which day and night are exactly equal. The solstices and equinoxes have, from earliest times, been major religious festivals.

The Zodiac and the Constellations

The horoscope notionally shows exactly where each planet (including the Sun and the Moon) is against the constellations behind it. This indication is notional because the position of the zodiacal constellations in the sky today is not the same as the astrological zodiacal signs. As well as being

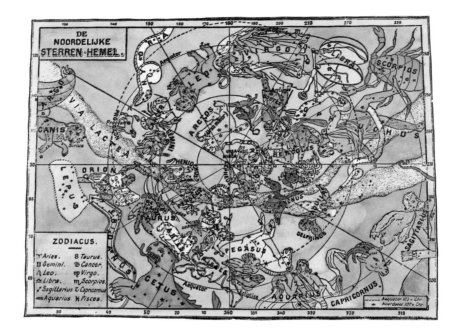

Right: *A relatively modern, c 1919, Dutch constellation chart after the edition of Libra's Astrology – Its Techniques and Ethics. The map places the animals of the zodiac in their places in the heavens.*

Below: *A charming eighteenth-century constellation map printed for Gerald Valk and Peter Schenk. The breadth and quality of astrological imagery, as evidenced by the planetary and constellation charts shown on these two pages, is extraordinary. These pieces are now widely and seriously collected as artefacts in their own right, and can fetch large sums at auction.*

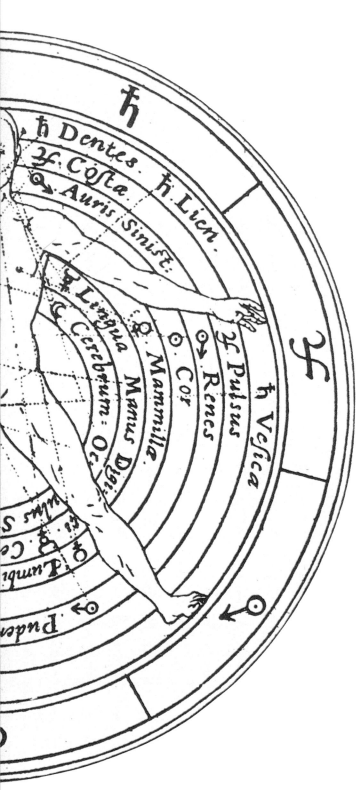

tilted, the Earth also wobbles on its axis, like a spinning top, and over the centuries the direction in which its axis is pointing has changed.

When the zodiac was first drawn up, some four thousand years ago, the Sun was just entering the constellation of Aries at the point of the spring equinox. The circle of the zodiac therefore began at 0 degrees Aries on around 21 March, and progressed through the signs during the year until it reached 30 degrees Pisces on around 20 March.

The Greek astronomer Hipparchus was the first to point out, around 120 BC, that this was no longer the case. By then, the Sun was moving out of Aries into Pisces; by now, another two thousand years later, it has moved on again, and is passing out of Pisces into Aquarius.

The position of the twelve signs on a horoscope is thus "out" by two, compared with the actual position of the twelve zodiacal constellations in the sky.

Critics of astrology claim that this "precession of the equinoxes" completely invalidates the whole thing; someone whom we call Scorpio because of their birth date ought really to have the characteristics ascribed to Virgo, which are quite different. The planets that we carefully place in certain signs in the horoscope ought to be somewhere else entirely. Astrologers, in response, say that the principles remain the same, and that the horoscope is a *symbolic* representation; it does not claim to be a photographic map.

The precession of the equinoxes has given us the terms "the Age of Aries", "the Age of Pisces", and the now famous "Age of Aquarius" which we are about to enter (or, according to some astrologers, have already entered).

It may be entirely coincidental that Christianity, one of whose symbols is the fish, began at the start of the Age of Pisces, but astrologers and new agers in general have made a lot of this. We are moving, they say, from the age of confusion and instability to the age of freedom of thought and brightness of attitude.

Drawing up a horoscope

Anyone wishing to construct their own horoscope from scratch should buy a book dealing with this in full detail, and also a copy of *Raphael's Ephemeris* or any other ephemeris (plural,

Napoleon Bonaparte (partial)

Aspects: Radix/Radix		
MC Sxt Mar	2 1	MC Tri Jup
ASC Sxt Ura	1 28	Sun Sqr Jup
Ven Sxt Ura	1 43	Ven Sxt Nep
Mar Sxt Ura	4 20	Sun Tri Nep
Jup Sxt Plu	4 36	Mar Cnj Nep
Nod Tri Sun	1 53	Ura Cnj Nep

11. 56 Cnc		
12. Regio Leo		
19 41 Leo		
17 6 Sco		
6 53 Sgr		

Node 20 48 Sgr R 3
Point 17 6 Pac 5

Sun	22 41 Leo	11
Mercury	27 51 Cap	
Venus	6 52 Can	
Mars	12 6 Vir	
Jupiter	12 0 Sco	10
Saturn	25 59 Can	9
Uranus	11 35 Cnc	
Neptune	3 41 Tau	11
Pluto	13 24 Cap R	11

MC Opp Plu 0 37
MC Sxt Ura 1 52
Ven Opp Plu 1 43
Mar Sxt Ura 5 27
Sat Opp Plu 1 24
Ura Opp Ura 3 53
Nep Tri Plu 4 44

Napoleon Bonaparte

Adolph Hitler

Radix
Adolph Hitler

Date:	20 Apr 1889 Sat
Time:	18 30 0
Zone:	1 0 E
Latitude:	48 15 N
Longitude:	13 3 E

MC	2 16 Leo
ASC	25 15 Lib
	Regio
11.	7 45 Vir
12.	3 29 Lib
2.	19 9 Sco
3.	21 25 Sgr

Sun	0 49 Tau	7
Moon	6 33 Cap	
Mercury	25 41 Ari	7
Venus	16 42 Tau R	7
Mars	24 Tau	7
Jup	Cap	3

Node 16 4 Cnc R 9
Point 1 0 Cnc 10

Aspects: Radix/Radix   Orb: 8 0

MC Sqr Sun	1 27	MC Sxt Nep	1 25	MC Sxt Plu
Sun Tri Moo	5 44	Sun Cnj Mer	5 8	Sun Tri Jup
Mer Opp Ura	6 11	Ven Cnj Mar	0 18	Ven Sqr Sat
Nep Cnj Plu	3 49	Nod Sxt Ven	0 38	Nod Sxt Mar

Adolph Hitler

Madonna Ciccione

Radix

Date:	16 Aug 1958 Sat
Time:	7 0 0
Zone:	5 0 W
Latitude:	43 36 N
Longitude:	83 54 W

MC	2 32 Gem
ASC	7 17 Vir
	Regio
11.	2 8 Cnc
12.	12 36 Leo
2.	9 32 Lib
3.	27 21 Lib

Sun	23 7 Leo	
Moon	11 30 Vir	
Mercury	5 39 Vir R	12
Venus	11 8 Can	
Mars	2 20 Tau	12
Jupiter	26 24 Lib	
Saturn	25 12 Leo	
Uranus	12 42 Leo	
Neptune	2 58 Sco	
Pluto	1 43 Vir	12

Node 25 20 Lib R 1
Point 25 40 Vir

Aspects: Radix/Radix   Orb: 8 0

MC Sqr Plu	0 49	Sun Sqr Mar	7 42
Moo Sqr Jup	3 59	Moo Tri Mar	7 40
Ven Sqr Nep	3 17	MC Tri Nep	
Mer Sxt Nep	2 9	Mer Sxt Plu	5 50
Nep Sxt Plu	0 15	Mer Cnj Plu	3 56
		Sat Tri Ura	6 26
		Nod Sxt Sun	2 13

Madonna Ciccione

Charles Chaplin

Radix
Charles Chaplin

Date:	16 Apr 1889 Tue
Time:	20 0 0
Zone:	0 0 E
Latitude:	51 31 N
Longitude:	0 5 W

MC	22 43 Leo
ASC	8 38 Sco
	Regio
11.	25 47 Vir
12.	18 31 Lib
2.	2 47 Sgr
3.	8 41 Cap

Sun	27 1 Ari	6
Moon	9 24 Sco	5
Mercury	17 50 Ari	5
Venus	18 7 Tau R	7
Mars	13 35 Tau	7
Jupiter	8 10 Cap	2
Saturn	13 26 Leo	R 12
Uranus	19 33 Lib	7
Neptune	0 44 Gem	8
Pluto	4 36 Gem	8

Node 16 16 Cnc R 9
Point 21 1 Tau 9

Aspects: Radix/Radix   Orb: 8 0

ASC Cnj Moo	0 46	ASC Sxt Jup	0 27	Sun Opp Ura 7 22	Moo Opp Mar 4 11
Moo Sxt Jup	1 13	Moo Sqr Sat	4 41	Mer Tri Sat 4 24	Ven Opp Ura 1 49
Ven Cnj Mar	4 31	Ven Sqr Sat	4 41	Mar Tri Jup 5 25	Mar Opp Ura 0 10
Nep Cnj Plu	3 52	Nod Sqr Mer	1 33	Nod Sxt Ven 1 50	Nod Sxt Mar 2 41

Charles Chaplin

Casting a Horoscope

These days horoscopes are very often cast on computer systems. These were made using electric ephemeris software. The horoscopes, cast by one of Sweden's best-known astrologers, John Alexander, are of Charlie Chaplin, Madonna, Napoleon, and Hitler.

Key

☉	Sun	♒ Aquarius	⚹ Quincunx	♉ Taurus	
☾	Moon	♓ Pisces	☍ Opposition	♊ Gemini	
☿	Mercury	☌ Conjunction	♅ Uranus	♋ Cancer	
♀	Venus	⚺ Semisextile	♆ Neptune	♌ Leo	
♂	Mars	∠ Semisquare	♇ Pluto	♍ Virgo	
♃	Jupiter	⚹ Sextile	☊ North Node	♎ Libra	
♄	Saturn	□ Square	☋ South Node	♏ Scorpio	
♐	Sagittarius	△ Trine	⚷ Midheaven		
♑	Capricorn	⚼ Sesquiquadrate	♈ Aries		

---

ephemerides) which gives the position of the Sun, Moon and every planet at different times on every day of the year. Whatever the times given in the tables, you can be sure that the exact time of your birth – which is what you need – will fall somewhere between them, which means you have to take the planetary positions at the nearest time, work out (for each planet) how far it will have travelled between then and your birth time, and add or subtract the degrees and minutes.

Before you can do any of this you need to know the exact longitude of your birthplace, so that you can convert the local time of your birth to Greenwich Mean Time (GMT). You also, of course, have to remember to take into account local variations such as British Summer Time or Daylight Saving Time.

All these mathematical workings-out can be very complicated, which is why many astrologers now use, and recommend, a computer program. There is absolutely no reason why not; after all, constructing a horoscope is nothing more than calculating what is where, when.

Do *not*, however, take note of any computer program which then goes on to "interpret" the horoscope for you. Interpretation is largely a matter of instinct and intuition which computers as yet do not possess. You will also need to know the ascendant and the *medium coeli*.

The ascendant is the sign which was rising on the eastern horizon at your moment of birth; this is almost as significant a factor in interpretation as your basic star sign. You not only need to know which sign it was, but how far it had "risen", so

the ascendant will be in the form of 8 degrees Cancer or 15 degrees Aquarius.

The *medium coeli* (MC) is the mid-heaven, the degree of the sign which was on the meridian, or due south, at that moment; again, this is in the form of 12 degrees Gemini or 23 degrees Libra. The *medium coeli* and ascendant are marked on the chart, followed by the houses.

The Houses

The astrological chart is divided into twelve sections, or houses. They represent the divisions of what is visible from Earth at any place and at any time. Also shown are the "invisible heavens", what is concealed beneath the Earth at the same time and from the same place. The houses do not have individual names but are allotted numbers. There is no one "correct" way of dividing up the horoscope into these houses. There are at least half a dozen completely different house systems in fairly wide use, all giving different results from the same data – as well as many others, less well-known. Although astrology is a complicated process and there are many variations of division and differences of opinion as to the exact positioning of houses, astrologers do agree on their meanings. Each house signifies one area of life, as follows:

1. The individual's appearance, temperament and overall potential.
2. Possessions and money.
3. Intelligence and close relationships.
4. Home, family affairs, parents.
5. Procreation, sexual relationships and pleasure, other pleasures.
6. Employees, hard work, chores.
7. Marriage, married partner, business partnerships.
8. Death, inheritance and secret wishes.
9. Expansion and exploration of the spirit and the mind; travel.
10. Career, ambition, reputation, honours.
11. Friendships, social life, associations and clubs.
12. Secrecy, the inner self, troubles, betrayals.

Above: This image, after Leonard Reymann's early sixteenth-century woodcut, depicts the twelve houses of the horoscope, which appear in red.

Opposite: A delightfully simplistic seventeenth-century schema – almost in the style of a needlework sampler – showing the twelve houses of the zodiac and their meanings.

his frinds
Unrelated
hopes

his Religion Long
Voyages Travel

his Mother &
Physick
also Reputation

his
Death
Legacies

his
Priuate
Enemies
Great
Cattle

the
Sick=
mans body
or
Person

The Sickmans Glass
Shewing What ~
Euery House Sig=
nifies in Case of
Sicknys or Other=
wise

his
wife
his Physi=
cian and
Publick.
Enemies

his
Esteate
or Substa=
nce

his Houses Land
Father and
Somtimes
Graue

his
Sicknes
and saruan
as

his
Kindred
& Short Iourne=
ys

his
Children
Sports Delights

Right: *A schema of the standard post-medieval sigils of the zodiac signs: this chart was produced in the* Aureus Tractatus de Philosophorum *in 1677.*

Interpretation

Whichever method is used for setting up the houses, once the framework is established all the planets (including, most importantly, the Sun and the Moon) can be put in place, with the degrees and minutes of each one. These show how the planets relate to each other.

With everything in place, the most difficult part of the whole business can begin: interpreting the horoscope. Again, there are many books which deal with this in far more detail than we can here, including long explanations of every planet in every sign, but we can outline the most significant factors to look for to obtain a meaningful reading. Different astrologers may take these in different orders, but the important thing to remember is this:

Nothing should be taken in isolation. You are looking for the overall picture. Any individual factor, however important, can be strengthened or weakened or otherwise affected by others.

1. The Sun. The sign this lies in is your "star sign"; this sign is the basic shape, the underlying foundation, of your personality. If it is in Leo, which the Sun rules, these qualities will be espe-

Left: *A highly stylized constellation map showing the places of the animals and other figures in the heavens. The artist has depicted all the constellations in a rather distorted and monstrous form. The close proximity of the astrologers to the firmament they are observing may be a metaphor for the huge influence the stars have in the life of Everyman.*

Below: *A medieval melothesic figure depicting a human form, and illustrating the qualities of the corresponding zodiacal signs. The text is Latin, and the plate almost certainly comes from a late fourteenth-century or early fifteenth-century treatise.*

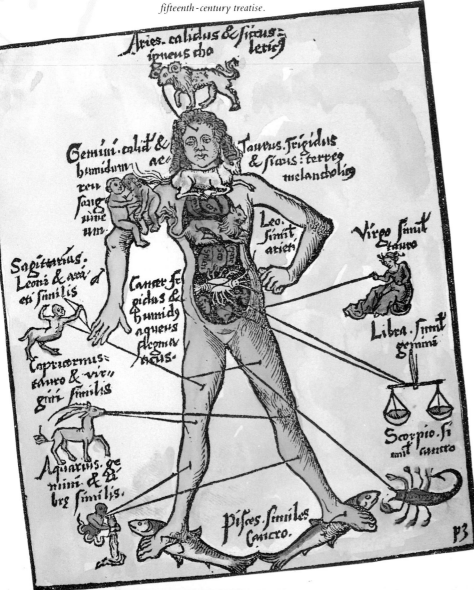

cially strong. The same applies, to a lesser extent, in the other two fire signs.

2. The Moon. This shows the characteristics of your subconscious – or, depending on terminology, your soul or spirit – the deepest, inner part of you. She governs your emotional responses, and represents all that is moving and changeable. It follows that the Moon has her strongest effect in water signs, most of all Cancer, which she rules.

3. The Ascendant. Often called the Rising Sign, the positioning of this sign indicates your temperament and instinctive attitude. Some astrologers also believe it gives an indication of your physical appearance, though quite obviously not all those with Taurus rising are short and plump with dark curly hair, and not all those with Sagittarius in the ascendant are tall and athletic-looking with a long nose!

4. The Ruling Planet. This is the ruler of the Rising Sign, the sign in which the ascendant lies. The Ruling Planet is one of the most important signifiers of character in the whole horoscope; indeed, it could be said to rule the horoscope. Where it lies – both the sign and the house – should be studied carefully, and it should be kept in mind throughout the interpretation.

Above: *This wonderful image from an early German woodcut could be an allegory for the pursuit of astrology. A scholar tears his way through the walls of the firmament to discover the mechanical workings of the stellar system.*

Right: *Mars, seen ruling Scorpio and Aries, and dominating a battlefield scene typical of his war-like attributes.*

5. The Elements: Fire, water, air and earth. For the rare fully-balanced person, the planets should be scattered amongst all the signs. If they are mainly in signs of just one element, then you are likely to be fiery and energetic, or earthy and practical, or quick-witted and imaginative, or emotional and intuitive. If you do not have any planets in a particular element then you will lack those qualities.

6. The Quadruplicities. The same idea applies. If the planets are mainly in cardinal signs you are likely to be strongly self-motivated, with leadership qualities. If they are mainly in fixed signs you may be solid but stolid, dependable but obstinate. If mainly mutable, you will be very adaptable, but can be selfish. Naturally, most people are some sort of mixture, but lacking one of them altogether shows a definite weakness in that quality.

R i g h t : A personification of Saturn. This planet rules Aquarius and Capricorn, and the people in the scene below are acting out Saturnian attributes, which tend to be solemn and serious.

7. The Planets in the Signs. Each planet has its own personality, each sign its own character. If any planet is in the sign it rules, those qualities will be strengthened: Mars in Aries, for example. Some planets and signs get on well together; others clash, and are weakening. Some combinations are particularly worrying: slow-moving Saturn in strong-willed Scorpio denotes great seriousness and heavy responsibilities. Many astrologers put special emphasis on where Mercury lies because of its speed and agility, and what it can show about your mind and your abilities.

There are seven "old" planets (including the Sun and Moon) and twelve signs; the eighty-four individual combinations would take up a number of pages. A quick bit of mathematical calculation shows that the total number of different combinations of all the planets in all the signs comes to 12^7, or 35,831,808 different personality types – a far cry from the standard complaint of the unin-

formed sceptic that according to astrology there are only twelve types of people! If you include the three "new" planets (and there are very good arguments both for and against) the total number of combinations comes to 12^{10}, or nearly sixty-two billion.

Obviously many of the combinations of planets in signs cancel each other out, and some are clearly far stronger and more significant than others. The factors already mentioned are crucial to determining the balance of the horoscope, as are two others.

8. The Aspects. The aspects are the angles between the various planets in the horoscope, and the interpretation depends a great deal on just which planets they are. Again the fundamental mathematical basis of astrology is highlighted. The main relationships are conjunction, opposition, trine, square and sextile.

Conjunction: two planets are very close – within seven degrees of each other. They combine their influences, intensifying whatever is good or bad.

Opposition: 180 degrees apart, ± 3.5 degrees. Again they combine their effects, but as they are pulling in opposite directions, this is usually bad.

Trine: 120 degrees apart, ± 3 degrees. If two planets are in trine, they reduce each other's influence in a good way, but if three are in a grand trine with each other, there is tremendous stability and balance.

Square: 90 degrees apart, ± 3 degrees. They diminish each other's effect in a bad way; if a third planet makes up a third corner of the square it is also in opposition to the first, and the overall relationship is very disruptive.

Sextile: 60 degrees apart, ± 3 degrees. This is generally favourable, in that the planets are seen to be working well with each other. It applies particularly to mental characteristics.

There are several other, less important aspects: semi-sextile (30 degrees), semi-square (45 degrees), quintile (72 degrees), sesqui-square or sesquadrate (135 degrees), bi-quintile (144 degrees) and quincunx (150 degrees). Generally, if the aspect divides the circle by 3, 5, 6 or 12, it is good; if it divides it by 2, 4 or 8 it is bad.

9. The Houses. The presence of a planet in a mundane house means that its influence will be especially felt in that area of life, either for good or for bad.

Popular astrologers often place an undue emphasis on this area of interpretation, probably because (compared with most other areas) it is relatively easy to make apparently clear (but actually vague) pronouncements: "You will be happy in love", "You will be successful in business", "Someone close to you will betray you", and so on.

Considering the disagreements amongst the experts, it is probably unwise to put too much faith in this part of the interpretation. There is a great deal of discussion about a planet being "on the cusp"; if astrologers would only agree about where the cusps (the dividing lines between the houses) actually are, this might make more sense.

10. In addition, the closeness of a planet to the ascendant or the descendant (180 degrees away),

A b o v e : *A copperplate engraved constellation chart by Andreas Cellarius 1660. It originally appeared in Schiller's* Atlas seu Harmonia Macrocosmica *in 1660.*

güt   mittel   böß

güt   mittel   böß

güt   mitttel   böß

gütt   mittel   böß

❡Der wyder bedeütet das haubte. vnnd der ochße den halß. als du vindeſt in der voideren igur gar klärlichen.

Above: *The twelve images of the zodiac signs. This hand-coloured print appeared in a German textbook on astrology c 1510.*

Right: *This is an astrological year chart, showing the various seasonal tasks that are carried out at different times and the zodiacal signs that therefore govern them. In the centre are personifications of summer and winter. This is a late fifteenth-century woodcut.*

or to the *medium coeli* at the top or the *imum coeli* at the bottom, or its presence (or more especially, the presence of several planets) in any of the quarters of the circle made by the lines drawn between these points – all these have significance.

The most important part of any interpretation, though, is the intuition of the astrologer. All the mathematical jugglings in a horoscope only point to potentialities; it is the astrologer's job to tease out the meaning.

One other vital point must be made. A horoscope does not, will not and cannot tell you what *will* happen to you in your life. It can paint a picture, of greater or lesser accuracy, of the qualities that make you the person you are; it is up to you to take those qualities, both good and bad, and make something of them.

Chinese Systems

ost Westerners think that Chinese astrology simply gives you a symbolic animal depending on which year you were born; but this is just as wrong as saying that you are a Cancer or a Leo and thinking that that is all there is to Western astrology. Chinese astrology is every bit as complicated to work out, both in the mathematical calculations and in the interpretation of the results.

Here we can unfortunately give only the basics, but even this much will show something of the richness of Chinese astrology.

It is said that one New Year the Buddha called all the animals to him, but only twelve came. To each of these in turn he gave a year to express its personality.

It is important to realize that the year has the characteristics of the symbolic animal, not just a person born in that year. Certain years are therefore more or less auspicious for beginning a new building, for example, or starting any major new

Above and left: These three figures are from a set of Chinese domino cards. This set uses as its theme the characters from the famous Chinese tale The Story of the River's Bank. Just as with Tarot in the West, these Chinese pieces are games-playing devices as well as part of a divination system.

Right: *An image of the double dragon, set between the Moon and the Sun, and standing on the Earth. There is an association between this figure and the lunar dragons of early astrology and alchemy.*

project. For individual people, the significance lies in the interplay between their own birth-year animal and that of the year in question. Some combinations are particularly fortuitous, others far less so, which is why people say they have had a good or a bad year. Your own year, every twelve years, provides excellent opportunities for your personality to flourish; the time is right for you.

Relationships obviously also depend on how the symbolic animals of each person interact with each other, and, traditionally, Chinese young men would present the details of their birth to the father of their intended young woman, who would see whether there would be a good match or not.

Chinese astrology is based on the cycles of the Moon, not those of the Sun, planets and stars. Because the lunar calendar does not fit in at all exactly with the solar calendar, the Chinese New Year is on a different date each year.

The year of each animal begins on the date in January or February shown in this chart.

Rat	24/1/36	10/2/48	28/1/60	15/2/72	2/2/84
Ox	11/2/37	29/1/49	15/2/61	3/2/73	20/2/85
Tiger	31/1/38	17/2/50	5/2/62	23/1/74	9/2/86
Cat/Rabbit	19/2/39	6/2/51	25/1/63	11/2/75	29/1/87
Dragon	8/2/40	27/1/52	13/2/64	31/1/76	17/2/88
Snake	27/1/41	14/2/53	2/2/65	18/2/77	6/2/89
Horse	15/2/42	3/2/54	21/1/66	7/2/78	27/1/90
Sheep/Goat	5/2/43	24/1/55	9/2/67	28/1/79	15/2/91
Monkey	25/1/44	12/2/56	29/1/68	16/2/80	4/2/92
Rooster	13/2/45	31/1/57	17/2/69	5/2/81	23/1/93
Dog	2/2/46	16/2/58	6/2/70	25/1/82	10/2/94
Pig	22/1/47	8/2/59	27/1/71	13/2/83	31/1/95

Over: *It is important to note that the Dragon is the only mythological animal among the twelve that make up the Chinese zodiac. Its inclusion probably dates back to its role in ancient Chinese astronomy.*

The usual criticism levelled at Chinese astrology (similar to the one levelled at Western astrology), that it says that everyone born in a particular year is of one type out of twelve, is quite inaccurate – though every school teacher will know that different years of pupils have quite different group personalities, some with a lot of pupils who are particularly bright, others very slow, others cheerful, others antagonistic. However, as we shall see, the season, the month, the day and the hour of birth also each have their own animal, and the complex interplay of several different animal characteristics – together with the five elements – is what makes up each person's individual personality.

In the ancient Chinese method of interpreting qualities as pairs of opposing but complementary contrasts (Yang and Yin) the symbolic animals in years ending in an even number (Rat, Tiger, Dragon, Horse, Monkey and Dog) are Yang, and those in years ending in an odd number (Ox, Cat, Snake, Sheep, Rooster and Pig) are Yin – very loosely, in Western terms, positive and negative, male and female, deductive and intuitive, hard and soft, thrusting and yielding, penetrating and receiving, etc.

The animals and their characteristics relate to each other in Yang-Yin pairs:

The Rat and Ox both appreciate the value of hard work in a project, the Rat at its conception and birth, the Ox as it grows through to satisfactory completion.

The Tiger and the Cat are the dark and light side of reconciling difficult problems, in an assertive or a conciliatory way.

The Dragon and the Snake both love the mysterious, the Dragon as a showman, the Snake as a mystic.

The Horse and the Sheep epitomize Yang and Yin: the aggressive, masculine Horse and the caring, sensitive Sheep.

The Monkey and the Rooster both achieve career success in an atmosphere of rapid change, the Monkey through versatility and skill, the Rooster through single-mindedness and ambition.

The Dog and the Pig represent the home and family; the Dog is protective, giving security, while the Pig cares for and nurtures the family.

Above: *Chinese astrology shares much of its imagery, symbolism and even meaning with the astrology of other Eastern and Oriental cultures: similar figures, gods, personifications and signs can be found in Persian, Arabic, Indian, and many other systems.*

Left: *This eighteenth-century woodblock print shows the twelve animals of the Chinese zodiacal system around the outer band, and the twelve corresponding character symbols on the inner band.*

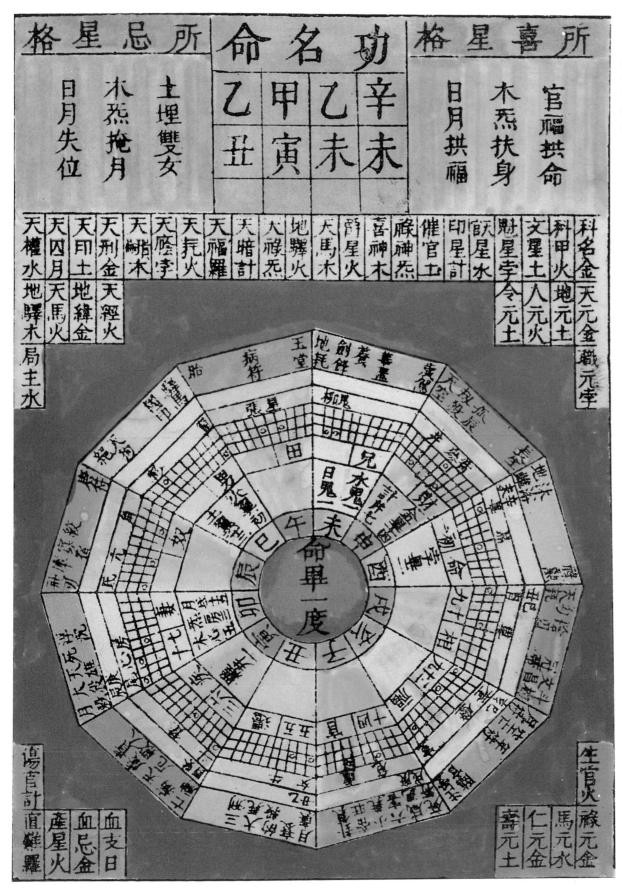

Left: *This hand-coloured woodblock print, which is shown courtesy of a private American collector, illustrates a horoscope diagram with the characters for the twelve animals in the central band.*

Chinese fortune-telling

Chinese fortune-telling stems from Chinese philosophy, at the heart of which is the idea of balance between opposites. Westerners often see Yang and Yin simply as masculine and feminine, but they are far more than this; they include the complementary ideas of positive and negative, active and passive, penetrating and yielding, ruling and submitting, hard and soft, bright and dark, heaven and earth, amongst many others.

The balance between these paired qualities is fundamental to Chinese astrology, the *I Ching*, and the adaptation of the game of Mah Jong for fortune-telling.

Natural phenomena, animals, flowers and different human occupation are seen in these modern Mah Jong cards, designed for use in fortune-telling.

The Animals

. . . .

Rat

Rats are intelligent, hard-working, assertive and ambitious. Their ambition is of supreme importance; Rats are usually careful with money – sometimes mean – but will spend it to further their career. They are also very generous to the object of their affections. They are friendly and extremely charming, but have a quick temper if they feel their plans – which they keep to themselves – are being threatened. Usually honest, they will lie to protect their career.

Compatible with Dragons and Monkeys.
Problems with Tigers and Dogs.

The Rat Year is a good time to start new plans. Creativity will flourish and artistry come to the fore.
Reorganization. Good for health and romance.

Ox

Ox people are patient, steady, methodical, reliable, solid, sometimes stolid, sometimes stubborn. They are very hard-working, but do not like innovation; the old ways are the best. Tradition and traditional values are important to them; they like order, and can be authoritarian. They are intelligent, but not terribly imaginative. They need security; they can be too materialistic. In love

they are slow to get started, but are then steadfast. Compatible with Snakes and Roosters.
Problems with Sheep, other Ox people, Dogs and Tigers.

The Ox Year is a time of stability and steady success. Any new projects should be initiated as soon as possible. A good year for farming.

Tiger

Tigers are born leaders: assertive, sometimes aggressive, very competitive. They are completely self-motivated, and can be selfish. They can easily dazzle others (and subdue them) with their brilliance and their magnetic personalities, but they also have a certain nobility. They are dynamic and enthusiastic, often reckless; they take risks, and can be dangerous to be with, though exciting; they can easily wear others out. In love they are passionate and have a wild streak, but tend to settle down later.

Compatible with Dogs and Horses, perhaps Pigs and Dragons.
Problems with Monkeys, Oxen and Cats.

The Tiger Year is a time of change and turbulence, for good or for bad. Love affairs are passionate, but health can be problematic; accidents can easily happen.

Above: *The Chinese zodiacal images of the Rat and the Ox are carved in relief on a highly-decorated column in the Chinese Garden in Sydney.*

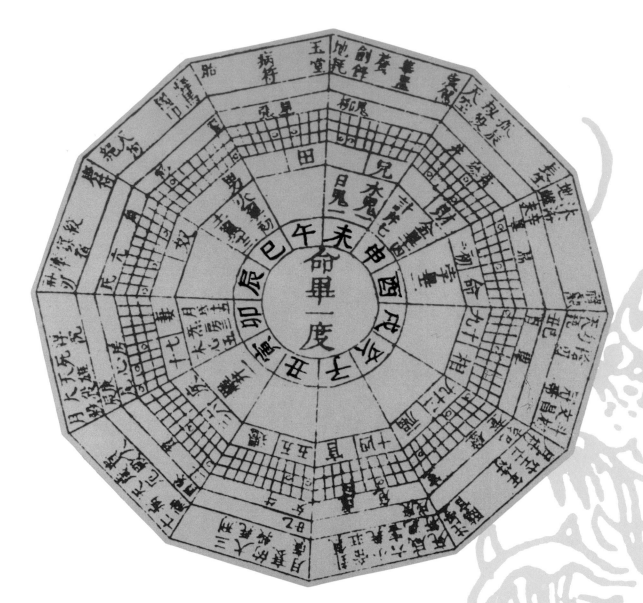

Above: *In many respects the Chinese horoscope illustrated here does not look greatly different from the Western horoscopes shown earlier. The inner, black band carries the characters associated with the twelve animals of the Chinese astrological system.*

Cat/Rabbit

Cats can be aloof from others; they tend to be quiet, and get on with things by themselves, though in fact they like the security of company and are good to be with, making excellent friends. They are survivors; they prefer sensible compromise to destructive confrontation. They are usually peacemakers, but if they have to fight they have tremendous courage. They are good judges of character; they are also healers. Cats are creative and artistic, but can be moody. In love they will flirt with fun, but are really looking for a warm and comfortable relationship.

Compatible with Pigs, Sheep and often Dogs. Problems with Roosters, Tigers, and often Monkeys and Horses.

The Cat Year is one of quiet progress in agreed

undertakings. Love can lead to procreation; a good time for recuperation in health particularly if there have been problems.

Dragon

Dragons tend to be successful. They are full of enthusiasm, and have the gift of inspiring this in others also. They are intelligent, imaginative, lively and independent; they hate being forced into a routine. They love the exotic and the unusual, including the supernatural; they also love show. They are not always easy to get on with, and can prove dangerous enemies; but they can be very good, supportive and helpful friends, if they are allowed to take the lead. They can easily be arrogant and proud.

Compatible with Rats, Monkeys and other Dragons.
Problems with Dogs especially, and with Horses and Sheep.

The Dragon Year will be unusually creative and innovative, especially in the arts and religion. High-risk projects are likely to succeed, but there will also be risks in love and health.

Snake

Snakes are deep-thinking and wise, but subtle; their success is often because they have manipulated other people, or made good use of their connections. They love finding things out, whether in gossip about other people, or in investigative research – but they are very secretive. They are critical and self-critical; they can be devious, and hold grudges. Like the Dragon, they enjoy mystery, but without the showiness; they are often mystical or psychic. They are often graceful and refined, and love luxury. In love they are sensuous; they will not take second best; they can be very jealous.

Compatible with Roosters and Oxen.
Problems with Pigs, Monkeys, Horses and often Tigers.

The Snake Year can be a time of deviousness and double-dealing, but should be successful if calmness prevails. Avoid potential scandal in relationships.

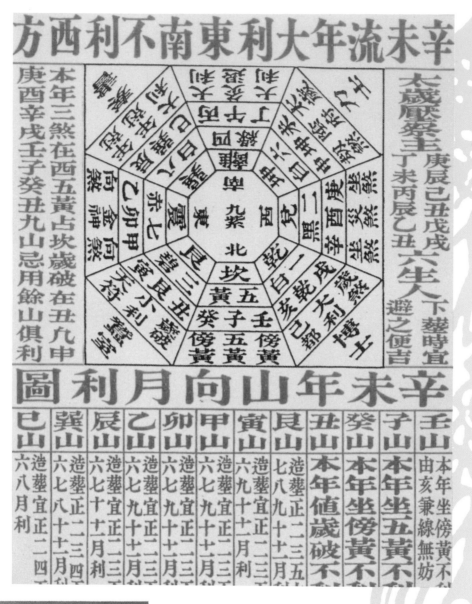

Right: *A Chinese "Feng Shui" chart from a modern almanac. One important element of Feng Shui is the art and science of fortuitous placement. When siting a new building, for example, the builders will first consult Feng Shui to confirm that the spirits are good and that the area is well-favoured.*

Below: *In Chinese astrology the Horse personality is sociable, competitive, gregarious, fairly solid and stable, healthy and robust. In Horse years consolidation is the watchword rather than excitement.*

Horse

Horses are sociable people, the sort who will belong to social or sports clubs, and take an active part in team sports; they are usually strong and healthy. Horses are not terribly inventive, but enjoy conversation. They are archetypally Yang, and like to be popular, and tend to be self-centred, though not selfish. They are hard-working and make good work-mates, and are naturally gregarious. They are quite well-liked by others, but their behaviour can be unpredictable and they can have nasty tempers. Their hearty exterior often masks an underlying weak and insecure personality. They fall deeply in love, but really they are "in love with love" – or with themselves – and fall out of love just as easily.

壬申年交節圖

方南利不西東利大歖事年流申壬

丙午丁未坤申寅八山忌用餘各山俱利

是年三煞在南五黃占坤歲破在寅九巳

太歲壓蔡壬辛巳庚寅己亥
戊申丁巳丙寅六生人
避之便吉 下蓡時宜

事用壬土

行姑得斷日局烏歲音屬太
雷把辛七張遇值德屬水歲
溫鸞四龍宿子年合金地名
元鸞牛治爲日鬼在歲支劉
帥食耕水暗虛金丁德屬珏
值三地二金宿羊畢在金天
年葉大日伏未管月壬納千

十九六三
二月月月
月廿十
廿五一五
五日日日

分初中末
伏伏伏
七六六五
月月月月
十廿十廿
四四四一
日日日日

全

秋社 曰母地 經母地 春社

Left: The so-called "geomancy" of the Chinese: the Geomantic Compass or Chart of Feng-Shui with a Spring Cow Chart. This is from an ancient "T'ung Shu" almanac. It is fascinating to compare it to the image on the opposite page, which is remarkably similar in style although these two charts were generated over five hundred years apart.

Below: Those who possess a goat personality are kind and considerate, yet can often be over-sensitive. Goat people tend to remain within a crowd rather than rise to a leadership role.

Compatible with Dogs, Tigers and Sheep. Problems with Rats, Snakes and Cats.

The Horse Year is one of strength and stability in both the business and the personal world. Health should be sound; any experiences of love will be active rather than deep.

Sheep/Goat

Sheep are vulnerable rather than insecure. They are archetypally Yin: good, gentle, considerate people, very caring, who make good listeners and offer a shoulder to cry on; but because they know how very easily they can be wounded they do not always reveal themselves fully to others. They react badly to criticism, always taking it personally; they can easily become depressed. They are diplomatic, and avoid confrontation. They are

Bottom, right: *The basic attributes of the Rooster personality are self-confidence, determination and pride. These can easily slip over into arrogance and aggression. Roosters are shrewd, well-organized and love a challenge.*

Below: *A charming domino card from* The Story of the River's Bank *set.*

artistic, though not creative in the sense of originality. They can appear vague and tend to be dreamers. In relationships they are more compatible with people who are tougher and less sensitive than themselves.

Compatible with Pigs, Cats, Horses – and other Sheep.
Problems with Oxen, Rats, Monkeys, Roosters.

The Sheep Year is one of peace, diplomacy and humanitarianism. The Arts are well-favoured; so is love.

Monkey

Monkeys can beguile anyone with their charm. They are clever, quick-witted and resourceful, but can be devious, deceitful and unscrupulous. They tend to be amoral rather than actively immoral: they are natural tricksters. They are fast learners, highly inventive, and extremely good at problem-solving. They thrive in an atmosphere of change. They are always able to get out of an awkward situation by quick thinking, and often by their innate humour. They are vivacious and friendly to everyone, which can be irritating for a new partner – and they are likely to change partners frequently. They are intelligent, but they tend to be vain, holding a low opinion of most other people. Overall, Monkeys are highly complex people.

Compatible with other Monkeys, Rats and Dragons.
Problems with Tigers and Snakes.

The Monkey Year is one of change, instability and confusion in business, love and health; it should be approached with care.

Rooster

Roosters often come over as abrasive, sometimes aggressive, throwing all their attention and energies into whatever they are pursuing, and ignoring or forgetting everything and everybody else. They are intelligent and intensely ambitious, and suffer fools badly; but they are very efficient, and good organizers. Like Monkeys they love variety and change, and thrive on activity. They can be great fun to be with if you can stand the pace – and

white, and they are born worriers. They tend to be suspicious of others and their motives until they get to know them. This can make it very difficult at the start of a relationship but once trust has been established, Dog people will be utterly loyal; they are natural home-makers and protectors. They do not, however, like public displays of emotion.

Compatible with Horses and Tigers.
Problems with Dragons, Roosters and Sheep.

The Dog Year is a time to think of defence, whether of the country, the business or the home. Health will be strong; love will be faithful.

Pig

Pig people are caring and loving people who work hard for the good of their family; they make excellent husbands, wives and parents. They are honest, sincere and tolerant, and expect others to be the same, which means that others can easily take advantage of them; in some ways they can be very naïve. Because they put their family before everything else they are unlikely to rise to the top of their professions; many of them work in "caring careers" where personal ambition is less important than the work they accomplish. They are also very practical people, who never leave jobs unfinished. They sometimes hide a warm heart under a bluff exterior, but anyone who knows them will quickly see beneath the apparent roughness, which, at times, can even appear to be rudeness. In love they are earthy and sensual.

Compatible with Cats and Dogs.
Problems with Snakes and Monkeys.

The Pig Year should be devoted to the welfare of the family; it is also a time of rest and reflection, and of drawing projects to a most satisfactory conclusion.

Far left: The Monkey is one of the most charming and seductive of the twelve animal characters. Perhaps best summarized in Western terms as a "lovable rogue", the Monkey is sharp, witty, streetwise, flexible, and ambitious. Its energy can also get it into trouble, however: it over-stretches, takes risks, and ignores the rules.

they are basically honest and straightforward, which is why they sometimes appear to be rude and tactless. They like to be the centre of attention, often performing to the gallery; they can be downright eccentric. In love, Roosters are all or nothing.

Compatible especially with Snakes, and also Oxen and Dragons.
Problems with Cats, Dogs, Monkeys and other Roosters.

The Rooster Year is one of determination, almost to the point of extremism. Business and career are in; love is out. All opinions will be voiced loud and clear.

Dog

Dog people are friendly, honest and likeable, and are steady and hard workers – but they are known for their occasionally sharp tongue. They are fair-minded, and have an exaggerated sense of fair play. They are very loyal, and will take the side of friends they feel have been wronged. But they do tend to see things in strict terms of black and

The five elements

Each year also has an element associated with it, and the Chinese have five elements, not the four of the Western world: wood, fire, earth, metal and water. Each element lasts for two years at a time, first exhibiting Yang characteristics, then Yin;

each element therefore covers a Yang-Yin pair of animals, a different element every twelve years. The combination of the animal and the element of each year, a twelve year cycle and a ten year cycle of pairs, offers sixty variants just for the year.

The same sixty possibilities are also available for the season, the month, the date and the time of birth. With this level of complexity, the Chinese horoscope is every bit as rich and detailed as its Western equivalent. The Chinese astrologer looking for the most propitious time for a new enterprise has a very wide spread of information.

The five elements affect the nature of the symbolic animal. To take the Snake as an example, it appears that the Wood-Snake is more considerate of others' feelings, the Fire-Snake is more suspicious and power-hungry, the Earth-Snake is more slow-minded and likeable and the Metal-Snake is both more secretive and more logical, while the Water-Snake is more artistic but more jealous – all these in addition to the basic Snake type.

The elements also relate to each other. Depending on the combination and positioning of the elements at different periods of someone's life in their chart, they have a tremendous effect on the personality, the directions one takes, and the relative success of different endeavours.

Wood burns, giving fire
Fire leaves ash or earth
Earth contains metal
Metal when heated flows like water
Water gives life to wood

Any adjacent pair of these has an overall good effect. But the elements can also go together in another order, and an adjacent pair of these would be destructive.

Wood sucks the goodness out of earth
Earth muddies water
Water quenches fire
Fire melts metal
Metal chops wood

In general, these are the characteristics of each element:

Wood is creative and inspirational, and denotes

health and happiness.
Fire is energy and excitement, but can be dangerous.
Earth is connected with stability and the land.
Metal denotes business efficiency – or strife.
Water shows change, intelligence, travel and communications.

Wood years end in 4 or 5 (plus, of course, the beginning of the following year), fire years end in 6 or 7, earth years in 8 or 9, metal years in 0 or 1, and water years in 2 or 3.

Wood	Fire	Earth	Metal	Water	
1934	1936	1938	1940	1942	Yang
1935	1937	1939	1941	1943	Yin
1944	1946	1948	1950	1952	Yang
1945	1947	1949	1951	1953	Yin
1954	1956	1958	1960	1962	Yang
1955	1957	1959	1961	1963	Yin
1964	1966	1968	1970	1972	Yang
1965	1967	1969	1971	1973	Yin
1974	1976	1978	1980	1982	Yang
1975	1977	1979	1981	1983	Yin
1984	1986	1988	1990	1992	Yang
1985	1987	1989	1991	1993	Yin
1994	1996	1998	2000	2002	Yang

Your other self

Many people find that they have two distinct personalities inside them; some people regularly have arguments with themselves. Perhaps they have elements of patience and irritability, or of caring and coldness, or they have conflicting urges to be impetuous or cautious. The theory behind Chinese astrology says that this is because the time of day at which they were born also has the characteristics of one of the symbolic animals; a similar idea, though for different reasons, to the Ascendant in Western astrology. Unlike Western astrology, though, the longitude is irrelevant – 2 a.m. is Ox wherever a person is born in the world – though local time adjustments such as British Summer Time or Daylight Saving Time should certainly be taken into account.

The animal of the time of birth could be called the other self, a companion, conscience or, at times, the darker side of the character.

Tiger, the equivalent tail end of February in the month of the Cat, and so on; if the New Year is in early February, then the month of the Tiger will extend into March, and this continues throughout the year.

There is a further complication in that each animal month may be the same or a day or two shorter than the equivalent calendar month, so that there is likely to be about a ten-day difference by the end of the year; here it is wise to work back from the next Chinese New Year.

Birth time	Other Self
11 p.m. – 1 a.m.	Rat
1 a.m. – 3 a.m.	Ox
3 a.m. – 5 a.m.	Tiger
5 a.m. – 7 a.m.	Cat/Rabbit
7 a.m. – 9 a.m.	Dragon
9 a.m. – 11 a.m.	Snake
11 a.m. – 1 p.m.	Horse
1 p.m. – 3 p.m.	Sheep/Goat
3 p.m. – 5 p.m.	Monkey
5 p.m. – 7 p.m.	Rooster
7 p.m. – 9 p.m.	Dog
9 p.m. – 11 p.m.	Pig

February	Tiger
March	Cat
April	Dragon
May	Snake
June	Horse
July	Sheep
August	Monkey
September	Rooster
October	Dog
November	Pig
December	Rat
January	Ox

B e l o w : *The Chinese call their astrological system "Ming Shui" – the reckoning of Fate. At every significant event – birth, marriage, and death – it plays its role. It is an ancient and revered philosophy, which plays a part in every aspect of the Chinese way of life.*

The month

Each month also relates to one of the symbolic animals, though it is not possible to equate them with the Western star signs because of the variable calendar already mentioned. It is made even more complicated by the fact that, to get the lunar year synchronized with the seasons of the solar year, seven times every nineteen years the Chinese "stretch" one of the months to double its length.

Very roughly, though, the following chart gives an idea of the relationship between the animal signs and the Western calendar months. If the date of the New Year is in January, then the tail end of January is included in the month of the

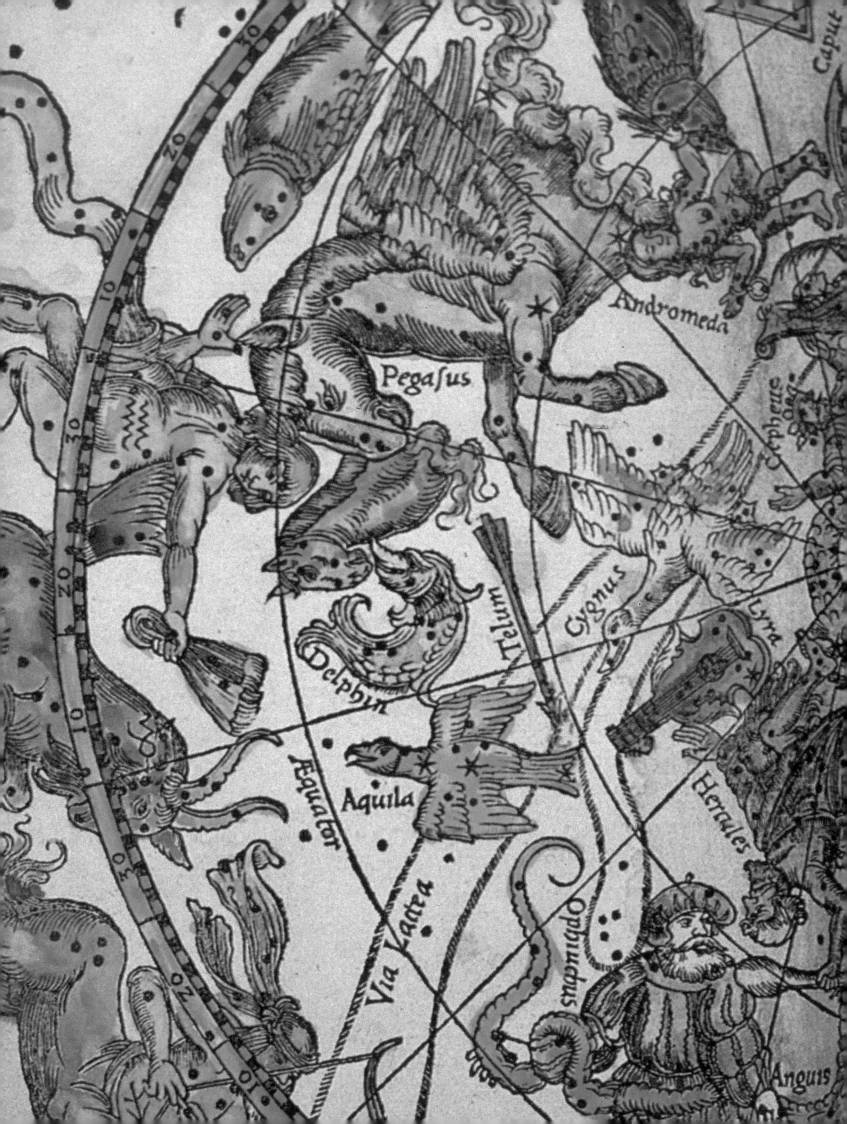

Personal Systems

*M*any systems of divination and prediction are concerned with the interpretation or manipulation of outside elements – Tarot cards, rune stones, I Ching stalks amongst them – but one of the finest mediums for divination is much closer to home: your own body.

Nothing is truer or more difficult to disguise than your physical attributes. The shape of the head, the features, the lines on the hand, and the way you write (even when you are attempting to conceal your identity) can all, to an experienced observer and interpreter, provide inescapable clues to the inner thoughts, the personality, and, through this knowledge, to likely future events in your life.

Phrenology and physiognomy, which were massively popular in the nineteenth century, today have a smaller following: but graphology is more credible than ever before as a revealer of character traits, and palm-reading will always be the most cherished and revered of divinatory skills.

Opposite: *Phrenology was never an exact science, with one agreed codification of attributes always associated with the same area of the cranium. As in many divinatory systems, different schools and theories grew out of the same basic idea. This image illustrates a system using 40 classifications.*

Palmistry

*T*he traditional image of a palm reader is of a raven-haired gypsy woman at a fair whose palm is crossed with silver as payment for revealing the secrets that she sees in her customers' hands. Part of this mystery still remains today, preserved through the art of both chiromancy, reading the future in the hand, and chirognomy, reading one's character in the hand.

Careful hand analysts will today look at far more than the lines on the palm of the hand; they will also examine the knuckles and the back of the hand, the shape of the finger-nails, the length of the fingers compared to the palm, the relative size and angle of the thumb, and even the colouring and texture of the skin. Both hands should be examined rather than just one.

As in the case of, for example, dreams, astrology, Tarot, and, in fact, any form of prediction or divination, the lines on your hand (and all the other factors) do not predict a fixed future; they tell you more about yourself, and thus reveal potentiali-

B e l o w : *In the medieval period, divinatory systems were intermingled rather than clearly separated mediums. This 1533 plate from Agrippa's* De Occulta Philosophia *illustrates a system combining palmistry and astrology.*

A b o v e : *This medieval zodiacal man illustrates the way that esoteric scholars of the time viewed the body. The theory was that each part of the anatomy was governed by external forces ruled by one of the astrological signs, thus linking individual physical properties with fate, destiny, and the cosmic forces.*

ties. Chiromancy is unlikely to tell you that you will definitely be married twice and have three sons and a daughter (though some palmists are remarkably accurate in such predictions); but it can tell you that you are likely to be a stable, loyal, loving partner, or that you are the sort of person who will rush headlong into relationships, or that you will be very close to children. It will not tell you that you will come into a fortune when you are thirty-five but it might tell you that you have a sound business sense, and should pursue (or avoid) certain career paths.

Similarly, to dispel a common myth, the length of the life line does *not* tell you how long you are going to live; but the line can give some indication of the strength of your life, especially your health. Again, the lines will not say that you will break your leg when you are forty; but certain things about them might point out childhood illnesses, and can (along with other factors) give an indication that you might have something wrong with your digestion or your breathing or your nerves.

Interestingly, such signs of illness in the lines will fade away once the illness is cured. One example is the presence of many thin vertical lines down the fingers, showing that someone is under a lot of stress. When the stress is lifted the skin on the palm side of the fingers may become smoother.

Health warning

Although a small number of Western doctors are beginning to take certain aspects of chiromancy seriously (as doctors in the past – and in the East – always have done), and to use hand analysis to detect the potential for certain illnesses, your own hand is not a diagnostic map for you to depend on yourself. If you think you detect signs of a particular medical complaint in your own hand or in anyone else's, consult a medical doctor. It is not your job to diagnose illnesses through esoteric or alternative means. All forms of divination should only be used for good – and occasionally the best good you can do is to persuade your friend or client to go to a doctor, without worrying them. Do not play doctor yourself.

A b o v e : *The great German chiromancer Johann Hartlieb, author of the earliest printed book on palmistry* Die Kunst Ciromantia, *which was published in 1475.*

O v e r : *Pietro della Vecchia's seventeenth-century painting,* Il Chiromante, *shows a nobleman having his future told by a palm-reader.*

Aspects of the Hand

The lines on your right and left hand will probably be fairly similar, but they will not be identical. Palm readers say this is because the dominant or active hand (the right hand for right-handed people, the left for left-handed) shows our living character, i.e. what we are actually making of what we were given to start off with – which is what is shown in the passive hand (the left for right-handed people, the right for left-handed). Another way of looking at it is that the dominant hand shows how we present ourselves in the world, while the passive shows how we really are inside.

It is essential to read both hands, and to note the differences between them. These can show, for example, a triumph of will over unpromising attributes, or a lack of development of potential abilities. They can also reveal internal personality conflicts, which is where skilled hand-analysts can find themselves (rightly or wrongly) taking on the role of a psychotherapist.

Above: *This hand-coloured woodblock plate appeared in Hartlieb's* Die Kunst Ciromantia *– the first ever chiromantic publication.*

Right: *In the seventeenth and eighteenth centuries, many aristocrats and influential people had themselves painted in the process of having their palms read: an ironic pose, considering that this is conceivably the only time a lady such as this would have ever come into such direct physical contact with a person of another class or background. Prediction is a great equalizer.*

Shape of the hand

There are two common nineteenth century ways of dividing up hand shapes. Casimir d'Arpentigny, a nineteenth-century French palm reader found seven hand shapes: elementary, square, spatulate, philosophic, conic, psychic and mixed. The brilliant palm reader (and charlatan) Louis Hamon, known as Cheiro, used this method, which accounts for its continuing popularity. The German Carl Carus preferred four divisions: elementary, motoric, sensitive and psychic. Another method used eight divisions: the Earth and the seven traditional astrological planets.

Perhaps the most straightforward is the modern esoteric authority Fred Gettings' four-fold elemental division, based on the length and breadth of the palm, and the relative length of the fingers; the fingers are said to be long if the middle finger from its tip to its join with the palm is three-quarters (or more) the length from the join to the top rascette, or bracelet on the wrist.

The Earth hand has a square palm and short fingers; these people are earthy, practical, sensible,

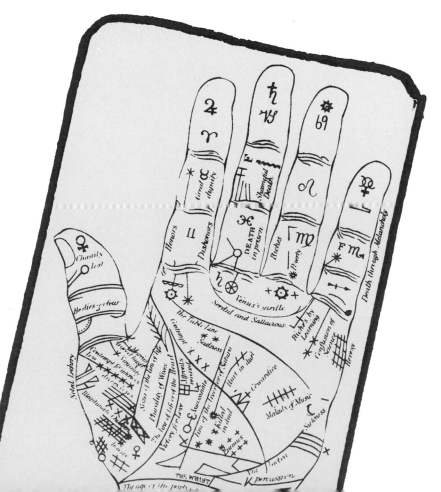

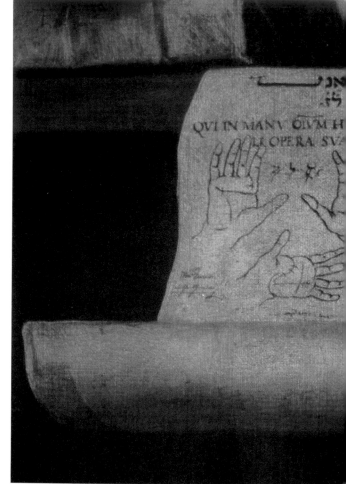

blunt and sometimes gloomy. The air hand has a square palm and long fingers; air people are intellectual rather than emotional, inquisitive, and good communicators, but can be cold. Fire hands have oblong palms and short fingers; their owners are active, energetic, extrovert, impulsive, and prone to flashes of fiery temper. Water hands have oblong palms and long fingers; water people are sensitive, emotional, caring, understanding, but easily led and easily wounded.

In all mentions of size, it is relative size that counts, rather than physical size. In general, small people have small hands, and large people have large hands; women's hands are usually smaller and less chunky than men's; children's are obviously smaller than adults'. But if a woman is sturdy and square-framed, she will probably have large, "masculine" hands; if a man is slender and fine-boned, his hands may look more "feminine". If you meet exceptions to these general rules, examine the hands carefully to see what more they can tell you.

The mounts

These are significant on two counts: how well-developed they are (rounded or flat, firm or puffy), and which lines run into them. Size is not everything; over-development is as significant as under-development.

At the base of the palm:
The Mount of Venus is the fleshy part of the palm at the base of the thumb. This rules, as might be expected, warmth, love and sex.
The Mount of Luna (or the Moon) is on the opposite side of the palm, by the percussive edge of the hand (the edge you would use to chop or strike something). This signifies imagination and creativity, and a romantic nature.
The Mount of Neptune lies between these two; those palm readers who use it say it signifies a strong, charismatic personality.

At the top of the palm:
The Mount of Jupiter is at the base of the index finger; it signifies power, good fortune and leadership.
The Mount of Saturn is at the base of the middle finger; it shows a quiet, prudent, thoughtful,

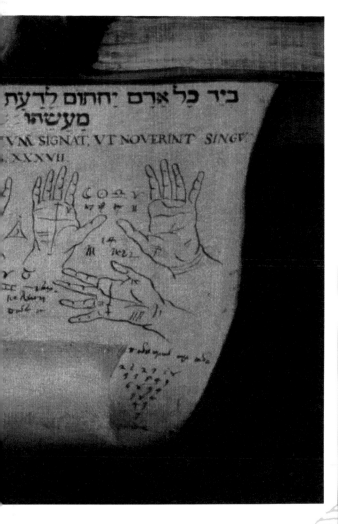

balanced .person, probably studious, possibly mystical.

The Mount of Apollo (or the Sun) is at the base of the ring finger; it signifies aesthetic appreciation, of both art and beauty, and also a happy personality.

The Mount of Mercury is at the base of the little finger; it shows liveliness and wit, versatility, and verbal communication.

In the middle:

The middle third of the hand is ruled by Mars. In the space between the base of the index finger and the inside base of the thumb, the Mount of Mars active (or positive) shows strength and courage, ranging from aggression to cowardice.

Opposite that, on the percussive side of the palm, the Mount of Mars passive (or negative) shows passive courage, the moral virtue rather than the physical strength.

Between these lies the Plain of Mars, the hollow of the palm, which shows capability and practicality if well-developed.

A b o v e : *An illustration showing the meanings of signs found upon the palm of the hand and their influence on the individual. This is the first page of Hartlieb's famous* Die Kunst Ciromantia.

The Fingers and Thumb

Each finger relates to one of the gods (rather than planets), as in their mounts except for Apollo whose characteristics are similar to those of the Sun. Apollo is also traditionally linked with medicine and music.

The length of each finger, and the length and prominence of each phalange or joint in relation to the others, indicates the presence and strength of each personality trait. Remember that it is as significant for a trait to be over-developed as under-developed. The first phalange (the joint with the nail) denotes mental characteristics and intuition, the middle practical, financial and business qualities, and the third material, earthy and sensual aspects. If any phalange is disproportionately long or short, it is likely to be a bad rather than a good sign.

A strong index (Jupiter) finger, then, would show strength of character and leadership qualities. If markedly long, it shows a domineering, arrogant personality; if markedly short, a reluctance to take responsibility.

A strong middle (Saturn) finger is likely to denote a serious, introspective, perhaps scientific character; if very long it shows coldness and a gloomy personality, if very short, flippancy and irresponsibility.

A strong ring (Apollo) finger shows emotional stability and artistic talent; if the finger is very long, vanity and a tendency to gamble, if very short, timidity, lack of creativity, and an inability to cope with money.

A strong little (Mercury) finger shows a powerful intellect and ability with words; very long implies a loud, garrulous, possibly dishonest person; very short shows a difficulty in expressing ideas in words. Because the little finger is often set much lower down the hand than the others, it is much more important to judge its length rather than where its tip lies against the ring finger. A little finger that has a natural tendency to lie away from the ring finger shows individuality; one that hugs the ring finger shows conventionality and dependancy on others.

The thumb is, literally and figuratively, out on its own. A strong, well-balanced thumb can offset defects revealed by other digits, and reinforce their positive points; a weak thumb weakens

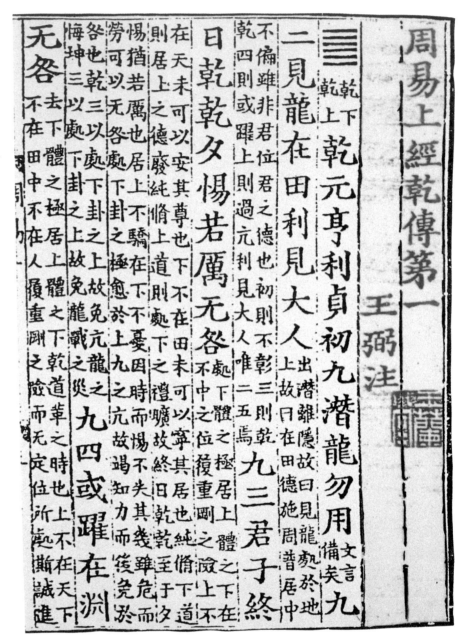

the whole hand. The first phalange represents will-power, the second the reasoning powers; the sensual Mount of Venus can sometimes be thought of as the third phalange. A well-balanced thumb lies between 45 and 90 degrees away from the index finger; closer than that shows someone who is tight-fisted, nervous or narrow-minded; wider shows extravagance, over-generosity and recklessness. A very large, bulbous first phalange, especially with a wide but very short nail, can denote a violent temper; it used to be called "the murderer's thumb".

Above and opposite: Chinese diagrams showing the locations of the "palaces" of the hand in Chinese palmistry, marked with the eight trigrams of the I Ching *system.*

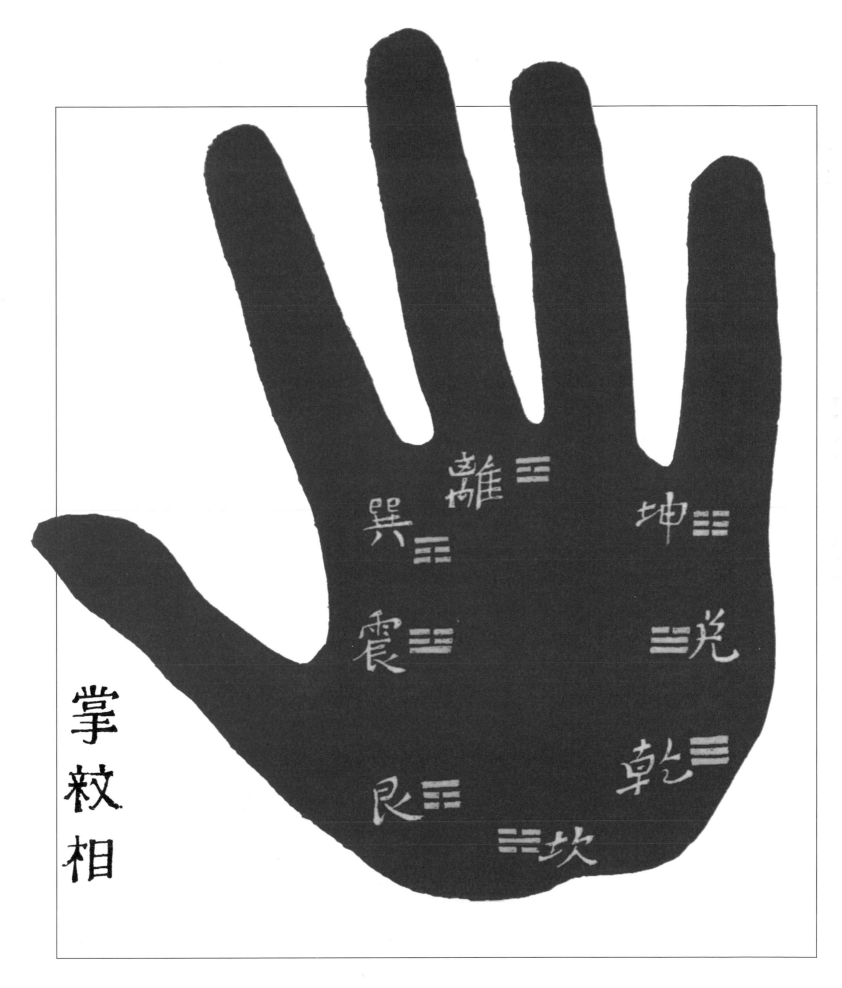

掌紋相

離 ☲
巽 ☴
坤 ☷
震 ☳
兌 ☱
乾 ☰
艮 ☶
坎 ☵

The Lines

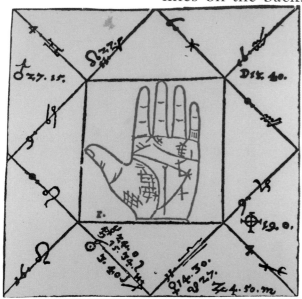

Above: *A print combining symbolism from palmistry and astrology, thus relating the hand to the horoscope. The horoscope itself was cast for 17 August 1507.*

Physiologically, the lines in the palm are simply where the skin folds and creases when we flex our hands, just as the tiny horizontal lines on the backs of our fingers, and the much more obvious wrinkles on our knuckles, are expansion creases. Skin is very flexible, but such creases, like the pleats of a skirt or the bellows of a concertina, enable it to adjust to a variety of stretching and contracting movements.

The basic pattern of lines will remain much the same throughout one's life, but individual lines will deepen or fade, lengthen or shorten, develop breaks, spurs, dots or stars. We have seen that the lines can be a very good health indicator; they can also develop as we become more or less assertive or compassionate, for example. Our characters change throughout our lives, and our hands reflect our characters.

Not everybody has all the minor lines, and in some people even some of the major lines are faint or absent; palm readers must work with what they are

Opposite above: The renowned palmist Barthélemy Coclès doing a reading for a client. This is an illustration from his own sixteenth-century chiromantic text.

Opposite below: Gypsies have always been associated with palmistry. Because of their life of perpetual travel, which in olden times was even more wide-ranging (encompassing the whole of Europe and the Middle East), they were rumoured to have acquired and mastered the esoteric mysteries of the world. This is a typically stylized eighteenth-century painting.

given. We will only deal with the five major lines here in this book.

The Life Line

This is the easiest to find and, in many people, one of the deepest. It is the curved line around the Mount of Venus, or, in more prosaic terms, the crease around the ball of the thumb. This starts at the edge of the hand, between the base of the index finger and the inside base of the thumb, and works down towards the wrist. Generally, the wider the swing of the curve into the palm, the better; it shows an open, generous, outgoing person, while a tight curve shows a more closed-in sort of personality.

The life line does *not* show how long you are going to live; a short life line or one that is broken does *not* mean you are going to die early. This is a popular misconception which should be discounted immediately.

What the life line does show is the strength or intensity of life, both in general health and in major and dramatic changes in one's life. It is quite common for a life line to break and restart, either with or without an overlapping section; this could indicate a major health problem, or a complete change in the way of life. A good, deep, strong line without any chains, islands, crossbars or breaks denotes rude health throughout one's life. Generally, islands and chains show health problems, and crossbars emotional upheavals.

The Heart Line

This is the higher of the two roughly horizontal lines, and runs from the percussive edge of the hand in the general direction of the index finger. The heart line is the indicator of emotional characteristics, particularly in regard to relationships; it is also supposed to show potential physical heart problems, though it must be stressed again that playing the amateur doctor is not a sensible game. Only if negative indicators in the heart line are supported by similar indicators throughout the hand (including the nails) should there be any worry at all, and then the best thing to do is to ask your doctor for a check-up. Self-diagnosis is like the person who reads a family health book from cover to cover and becomes convinced they have eighteen different diseases.

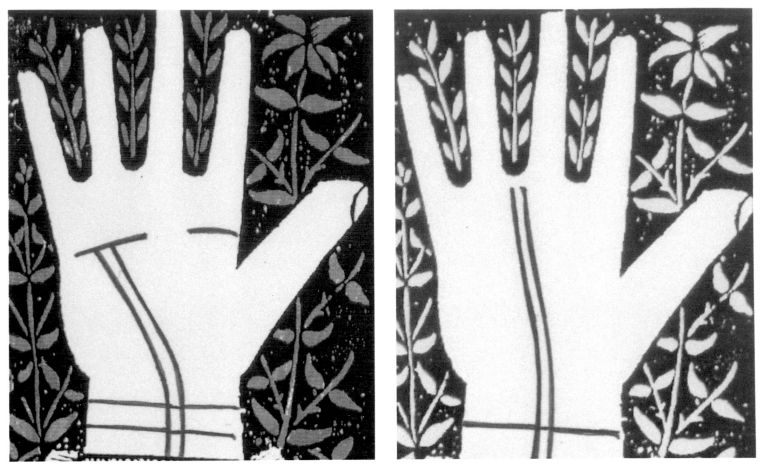

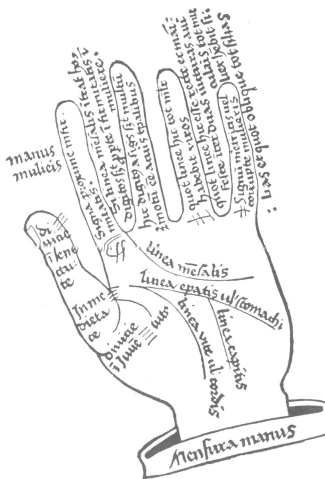

The ideal heart line starts cleanly at the edge of the palm and progresses without any fading, breaks or crossbars, in a smooth curve, to end up near the index finger. This is a warm, loving, dependable, emotionally well-rounded person without any major hang-ups. Few of us are that lucky. A fairly straight line shows that the heart is ruled by the head; "logical lovers" may be clear about how they feel, but their partners tend to find them infuriating. A weak, faded line denotes emotional insecurity. Chaining shows a tendency to fickleness and infidelity. Breaks are supposed to show a broken heart; but the line usually restarts before too long! Forks at the end can be good or bad, depending on where they go: the mounds of Jupiter and Saturn indicate strength and leadership, and deep-thinking (or moodiness) respectively; a fork joining the head line means conflict between the heart and the head, emotion and reason, which is usually bad news.

Above: *The four coloured illustrations on these pages are examples of readings by the sixteenth-century palm reader Barthélemy Coclès. They were first published in his book* Chyromantiae.

The Head Line

This is the lower of the two horizontal lines, and starts near to, or often joined to the life line,

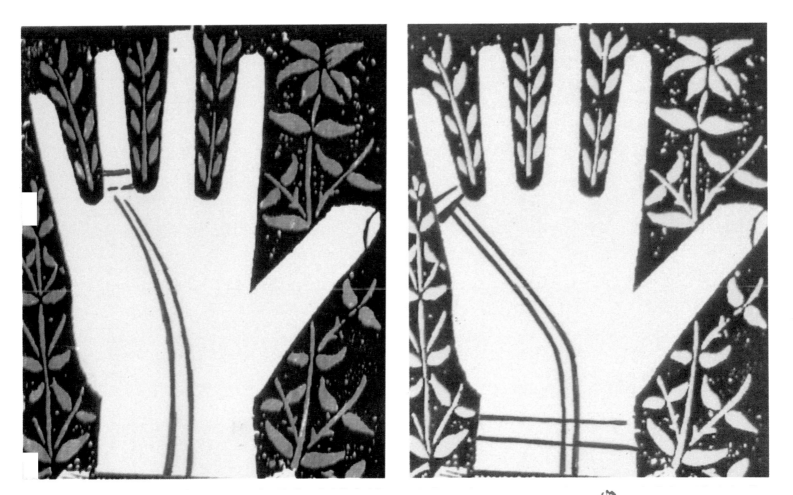

working its way over to the percussive edge. Along with the thumb, the head line gives the strongest indication of the mind and the will. Generally, the straighter it is, the more analytical the mind; straight head lines are often found on practical, square hands. If it curves down towards the Mount of Luna on the lower percussive edge it shows a more intuitive and imaginative approach. If it starts well above the life line it shows independence, even recklessness; if below it shows nervousness and timidity. If it is joined to the life line, an early separation is fine; but a late separation means a late developer.

Forks show diversity, but can bring confusion. A fork up to, or starting beneath the middle finger is associated with intense study, a fork under the ring finger with writing talent, and a fork under the little finger with business success.

The Simian Line

There is a rare case where the heart and head lines are one line, a horizontal slash across the palm known as the Simian line. It usually denotes someone with extreme intensity, of concentration

or emotion or purpose, who works with single-minded devotion for what they want. They love and hate and believe absolutely, with no room for doubt; everything is either black or white.

The Fate Line

This is a vertical line, usually starting at or near the wrist and going up through the middle of the palm to end near the base of the fingers. It is sometimes called the Line of Saturn, though the chances are that it will not reach that far, or that it ends somewhere else. It can also be called the destiny line.

Despite its name this line does not predict one's fate. Although more than any other line it is supposed to indicate success or failure in life, what it really shows is the effect of external influences on our lives – and this, as always, is up to us. Indeed, some palm readers say that a complete absence of the fate line means that we are in full control of our own pattern of living, without any help from anyone else; others say that an absent or very faint fate line shows a happy-go-lucky person, unconcerned with the direction of their life. The fate line, like all lines, must be read in conjunction with the rest of the hand.

The start and end points of the fate line are particularly important. If it starts at the wrist it indicates self-reliance: making your own fate. If it starts from the life line it shows strong family influences, which could be working in and inheriting the family business, or having your life ruled by a domineering parent. Starting from the Mount of Luna shows a changeable, uncertain career, perhaps in the public limelight: the arts, for example. If the fate line starts high up, near the head line, it shows a late start, and perhaps a hard slog before success occurs.

The classic fate line runs up to the Mount of Saturn at the base of the middle finger, showing responsibility and success in a settled, conventional way – a family man with a safe and steady but unexciting job, for example. If it ends on the Mount of Jupiter it shows ambitions and self-motivation, and on the Mount of Apollo creativity and a leaning towards the arts.

The Apollo Line

Known also as the Sun, success, fortune or fame line, this runs parallel to the fate line, closer to the percussive edge of the hand; it is usually shorter, starting higher up the hand, and it ideally runs towards the Apollo or ring finger. This line is often missing from a palm, but this does not mean a complete lack of success; the line is more to do with unusual success.

The fact that it usually starts fairly high up the hand shows that such success or fame should not be expected young, unless it is recognized early on that a person is exceptionally gifted and talented. More usually success and renown are built up as abilities develop through life.

Timing the Lines

This is a highly contentious issue, as there are many different methods of turning palm-lines into time-lines; most of these methods contradict each other and none of them (given the size of the hand as a life-calendar) can be entirely accurate. Line-timing lays a heavier emphasis on foretelling the future (for example "You will have an unhappy love relationship or an abrupt change of job or a serious illness when you are thirty-five or forty-two years old"); this can lead to the popular misconception about a short life line meaning an early death.

Some palm readers determine a mid-life point on each line, and work backwards and forwards; others start at the beginning. As a general rule, given the dimensions of the hand, a millimetre (or $\frac{1}{32}$ in) a year is the accepted measurement. This depends on accurately establishing a base-point, and any miscalculation or blunt pencil will throw it out. The fate and Apollo lines are measured from the bottom upwards, and the life and head lines from the thumb side of the palm towards the percussive side; the heart line used to be measured from thumb side to percussive side as well, but modern palm readers usually say that instead it starts at the percussive edge and progresses towards the index finger.

Some general idea can be given, of whether something is earlier or later in life – but do not forget that lines change through your life, deepening, fading, lengthening, shortening, breaking, forking, growing or losing cross-bars, and so on. The lines change as your life changes.

The future is not fixed in your hands – but your character may well be revealed there.

Mount of Venus

Life Line

Heart Line

Head Line

Health Line

Phrenology and Physiognomy

Phrenology

Phrenology is the art – or science – of judging personality types and traits (and hence divining elements of the subject's future) by way of examining bumps on the head. It was devised – or at least codified – by a doctor, Franz Joseph Gall, who was born near Baden in 1758. He began lecturing on his theories in Vienna around 1796. In brief, the idea of phrenology is that the shape of the skull reveals the shape of the brain beneath it, and that over-developed or under-developed parts of the brain are responsible for character differences. Gall identified thirty-seven different parts of the brain which he called "organs".

He divided the organs into two main sets, affective and intellectual. The affective organs he divided into eleven at the back of the head and over the ear which controlled propensities, or essential qualities, and twelve on the top of the head controlling sentiments or emotions; the intellectual organs were twelve above the nose and eyes to do with perception, and two high on the forehead to

Below: A nineteenth-century phrenology chart showing the main distribution of the areas relating to attitudes, temperaments, and the other characteristics.

Above: An illustration from Jean Belot's 1649 publication Oeuvres *indicating the location of the planetary parts of the human face.*

do with reason. The Table of Phrenology gives a reference to the thirty-seven affective organs. The brain being made up of two lobes, these thirty-seven organs are repeated on each side.

As in palmistry, if an organ is under-developed, the person may have a deficiency in that particular property; if over-developed, an excess. Number 12, for example, if under-developed would show someone with an inferiority complex; if over-developed someone who is arrogant and egotistical. Similarly number 13 shows the range from vanity to a total disregard for what others think. Number 20 ranges from fanatical religious or superstitious belief to utter scepticism about everything to do with the spiritual or supernatural.

The proportions of different organs or groups of organs is supposed to be able to reveal not only the character but the abilities of the person. Clearly someone with 33 and 34 well-developed would make a good musician, while those with 37 make excellent philosophers or politicians.

Modern science has gradually revealed that the whole basis of Gall's theory is fallacious. The brain does not actually touch the inside of the skull at any point, so hillocks and hollows on the head bear no relation to what is inside.

Similarly, the size and shape of the head in fact says little about the brain, and the size of the brain has no proven relationship to the intelligence or ability of its owner.

However, phrenology has been with us for two centuries, and many brilliant men and women have devoted a significant part of their lives to it. Could this be a situation where the right results were achieved by the wrong methods? *Is there any truth in phrenology?* Even if this is in doubt, the experimentation can be entertaining.

Table of Phrenology:

Affective organs

Propensities or Essential Qualities

1 Amativeness: love and sexual energy
2 Self-preservation
3 Parental instincts
4 Inhabitiveness, domesticity
5 Friendship
6 Combativeness, competitiveness
7 Destructiveness, impatience
8 Secretiveness
9 Acquisitiveness
10 Alimentiveness, appetite
11 Constructiveness, achievements

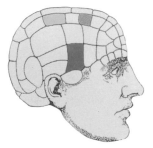

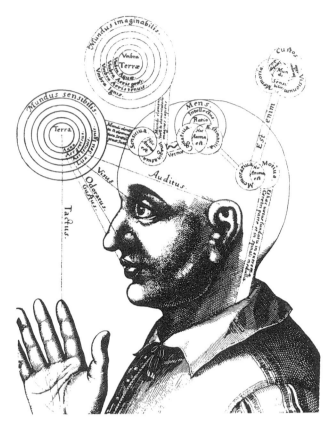

Sentiments or Emotions

12 Self-esteem
13 Approbativeness, desire for approval, vanity
14 Cautiousness, prudence
15 Benevolence
16 Veneration, respect
17 Firmness, determination
18 Conscientiousness
19 Hope, optimism
20 Wonder, belief
21 Ideality, beauty
22 Mirthfulness, humour
23 Imitation, emulation

Intellectual organs

Perception

24 Individuality, perspicacity, observation
25 Form, shape, spacial awareness and memory
26 Size, appreciation of measurement and proportion
27 Weight, physical awareness and balance
28 Colour and tone appreciation
29 Locality, place memory
30 Number, arithmetical ability
31 Order, methodical nature, tidiness
32 Eventuality, memory of events
33 Time sense, chronological perception, rhythm
34 Tune, melody, harmony appreciation and musical ability

35 Language, verbal, oratorical or true linguistic ability

Reason

36 Comparison, analysis, constructive thinking
37 Causality, logical thought

Physiognomy

If the probity of nineteenth century phrenology, as developed by Gall, is in doubt, there may well be clues to the character from the general shape of the head and the distribution of features on it. "I wouldn't trust him, his eyes are too close together." "He's a vicious-looking brute." "You can tell she's artistic just by looking at her." Very often these instant assessments are accurate, a fact that television and film producers make use of in casting actors as characters. "Character" actors often complain that they are being typecast, but there are faces that we can instantly recognize as portraying a villain, an intellectual, or a sultry lover.

It is not always the case, however. "You wouldn't think it to look at him, but he's one of their top scientists." "I know he looks rough, but he's one of the gentlest people you'll ever meet." Those same film producers delight in fooling us by turning the character with the most soft, friendly, unassuming and pleasing face into a cold-blooded murderer.

Above left: A famous seventeenth-century illustration by Robert Fludd which shows the significance of parts of the head, external and internal influences and supposed mental abilities.

Above: In the nineteenth century phrenology experienced an enormous wave of popularity; not just with students of the esoteric, but also with a much wider general public. So voguish was it that it infiltrated every type of social and cultural medium – as illustrated by this magazine cartoon.

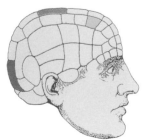

Above: *The title page of the
famous chiromantic,
physiognomical and* phrenological work,
Ludiculrum Chriomanticum
Praetoris.

Having close-set eyes, a receding chin, small, large, high or low ears, a nose of a certain shape and size, prominent cheekbones, a wide mouth, full or thin lips – do these characteristics show character? Or is it more what we do with these physical features rather than the features themselves? With the same features we can look full of hate, angry, serious, sullen, bored, relaxed, pleased, happy, excited, loving. We can spot these signs in other people at a glance. Actors, again, are well trained in this use of their features.

Some people are extremely skilled at reading the more subtle signs of what we now call "body language": a good priest or counsellor, psychotherapist or doctor, for example – and also fortune-tellers of all kinds. The best palm or Tarot readers, for example, probably pick up just as much, if not more, from their reading of the whole person as from the palm or the cards, and often quite unconsciously.

This is especially helpful when the reader has to make a choice between quite different inter-

The illustrations on these two pages are from early physiognomical works which compared human types with types from the animal world. Facial traits were often compared to animals representative of signs of the zodiac, such as Taurus the bull or Capricorn the goat, as an indication of the corresponding characteristics in people born under a particular sign. However, modern sensitivity to the quite unacceptable racist overtones of the comparison between certain racial types and animals accounts for some of the lessening in popularity and credibility of physiognomy as a fully-fledged science.

pretations of the palm or cards; one feels right, while the others do not seem to apply. Intuition is the most valuable asset for any reader.

One of the major causes of inter-racial distrust and misunderstanding is that we find it more difficult to read the more subtle of these signs in the faces of people of other races.

Interestingly, there is also inter-species misunderstanding. Why do cats always jump on the lap of the one person in the room who actively dislikes cats? For a cat, wide-open, staring eyes mean a challenge, a possible threat; narrowed eyes are a sign of welcome and trust. Although a cat will know the friendliness of people it is familiar with, it will misunderstand a cat-loving stranger's wide-eyed, happy face. But the person who dislikes cats will shrink back, automatically narrowing their eyes; to a cat this may mean "Hello, I want to be friends."

The eyes, in fact, are one of the best things to look for in judging what a person is really thinking and feeling. It is easy enough to fake a convincing smile but it is a lot more difficult to make eyes sparkle with feigned interest and friendliness while wishing not to be bothered by someone. "The eyes are the windows of the soul," wrote Max Beerbohm, misquoting William Blake. If people will not meet your eyes, traditionally this indicates that they may be hiding something, or are ashamed of something. If they stare brazenly they might be a good actor, but you can often detect either a cockiness or a shiftiness that gives the game away. Compare bright, keen eyes with eyes that are dull and lack-lustre. Notice if someone's eyes are watching your own; remember that they are reading you as well, looking for your own signs of nervousness, boredom or rejection – or friendliness, interest and hope.

The art of physiognomy

The ancient Greeks placed a high reliance on physiognomy, the judging of character by the overall shape of (largely) the head. In the sixteenth to nineteenth centuries a number of people, from poets and pastors to anatomists and physiologists, made studies of physical form, and what it can show of the personality. There are several different methods of analysis in physiognomy; here we shall just look at some of the basics.

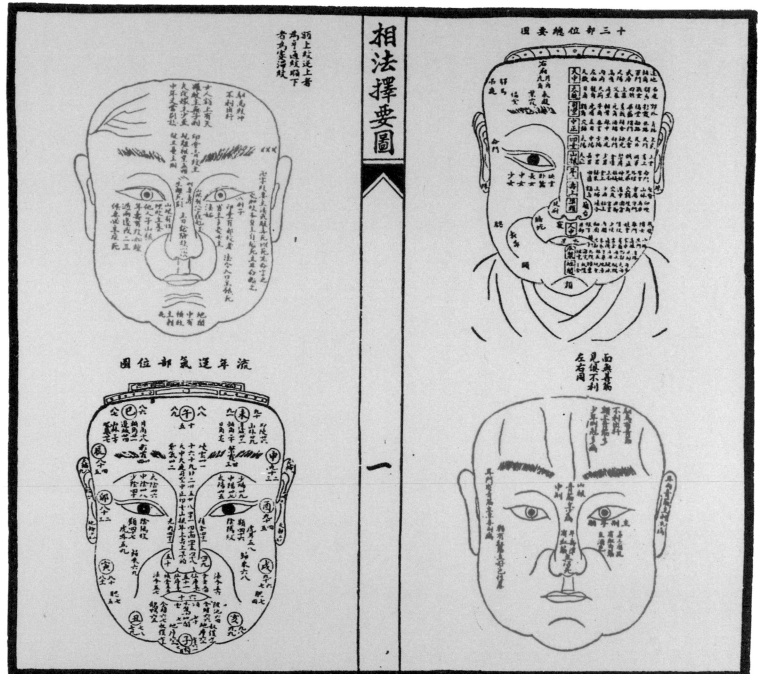

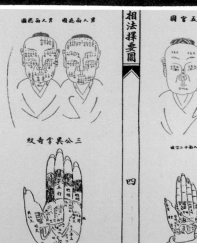

Left : *Animal-human faces surrounding the head of the famous early physiognomical scholar Giovanni della Porta (1538–1615). This illustration was first published in his book* Physiognomia *in 1650.*

Left and above: *The Chinese were interested in physiognomy centuries before any codification of systems was formalized in the West. These illustrations first appeared in "T'ung Shu", an ancient Chinese esoteric almanac.*

It must be pointed out that physiognomy is an old art, and because of its Western origins the majority of studies of physiognomy have been on Caucasians, mainly Western Europeans and white Americans. Because the underlying structure of the head is a different shape for non-Caucasians, whether Chinese, Polynesian, Afro-American, or other racial types, the following cannot be applied as readily to them. As physiognomy has not been widely adopted in current scientific thinking, regrettably no modern studies are available incorporating a contemporary cultural mix of subjects.

The profile is particularly important. The facial angle can be measured against the horizontal by drawing a line from the forehead to the chin, or more generally, the profile can be described as convex, plain or concave.

A convex profile has an outward curve, with the forehead and chin set further back than the nostrils (*not* the tip of the nose); people with this profile are thought to be quick-thinking and quick-tempered. The plane profile, more or less a vertical line, denotes a well-balanced person not given to excesses. The concave profile, with a projecting forehead and chin, shows an unhurried, patient person.

Looking at the front of the face, it can be divided into three sections by drawing a horizontal line at the very top and bottom of the nose. If the three sections are of equal height, the person is well-balanced. If the forehead section is longest, this represents considerable intellectual powers; a long middle section shows a practical, energetic, active person, while a long mouth and chin section denotes determination.

The forehead can be high or low, and narrow or broad. High again indicates intelligence, if narrow the person is good at learning; if broad, it shows inventiveness and creativity. A person with a low forehead is thought to be less intellectual; if narrow it indicates a somewhat dull, conservative narrow-minded personality; if broad it represents a constructive and persevering determination.

Large ears are supposed to show a vibrant, active person; medium-sized ears indicate someone who is open-minded and fair, and small ears someone who is cautious and conservative. If the ears lie flat against the head the person is cautious; if they are projecting the person has more verve.

A protruding chin denotes stubbornness, a

R i g h t : *These six "types" come from J K Lavater's eighteenth-century book* Physiognomical Fragments. *Belying its title, this is one of the most ambitious works on the subject ever produced, as Lavater struggled to create a definitive and comprehensive codification of his discipline.*

receding chin weakness and lack of determination; these can be countered by a broad chin showing strength and conscientiousness, or a narrow chin showing fragility and lack of will power.

Similar theories can be applied to the nose, the eyebrows, the eyes, the cheeks, the mouth and the lips. Some physiognomists also consider the colour of the eyes and hair. Although it can be said that these, like other physical characteristics, are inherited factors, it can also be argued that character and temperament are also partly inherited. Brown eyes traditionally show someone with depth of emotion, both good and bad, and also given to spells of moodiness; blue eyes show self-control and practicality, but also coolness of emotion; green eyes show great intelligence and intensity of emotions, particularly the legendary wild love, artistic nature and fiery temper of the green-eyed redhead.

How much can be read into such "analysis" is open to debate. We all know people whose personality fits in exactly with the small selection of physical attributes discussed here – but we also probably know people who run counter to some or all of these "rules". A physiognomist would say that this is because we are ignoring all sorts of other characteristics. One system uses a table of

sixty pairs of attributes such as boldness and timidity, industry and laziness, modesty and shamelessness, self-indulgence and ascetisism. Each aspect of the appearance – drooping eyelids, high cheekbones, pointed ears – is given anything from three or four up to over a dozen of these attributes, whether positive, average or negative. All the marks for each attribute are then totalled, giving an extremely detailed personality picture.

But the best guide is often simply the gut reaction: "I think I like this person; they seem to be strong-willed without being domineering, and kindly without being cloying," or, "I'm not sure I trust this person; there's something about them that doesn't ring true." Often it is possible to get a pretty good impression before they even begin to speak; whether you call it physiognomy or body language, it is instinctive, and very often surprisingly accurate.

T o p a n d a b o v e : *Pre-eighteenth-century physiognomical texts were of a quaint and general nature. Even in Barthélemy Coclès's* Physiognomonia, *commentaries tended towards personal subjective comment rather than objective investigation.*

R i g h t : *This illustration comes from Richard Saunder's book* Physiognomie, Chiromancie, and Metoposcopy, *which was published in 1653. Metoposcopy is the science of relating the positioning and occurence of moles on the body to attributes and personal characteristics. It is little practised today.*

Graphology

*H*andwriting analysts are very quick to point out that there is nothing occult or esoteric about their work. Graphology is a rational, scientific method of analysing people's characters, they say, and should not be put together with such things as astrology and palmistry.

For those who give some time to things like astrology and/or palmistry, for example, there is no problem: handwriting analysis is just one more way of examining someone's character. Handwriting has been studied for thousands of years. Aesop, Aristotle, Virgil and Julius Caesar all saw merit in examining it; the Roman historian Suetonius, in his biographies of the emperors, always described their writing style. Shakespeare, Sir Walter Scott, Robert Browning and Benjamin Disraeli, amongst many others, practised graphology in one way or another.

In the last few decades, handwriting analysis has become more and more widespread for the two

Above: *Runes were one of the earliest of writing systems; consisting of combinations of straight lines, they were used extensively by the early Norsemen whose literature is today the subject of philological research. In modern times, runes have taken on a more esoteric meaning and are believed to have predictive powers.*

Left: *An impressive marble
statue of the great playwright
and poet, William Shakespeare.
He wrote in an age when there
was no set style of English;
consequently he was able to
experience great freedom of
expression while at the same
time acting as a strong influence
on his readers and audiences. He
says in* Henry IV, Part 1: *"I
once did hold it, as our statists
do,/A baseness to write fair, and
laboured much/How to forget
that learning; but, sir, now/It
did me yeoman's service."*

Right: *A satirical eighteenth-century portrait of an astrologer, Partridge, with his chart as symbolic of superstitious belief. Opposite stands the satirist, Swift (here called Bickerstaff) who represents logic as portrayed through handwriting.*

PATRIDGE | BICKASTAF

main purposes of screening job applicants and detecting forgeries.

In the first case, it is more widely used in the USA and continental Europe (especially in Germany and the Netherlands) than in the UK; people are often asked to write their letter of application by hand rather than use a typewriter or word processor. Clearly undesirable character traits revealed by analysis – unreliability, carelessness, untidiness – will cause rejection without even an interview, while for shortlisted applicants, a more detailed analysis will give the interviewers a lot of useful information about the applicant.

Graphologists claim that they can spot whether someone has a critical mind, shows informed judgement, has mental agility, a methodical approach to work, perseverance, or reliability, or if they have confused ideas, or show traces of dishonesty, stubbornness, rigidity of thought, nervousness, evasiveness, egocentricity, hypocrisy, or any mental or emotional imbalance.

In the second case, that of detecting forgery by comparing a questionable piece of writing with known examples, graphologists can prove that a letter, suicide note, will or signature was or was not written by a specific individual. They are also able to point out if the writer's state of mind was seriously disturbed at the time of writing.

It is supposed to be impossible for even an

expert forger to fool an expert graphologist – or a well-programmed computer. Computer analysis of signatures has advanced to such a degree that before long banks are likely to have verification machines on their counters, to compare a customer's on-the-spot signature with that on a credit card, or in the bank's own records.

There is no doubt that graphology works – but how is it done? Different graphologists may concentrate on different areas, but all of them look at the overall impression given by a page of writing before they focus in on any individual characteristics.

The page as a whole

Before looking at the handwriting itself, and the formation of individual letters, the graphologist stands back and looks at the whole page. The way that the writing is arranged on the page gives important information in itself.

The first things to look at are the margins, the slope, the size, the movement, the tension and the pressure of the writing. Then the slant, the weight, the speed, the spacing between words, the general shape or style of handwriting, and next the three zones or levels are carefully examined. And only then is the formation of individual letters studied.

No one sign can be taken as conclusive; as with all forms of character analysis, it is the overall picture, made up of all the signs working together, which counts. Note also that people write in different ways under different circumstances: scrawling a note to the milkman, writing a letter to a friend or lover, applying for a job, making a fair copy for public display – all are different, but a graphologist claims to be able to identify them all as being from the one hand.

Margins

If the writer has been instructed to leave wide margins all around (for example, in an examination paper), this does not apply as much. Similarly, journalists and other professional writers may automatically leave wide margins.

No margins at all may mean that the writer wants to fill every bit of his life (and everybody else's) with himself, or he may be mean, or he may feel rather trapped.

Well-balanced margins could show a well-balanced mind.

A very wide left margin can show a fear of contact or a lack of caution.

A very narrow left margin can show cautiousness and economy, perhaps stinginess.

A left margin that grows wider down the page can

Above: Graphologists are called in to authenticate documents in a wide variety of situations. Here a graphologist examines a court document from the heresy trial of Joan of Arc.

Right: *The Metropolitan Police of London issued this poster in 1886 in an attempt to track down the infamous murderer, Jack the Ripper. The police hoped that his acquaintances would recognize his distinctive style of handwriting.*

show someone who is forward-looking, or becoming less cautious in life.

A left margin that grows narrower can show a developing caution.

A very wide right margin might show a fear of the future.

No space at all on the right might show that the writer is bubbly and effervescent.

The slope

The slope of the lines, including variations in the sloping, might simply show that the paper was badly positioned for the writer. The following are possible indications, but by no means invariable.

If the lines are horizontal (on unlined paper) it could show a clear and orderly mind.

If the lines slope upwards it can show optimism, ambition and enthusiasm.

If they slope downwards it might show pessimism and discouragement, or simply that the writer is tired.

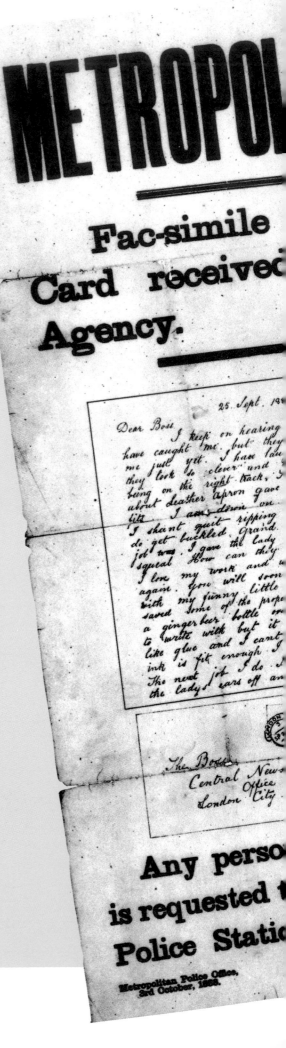

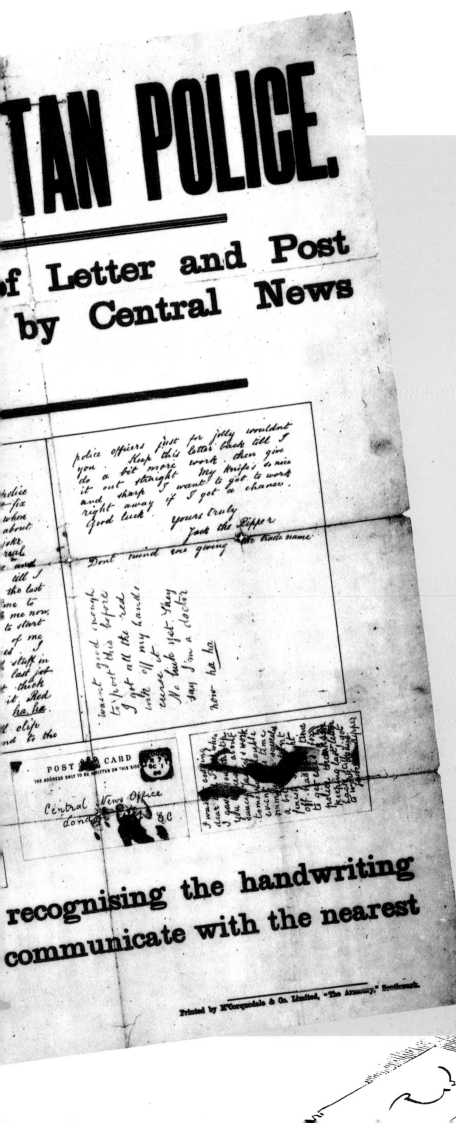

If they rise then fall, so they are hump-shaped, it might show someone who has initial enthusiasms, but no persistence.

If they fall, then rise, it could be that the writer is discouraged, but is determined to stick it through.

If they undulate, they might denote an unstable character, or someone who is always battling against life's problems.

Size

Large writing can show an ambitious and expansive personality, full of confidence and enthusiasm; this can also indicate someone who is proud, arrogant and domineering.

Small writing can show someone who is intelligent and tidy-minded, but quiet and withdrawn, not wanting to draw attention to herself.

Connections

In continuous writing it is very rare that *all* the letters are joined up. Groups of three, four or five letters show mainly positive characteristics, though poor grouping may indicate a disconnected state of mind. Consistency and phraseology are more important than the actual numbers of letters connected.

If words are connected, it can show inventiveness, someone whose thoughts are ahead of the pen, but if overdone it can show carelessness and lack of precision.

Slant

Generally, upright writing can show independence, straightness and self-control.

Slanting forwards can show a creative mind, often extrovert. If extreme it might show someone out of control, probably over-emotional.

Slanting backwards can show reserve, pride or introversion. If extreme it may indicate someone who feels isolated, wrapped up in himself or repressing his emotions.

Weight

A strong hand can show energy, but this also depends on the speed and dynamism of the writing in general.

Too heavy a hand, leaving a deep impression or even slashing at the paper, might show someone not fully in control of himself or of his emotions, and possibly full of his own self-importance. This is apparently more often seen in a male hand.

A very soft, light hand can show someone writing with the minimum expense of energy, maybe because of a naturally economical personality or because of weakness and timidity.

Speed

This obviously depends on how skilled at writing the writer is. Slow writing can show someone who simply finds writing difficult – someone partially illiterate, a child, or someone writing in a language (or a script) with which they are not familiar. But in normal cases, slow writing could show someone who is careful and deliberate, or perhaps unsure of himself.

Fast writing might show confidence and spontaneity, but can denote sloppiness and lack of attention to detail.

Spacing

This will vary to some extent throughout a piece of writing, depending partly on the sense of the words themselves. The average space left between words is usually about the width of a wide letter. Very wide spacing might show a sense of isolation from other people, possibly through pride, aloofness or snobbery.

Very narrow spacing could show warmth and spontaneity, but also perhaps a clinging person, who needs other people a little too much.

Style

Although schoolchildren through the years have had particular handwriting styles hammered into them, by the time they reach their teens they may be making a rounded style more pointed, or vice versa; they may be adding ornamentation to a plain style, or simplifying the more ornate style

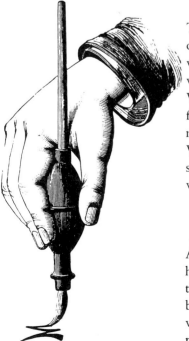

they were taught. Graphologists look particularly at how letters are joined, because this is where individuality most alters a taught hand.

Garland is the most simple, easy form of connection in rounded writing; it might show a receptive, friendly person.

Arcade connections are fussier. The writer makes a point of showing the connections, often swooping over the top of the next letter before forming it. It might show someone who is conscious of their position, who is perhaps somewhat guarded, reserved, maybe formal, but courteous.

Angular writing could show firmness, reliability and persistence, someone who will get a job done properly, whatever the inconvenience.

Double-curve writing is a mixture of arcade and garland, looks like a ribbon waving across the paper, and seems to be full of "m"s, "n"s, "u"s and "w"s. If the writing is otherwise energetic and intelligent it might easily show diplomacy and adaptability, but in a weak hand it might show irresolution.

Thread writing sprawls, often untidily, across the paper. It can show a fast-thinking, creative person, but it could mean a capricious, changeable, even hysterical personality.

Zones

Letters, and lines of writing, can be divided into three zones: upper, middle and lower. The middle zone is the vertical space taken up by a lower case "a" or "o", or the rounded part of a "d" or "p"; the upper zone is the ascenders, or upright stalks, of the written letters "b", "d", "f", "h", "k", "l" and "t"; the lower zone is the descenders, or downward strokes, of the written letters "f", "g", "j", "p", "q", "y" and sometimes "z". Note that in handwriting the letter "f" usually has both an ascender and a descender.

The middle zone shows our everyday concept of self, how we fit into the world, our social attitudes and normal emotions.

The upper zone shows our ambitions, imagination, flights of fancy and whim, quests and spiritual awareness.

The lower zone shows our materialism and sensuality, the earthier side of our personality and our emotions.

Ideally the three zones should be of similar

Identifying connections in writing

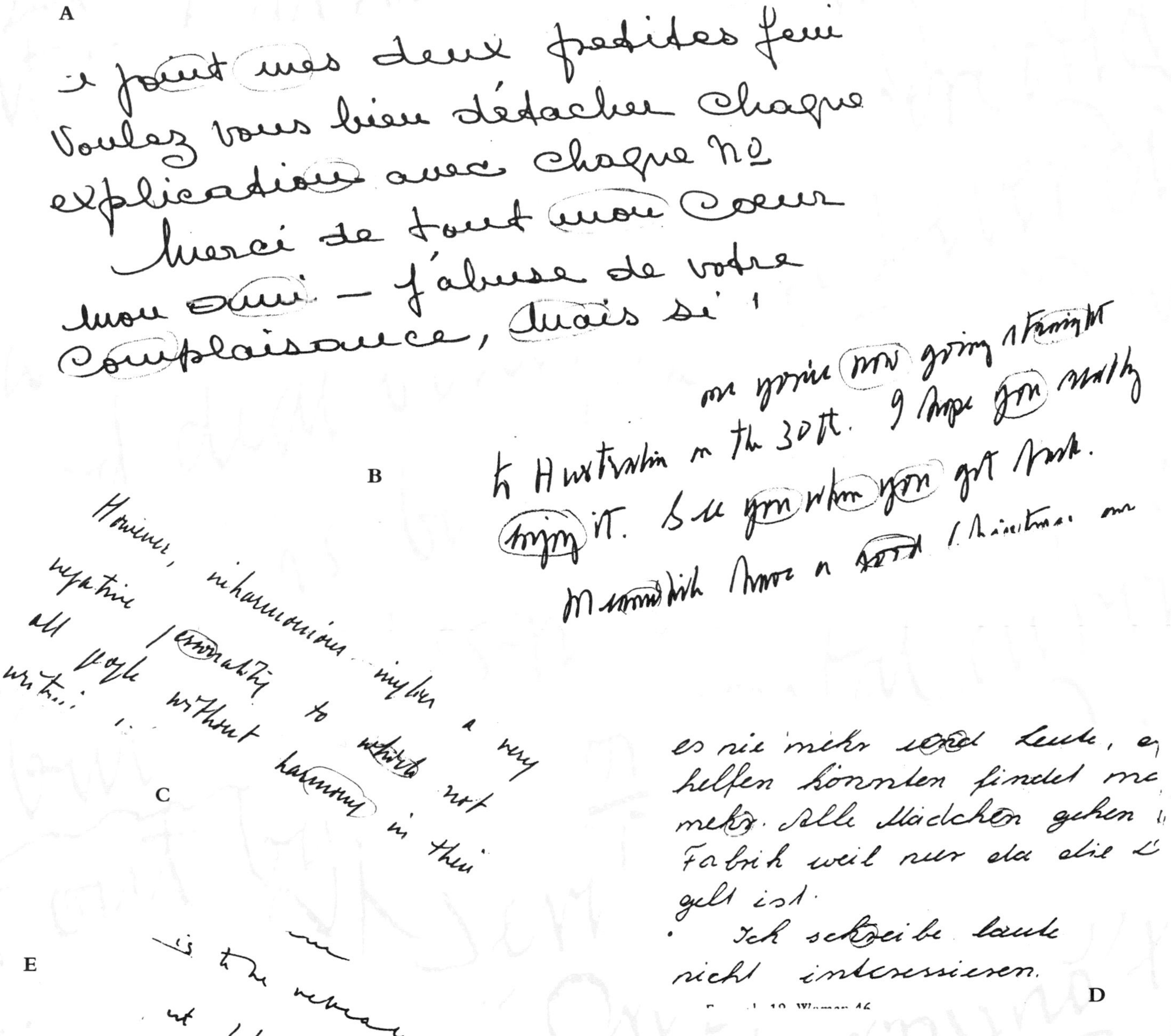

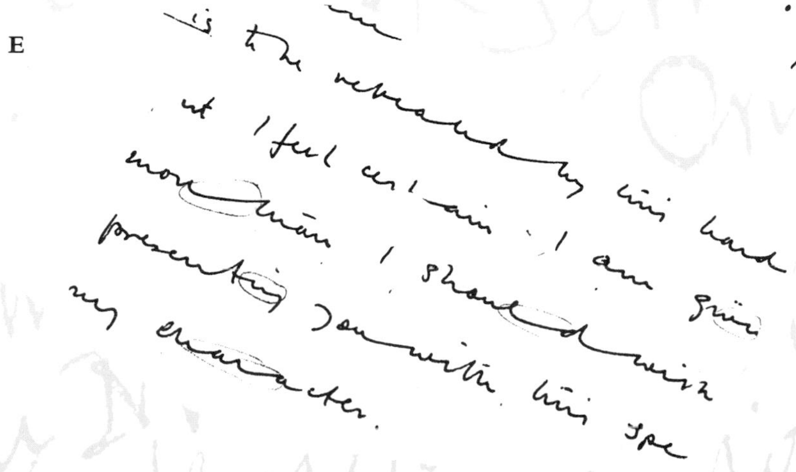

Various styles of handwriting can be identified by the connections made between letters, or even between words. Here are examples of distinct types: A=Garlands, B=Arcades, C=Angular, D=Double Curve, E=Thread or Freeform.

heights, whatever the overall size of the handwriting: the mythical well-balanced person.

Large and small here represent size in relation to the other zones.

A large middle zone can show someone who is solidly at the centre of their own world.

A small middle zone might show a lack of self-confidence or self-awareness.

A large upper zone could show someone who is reaching as far as they can, possibly spiritually-orientated, maybe an habitual day-dreamer.

A small upper zone could show a lack of imagination, a lack of striving after higher things.

A large lower zone might show someone very sensually-orientated, maybe with an appetite for home comforts (and therefore money), good food and wine, and sex; alternatively someone who is very physical, such as a sportsman or a dancer.

A small lower zone might therefore show sexual inhibitions, or a non-physical person.

Individual letters

Graphologists who work with the latin alphabet concentrate particularly on letters such as "d" and "g" with their ascenders and descenders, their connectivity and their propensity for loops; "i" and "t" quite literally for dotting the "i"s and

crossing the "t"s; and the personal capital "I" (in the English language), which in itself can tell a great deal about how the writer views his or her own character.

However, no one indicator of character should ever be taken in isolation; a careful graphologist will spend many hours and sometimes days building up an overall picture of someone's character from handwriting, taking all indicators into consideration, and balancing out contradictions.

Differences in interpretation

The precise "meaning" of any one characteristic of handwriting might vary from place to place in a piece of writing, depending on its immediate context. A graphologist might decide that a characteristic that usually means one thing might mean another in an individual person's handwriting, because of other factors.

A large loop in a lower-case "g", for example, might imply romanticism or earthiness, or it might indicate showiness in another person's hand; it could reveal an imbalance in character if it does not fit in with the rest of the handwriting.

In addition to this, different graphologists, and their textbooks, seem to find different meanings in the same characteristics. This could partly be because the "science" of graphology has developed considerably in the last couple of decades.

Differences of opinion might also stem from different countries; handwriting styles and habits are not the same in every country, and a graphologist from one country cannot pronounce on the writing of someone from another country with anywhere near the same degree of accuracy, until he has immersed himself completely in the writing of that country.

A good graphologist will also constantly be revising his techniques in the light of experience; if he finds a hundred cases of insensitive and unimaginative people displaying signs he has always interpreted as sensitivity, imagination, brightness and artistic creativity, then he should take a good look at his interpretation of these characteristics. Of course, at times, graphologists disagree simply because they hold different opinions. As in other forms of character analysis, intuition combined with knowledge and study holds the key to much of interpretation.

Sandwich, February 11

Dear Julia,
Well, this is where we're
staying. But actually is this old-fashioned.
even though this is in fact a modern
town. Somehow they forgot to raze this
part — lucky for us, as it's very quiet,
with wonderful food. We really needed
a rest after the New York part of the trip
which was really quite hectic. I did
like New York but found it very
run down in parts. The Met was amazing —
I could have spent all week there if
Robert had let me. I found you the
most wonderful birthday ____ in
the shop there (so much ____
that one we were ____ to
exhibition) — but I'm ____
clues!   We'll be ba____
Don't worry about ____
149 Main Street, Sandwich, Mas___

April 19, 1991

Dear Julia,
Thanks very much for
the curtain samples. Which did
you prefer? I rather like the
deep blue, although perhaps
it's a bit overpowering for the
room. I shall need about
5 metres for the sitting room.
Are you still in touch with Mrs.
Bately? She did such a
wonderful job on Jane's
blinds that I'm hoping she
can run up the curtains for
me.
     Oh yes. I forgot to tell
you — we're going to Chile!!

Analysis of handwritten letters

A graphologist's comments on the style of hand-writing in these letters:

"The margins are well kept, and so, generally, are the distances between the words and the lines. However, the distance between the letters is very irregular, and the letters are connected clumsily.

The writing is quite loose with a watery aspect. The slant is also regular, predominantly towards the right. The lines descend gently. The movement is agile and quite supple. The structure seems to lack backbone."

Signatures

The signature is different from a writer's other handwriting. A page of writing can be about anything – work, study notes, holidays, hobbies, friends, memories, plans, and so on – but a signature is "about" the writer. Each signature is its writer's personal statement to the world: "This is who I am; this is how I want to be perceived by you, the reader."

But do our signatures always say what we want them to? Although one may quite consciously develop one's signature so that it looks attractive, strong, or interesting, it will also contain many clues from the subconscious, revealing secrets to the trained eye that the writer would probably prefer were kept hidden.

Although the signature stands apart from the writer's other handwriting, it must also be compared with it; they are, after all, written by the same person, and any major discrepancy shows a conflict between the "true" character and the public persona of the writer. The signature is quite likely to be a little larger than the rest of the writing, but should not be disproportionately so; similarly, although it is often a little fancier, it should not leap out from the rest of the page. For example, a large flourish of a signature following a

page of small, tightly closed-in writing is fairly unusual.

Just as with the rest of handwriting, no one sign should be taken on its own. The graphologist, like any reader, may form from a signature an overall impression of kindliness, quietness, forcefulness, or pretentiousness. However, a careful consideration of a dozen different indicators may reveal to the expert that the writer is forceful, ambitious, thrusting and overbearing, or, on the other hand, is trying to appear forceful while actually being very timid or indecisive.

Generally speaking, it is true to say that a plain, unadorned signature shows the writer to be straightforward, honest and self-confident without being arrogant. Again generally, the more flourishes and fancy strokes, the more affectation and falseness.

If the signature is largely illegible, it can show that the writer has a very low opinion of his own self-importance; or it could show the complete opposite, that he expects everyone to know exactly who he is, and sees no reason why he should take the trouble to reveal himself neatly to people who are less important than himself.

If the signature is much larger than the other writing on the page, it shows that the writer thinks highly of himself, though this is likely to be self-deception; if it is much smaller, it usually shows low self-confidence, without expecting high regard from others.

If the first name is larger than the surname, it shows more informality and a willingness to be friendly; if the surname is larger, it shows a more formal person.

If any part of the signature is underlined, it draws attention to that part of the name and may denote a degree of self-importance. It may well also be compensating for insecurity. Over-tracing of a signature shows nervousness and a lack of self-confidence.

A loop around part of the name, or a large capital letter enclosing some of the rest of the name, reveals a tendency for self-protection, wariness, or sometimes secrecy.

Lines crossing through part of the signature show a self-critical or self-destructive tendency.

A dot at the end can show finality, firmness, pedantry, and a refusal to consider other people's viewpoints.

Declaration of Simon Fraser 10 April

The Great Seers

*P*redictive and divinatory skill is such a strange concept to modern man that almost any lengths are taken to prove it bogus or inaccurate. This is not scepticism, or even cynicism, but just good sense: it is beyond our comprehension, therefore there must be some other explanation.

And yet, in the course of history, there are dozens, if not hundreds, of well-documented cases where accurate predictions have been made, recorded and circulated years before the prophesied event has taken place. There is no argument: this has happened over and over again, and it is only the hyper-rationality of twentieth-century mankind that blinds us to this obvious fact.

Some men and women are undisputedly given the gift of the future: with faith, it is open to all. In this section are noted a few famous examples to illustrate that destiny can be revealed – that it is possible to tear through the veils of time.

Opposite: *This Rembrandt etching shows a magician predicting the future using a magic mirror. The magic qualities of mirrors stem from the early art of hydromancy, foretelling the future by gazing into water. In medieval Europe mirrors were considered lucky in that they kept away evil spirits. Even today mirrors are associated through folklore with predicting the identity of young girls' future husbands.*

Nostradamus

Above: *Nostradamus at the centre of an engraving that shows him aged fifty-nine, at the height of his fame. His extraordinary collection of predictive poems,* Centuries, *had been published seven years previously and his fame had spread wide, reaching even royal circles.*

Michel de Notre Dame (or Nostre-Dame according to some sources) was born into the great Jewish community that thrived in Provence during the sixteenth century. Both of his grandfathers were court physicians to King René of Provence – Jean de Saint-Rémy and Pierre de Nostre-Dame: their offspring married, and Michel was born in 1503. He came under the influence of his grandfathers at an early age. At that time physicians would have been well-versed in all of the esoteric and arcane disciplines that were at the fringe of medicine – alchemy and astrology among them – and the boy, tutored in particular by Jean de Saint-Rémy, would have received instruction in these subjects along with his quota of more usual lessons in Latin, Hebrew, mathematics and Greek.

Nostradamus (as we will henceforward call him) completed his basic studies in the Humanities at Avignon, and then, naturally enough, given his family background, moved on to the great medieval University of Montpellier, where he joined the medical school. This was at the time of the black plague in Europe, and much of his early experience came in the treatment and attempted prevention of the disease. As the story goes,

he had an extraordinarily high rate of success compared with his colleagues: his fame spread, and he began to be summoned to the bedsides of the wealthy and influential. At this stage he had still not officially qualified as a doctor – this came later, after the plague had ended, when he returned to Montpellier to take his examinations.

In his healing travels, he had developed a taste for the countryside, and now settled in the small town of Agen, where he married Adriète de Loubéjac, and fathered two sons. Unfortunately all three members of his family died suddenly, and the depressed physician once more took to an itinerant existence. This was a transitional time in his life: most now believe that it was this period of intense grief and existential re-evaluation that transformed a learned but staid physician into the most extraordinary seer and prophet of recorded history. Certainly, little is known of his movements at this time (though it is rumoured that he travelled widely in Italy and France to meet some of the greatest esoteric scholars of the age), but when he returned to view, he was a different man. One story, possibly apocryphal, told of his "missing" period in his life is that while in Italy he mystified his companions by falling prostrate before an undistinguished junior monk. In response to their astonishment, he would say only, "I had to bow before His Holiness". The action only became logical many decades later, when the monk was made a Cardinal, and finally became Pope Sixtus the Fifth in 1585. If true, this is the first recorded exemplification of Nostradamus's divinatory gift.

At the age of forty-four he married for the second time and settled once more in Provence, this time at Salon. He still practised as a physician,

and his reputation and fame were as strong as before. So famous did he become, that the rich and powerful beat a path to his door, and his presence in Salon did a great deal to make it a popular and wealthy town. Yet his great skills, combined with the lifestyle he had adopted, also caused the rumour to spread that he was an occultist and practitioner of witchcraft. Although he was devoutly Catholic (his parents having had to convert to Christianity to comply with the draconian religious laws prevalent in France at the time), he would spend days at a time in his dusty study surrounded by huge and obscure books – the great works of medieval learning – and his magnificent collection of strange instruments, including astrolabes, alembics (glass implements used for distillation), wands, mirrors and other alchemical equipment. It is perhaps no small wonder that the simple folk of Salon misunderstood his purpose: learning in the sixteenth century inevitably encompassed subjects closely associated with the occult.

It was at this time that Nostradamus himself added to the flames of rumour by admitting for the first time that he believed himself to be endowed with the gift of prophecy – that he had been born with an extra sense which allowed him to foretell future events. At the same time, he also made it clear that these prophetic visions did not just visit him at random: he had developed a scientific system which allowed him to enter the future under the right circumstances. The system, together with his inherited sixth sense, combined to allow him to record events yet to take place. To this day, nobody has managed to discover what processes, materials, or substances the system embraced, though many have sought for years to "break the code" of Nostradamus's methods.

One clue may be in Nostradamus's ancestry. His forefathers fled persecution and slaughter as Jewish refugees, and one theory is that, over the generations, old manuscripts and books from the ancient Egyptian libraries may have been passed from father to son until they reached Michel. His grandfather's learning, and the nature of their profession, could well serve to reinforce this argument, as does Nostradamus's own confession that he had learned several ancient Egyptian documents by heart before destroying them. The whereabouts of the knowledge and artefacts from the ancient libraries destroyed by the barbarians is, of course, one of the central preoccupations of all those interested in occultism and the mysterious arts: it has also been associated with the wisdom inherent in the Tarot pack. It is therefore perhaps not surprising that this theme should again have been infiltrated into the story of Nostradamus. Whatever the truth about these rarer books, he is certainly known to have possessed a copy of *De Mysteriis Egyptorum*, Iamblichus's fourth-century esoteric guide, an edition of which was produced in Lyons in 1547.

Whatever the origin of his skills, his proclamation of them, and his demonstration of their veracity, soon made him a wonder of his age. His routine was now set: every night he would sit before a brass bowl filled almost to overflowing with water. He would then record his visions in quatrains (four-line poems). The reading and interpretation of these poems would provide the key to the future. The poems were gathered together in book form and called *Centuries*, and the first edition was published in 1555 (by M. Bonhomme, a printer at Lyons).

The circulation of Nostradamus's verses caused a sensation. They quickly reached all the civilized courts and corners of the world, and became vastly influential. An argument could be made that Nostradamus had become the first "popular" bestselling author in publishing history. Salon, already changed by the influx of notable "tourists" who had come to consult the great physician, was transformed virtually overnight into one of the most remarkable and famous locations in Christendom. Even the boy King of France, Charles IX, visited Salon, braving a new outbreak of plague in the region, to meet the great prophet.

Nostradamus's fame and success bred jealousy in his rivals, and many pamphlets were published attempting to make him out to be a charlatan. At the same time, the accuracy of his predictions further increased the rumours that he was a witch – and in retrospect, given the atmosphere and attitudes of the time, he was lucky to avoid being officially accused or physically attacked by the mob. He lived on in Salon, revered by some and reviled by others, until he died beside his bench, as he himself had foretold, on the night of 1 July 1566.

The Predictions of Nostradamus

As has been mentioned, great mystery surrounds the work of Nostradamus, and little is known of his methods. The quatrains themselves have provoked enormous controversy over the years. A typical reaction is that "they are so vague they could be applied to any event", and, indeed, it is the case that names are changed, generalizations are common, and the verses often look, on first reading, quite meaningless.

Nostradamus's own explanation for this is simple and reasonable: it is given in the foreword he placed in the second edition of the *Centuries*, in which he dedicates the book to King Henry II. "The danger of the times, O Most Serene Majesty, requires that such hidden events be not manifested save by enigmatic speech: . . . did I so desire, I could fix the time for every quatrain . . . but that it might to some be disagreeable." This implies two additional reasons: firstly, for the most contemporary predictions, Nostradamus feared that knowledge of events in the short term future might provoke unrest or even violence. If someone knows that an invasion is planned, or a war is to take place, that information alone might be enough to put a spark to the flame. And secondly, it clearly touches on the central dilemma of all predictive endeavour: namely the advisability or otherwise of revealing the future, once known, to those whose lives are to be affected. To put it simply, Nostradamus was aware that most people cannot cope with prior knowledge of their own destiny – whether good or bad. It is for this reason that his quatrains are packed with anagrams, slight misspellings and synonyms (Hister for Hitler; Nizaram for Mazarin and so on). For those who doubt, it is interesting to note that one of the most respected mathematicians and statisticians in the world once calculated that the probability of such transpositions being accidental (i.e. that Nostradamus invented random names and references which just happened to closely fit later historical figures) is, on close analysis of the texts, so many millions to one that it is infinite. In other words, there is no statistical chance that Nostradamus's work is bogus.

Students of Nostradamus should not look on the quatrains purely for obvious and direct advice,

Dieu convert icy de ma bouche, Pour tancoucer la verité, Si ma prediction te touche Rendy grace à sa Divinité,

A b o v e : *Michel de Notre Dame, better known as Nostradamus, believed he was endowed with the gift of prophecy. He is pictured here at his desk, surrounded by books and astrological instruments. The verse beneath reinforces the belief that his keen talent is a divine one; he saw himself as God's mouthpiece for the truth.*

but should approach the verses as they would any other type of divinatory reading: the information is provided, but personal analysis and interpretation is the final part of the process. As Le Pelletier, the most distinguished scholar of the quatrains, has noted, they are "a sort of . . . Tarot in verse, a cabbalistic kaleidoscope". Nostradamus, like the great ancient oracles, creates a divinatory framework which, for the sympathetic and mentally-atuned interpreter, lays bare the future: each quatrain is, in those terms, like a cast of the runes or a layout of the Tarot which needs to be read with the same degree of depth and sensitivity to discover the truth. Nostradamus summarized the system succinctly: "To understand my [verses] is as easy as blowing your nose, but the sense is more difficult to grasp".

To take just one example in detail, this is the quatrain most often interpreted as Nostradamus's prediction of Napoleon's rise to political power:

> *Un Empereur naistra près d'Italie,*
> *Qui, à l'Empire, sera vendu bien cher;*
> *Diront avec quels gens il se ralie,*
> *Qu'on trouvera moins prince qu boucher.*

This is only one of many of the quatrains associated with Napoleon, who lived three hundred years after Nostradamus. Translated, it reads: "An Emperor will be born near Italy, whose empire will cost France very dear. They will say of those who he gathers around him that they are butchers rather than princes". Napoleon was born in Corsica – close to Italy; his expansionist dreams effectively drained and destroyed France, eventually leading to its defeat in a succession of wars; and his generals and political associates were certainly not princely in revolutionary France. The phrase "moins prince" is perhaps the most significant: in Nostradamus's time, the thought of an Empire without princes was unheard of – foreseeing an Empire may be a lucky guess, but foretelling Republicanism is divination almost beyond the realms of imagination. If this were a single prophecy it might be explained away by chance, but there are "Ten Centuries" of quatrains – over one thousand, set in chronological order. It is no wonder that Goethe, in *Faust*, shows his protagonist reading the *Centuries* of Nostradamus and proclaiming, "Was it a god who penned these signs?"

A b o v e: *"The London Senate will put to death its King", decreed Nostradamus, and indeed Charles I was condemned to death for the crime of high treason by his parliament; he was taken to his execution in Whitehall, London, in 1649.*

L e f t: *Nostradamus's gift of predicting events was uncannily accurate; he prophesied the destruction of the great force of the Armada sent by Spain against the British. The British fleet was led by Sir Francis Drake in 1588 and victory was swift.*

L e f t : *The description of Nostradamus's "Empereur", mentioned in one of his Centuries, fits the figure of Napoleon with astonishing accuracy. Napoleon has been the subject of much esoteric analysis, particularly that of numerology; having been connected with the prophecies of Nostradamus he remains a fascinating figure for the application of other forms of predictive research.*

The Astonishing Accuracy of Nostradamus's Verses

Nostradamus's quatrains are now thought to have accurately predicted the following events and circumstances, among hundreds of others:

★ *The blinding and death of King Henry II of France*

★ *The ascension to the throne of France of all three of Henry II's sons – Francis II, Charles IX, and Henry III*

★ *The Spanish Armada and its destruction by the English*

★ *An English colonial Empire of three hundred years, commencing in the last quarter of the sixteenth century, and beginning to deteriorate at the end of the nineteenth century*

★ *The French Revolution*

★ *The English Civil War ("The London Senate will put to death its King")*

★ *The life and achievements of Oliver Cromwell ("Twenty months he will hold the Kingdom in utter power. A dictator, cruel, but leaving a worse cruelty behind")*

★ *The scandals of the reign of Louis XV ("The great monarch who will succeed . . . will give an example of an immoral and adulterous life")*

★ *The atrocities and carnage in Nantes in 1793, when over one thousand people were slaughtered*

★ *The harnessing of electricity for man's use, and the coming of telegraphic and wireless communications*

★ *The world-wide 'flu epidemic of 1918–1919*

★ *The rise of Hitler and the Third Reich in Germany*

★ *The political power of Charles de Gaulle in France*

★ *The atom bombs dropped on Hiroshima and Nagasaki at the end of World War II in the Far East ("At the port and in two cities, two scourges such as have never been seen")*

★ *The assassination of two of the Kennedy brothers, John and Robert, and the political demise of the third, Edward*

Above and left: *The rise to power of Hitler and the German Third Reich was foretold by Nostradamus in his collection of poems, Centuries. The reference that is relevant to Hitler is actually spelt "Hister", yet, statistically speaking, the probability of the similarity being mere coincidence has been found to be nearly impossible.*

Right: *The extensive use of electricity was also foretold by Nostradamus; Thomas Alva Edison invented the incandescent lamp and brought electric light to many millions of homes.*

Cheiro

Count Louis Hamon was born in Ireland in 1866. Moving to London, and adopting the pseudonym Cheiro, by the 1890s he had established himself as the darling of society and the most famous palm reader in the world. He was fortunate, in that his appearance on the scene coincided with an enormous upsurge in the popularity of and interest in predictive skills, but he takes credit for having the looks, charm, and genuine divinatory talent to take full advantage of the mood of the times. The books he published at the time, some of which are still available, were instant successes, and he also made a series of films for the early cinema on the subject of chiromancy. His personal history remains hazy – leading to the feeling among some that he was no more than a con-man who made more than his fair share of lucky guesses. However, as can be seen from the list of just some of his predictions given here, statistical probability sides with Cheiro in confirming that his work was much more than opportunistic flammery.

One of the best descriptions of Cheiro's fame comes in the "Publishers' Preface" to his early work *Read Your Past Present and Future*; though hardly likely to be completely objective, all of the examples given are confirmed by other sources.

"The name 'Cheiro' covers one of the most remarkable personalities of modern times, a highly-gifted man who, had he desired, might have won fame in many other pursuits in life, but who chose at the very threshold of his manhood to live in the East, so that he might be able to study the forgotten wisdom of those wonderful races such as the Hindus, the Chinese and Persians, and returning to Western civilisation he took a sacred vow that for twenty years he would devote himself to converting the most intellectual and highest personages in the world to believe in the strange Science of which he had made himself the Master.

In carrying out his vow his success has been phenomenal. He has read and taken impressions of the hands of most of the crowned heads of Europe, together with Presidents of Republics and Kings of Commerce. One and all have borne witness that 'Cheiro's' powers of predicting events years in advance from the lines in

A b o v e : *The American author Mark Twain was facing bankruptcy when he was told by Cheiro that he would receive a great sum of money when he reached the age of sixty-eight. Although he received this prophecy with scepticism, he did indeed enter into a lucrative publishing contract exactly as predicted by Cheiro.*

R i g h t : *Cheiro's best-selling book on the predictive strengths of palm-reading. Some of his works are still available today and his followers are dedicated and widespread.*

Left: Count Louis Hamon, better known as Cheiro, was responsible for a tremendous upsurge in the popularity of palmistry at the turn of the century.

Left: Count Louis Hamon, better known as Cheiro, was responsible for a tremendous upsurge in the popularity of palmistry at the turn of the century.

Left: One of the earliest proponents of palm-reading was Johann Hartlieb. His book Die Kunst Chiromantie was the first ever to be published on the subject and appeared in 1475.

Below: Queen Victoria as a young woman in 1838, wearing her Coronation robes. Cheiro's predictions even touched upon royalty: he foretold the date of the Queen's death in 1901.

their hands has been something akin to the marvellous.

Taking one or two illustrations at random: 'Cheiro' predicted the date of Queen Victoria's death, the exact year and even the month when King Edward the VII would pass away, the terrible destiny that awaited the late Czar of Russia, the assassination of King Humbert of Italy, the attempt on the Shah's life in Paris, and in thousands of well-known persons' lives with equal accuracy, the leading events of their careers.

It is on record that one of the most dramatic predictions ever made, was, when in 1894 (twenty-two years before the tragic event) 'Cheiro' foretold to Lord Kitchener the exact year of his death – and *the likely form it would take*. The words of this remarkable prediction made by 'Cheiro' at the War Office, was the following:

'That he, Kitchener, would meet his death in his sixty-sixth year – not the end that a Soldier might naturally expect on the battle-field – but that his death would be caused by water, most probably by storm or disaster at Sea, with the attendant chance of some form of capture by an enemy and exile from which he would never recover.'

When this prediction was made – the great Kitchener was only a plain Colonel and in that year 1894 he gave 'Cheiro' a signed impression of his hand which had strangely enough the Seal of the War Office imprinted on it, which may be seen at the top of the second finger in the Film reproduction of Kitchener's hand, which is now being shown at all the principal Cinemas in England.

Lord Kitchener never forgot this prediction. During the Great War, while at the Front, as related in the Press, he mentioned it to General de Ballincourt and members of his Staff.

The tragic sinking of the battleship 'Hampshire' on the evening of the 5th June, 1916, in Lord Kitchener's sixty-sixth year, and the chance that the great Soldier might have been captured by an enemy submarine, bore out 'Cheiro's' prediction to the letter, and is a remarkable example of the accuracy of his system in reading the lines of the hand.

A similar prediction was made by 'Cheiro' to the celebrated journalist, W.T. Stead, and with equal exactness, when he went to his death in the disaster to the 'Titanic' on her first voyage.

It can be said without exaggeration, that 'Cheiro' has become world-famous through the perfection to which he had brought this Study of the Hand. In London, Paris, New York, Boston, Chicago, in all the great Towns of America, in Petrograd, Rome and the principal Continental cities, he has demonstrated that the lines of the hand are a veritable chart of life, his success has been certified to by all classes and in his Visitor's Book autographed testimonies may be seen that are *without a parallel* in the history of the World.

In this small but concise work that we now issue to the public, the reader will find clearly drawn illustrations of the various lines that seem so bewildering when glanced at in ignorance of their real meaning. The Author, however, illuminates the whole subject in a lucid style peculiarly his own, and in such a form that the reader can 'Know Himself' or Herself, in a way that would be impossible by any other study.

Above: *Lord Kitchener in the now-famous poster appealing for army recruits. In 1894 Cheiro examined a palm print given to him by Kitchener and predicted his death by drowning in 1916.*

We have no hesitation in saying that this book places in concise form rare knowledge that cannot but be found of benefit to all."

Predictions by Cheiro

★ *Mark Twain records that in 1895, when he was sixty, Cheiro told him in a reading that he (Twain) would suddenly come into money in his sixty-eighth year. Bankrupt at the time, and in debt to the tune of over $90,000, Twain viewed this with amusement. But in November 1903 he was, out of the blue, offered a contract with Harper, the publisher, which cleared his debts and ensured him thereafter an income of over $100,000 per annum.*

★ *He accurately predicted to King Edward VII that he would die in his sixty-ninth year. He also accurately foresaw the time of Queen Victoria's death, and told others of his prediction.*

★ *In an exhibition reading at which he was unaware of the identity of his subjects (being separated by a cloth screen), he told Oscar Wilde that he was a well-known man at the height of his fame, but that he must avoid rash actions in seven years' time or he would be ruined. Seven years later, Wilde was jailed, after two infamous legal actions which he himself initiated, for homosexuality.*

★ *He visited Russia in 1904 to do a reading for the Czar in which he foretold that Russia would be involved in a calamitous war between 1914– 1917 and that the Czar would then lose all he loved most.*

★ *His most famous and well-documented prediction was in a reading for Lord Kitchener, over twenty years beforehand, that he would die by drowning in 1916 unless he avoided all forms of sea travel. Kitchener went down on the Hampshire in 1916 during World War I.*

★ *He told the killer, Meyer, when he was on death row that he would not be executed as his life line continued for many more years. This seemed impossible at that time, but, sure enough, Meyer received a last minute reprieve.*

William Lilly

William Lilly (1602–1681) was the most famous and revered astrologer of his time. Born shortly after the death of John Dee, he followed in Dee's

tradition, and was one of the last of the great "occult" astrologers. He was closely aligned to the Parliamentarian cause in the English Civil War, and lost his patronage and fell out of favour when the Monarchy was reinstated.

Lilly's divinations were expressed in the form of mystical symbolic drawings and astrological pamphlets. His two most famous predictions were of the Great Plague in 1665 and the Great Fire of London in 1666: both predictions were made ten years before the events he accurately described, and were recorded and circulated at the time of prediction.

Lilly, the Great Plague, and the Great Fire of London

Lilly's book of *Astrological Predictions*, published in 1648, contains the following passage:

"In the year 1656 the Aphelium of Mars, who is the general signification of England, will be in Virgo, which is assuredly the ascendant of the English monarchy, but Aries of the Kingdom. When this absis therefore, of Mars, shall appear in Virgo, who shall expect less than a strange catastrophe of human affairs in the commonwealth, monarchy, and Kingdom of England? There will then, either in or about these times, or near that year, or within ten years more or less of that time, appear in this kingdom so strange a revolution of fate, so grand a catastrophe and great mutation unto this monarchy and government, as never yet appeared; of which as the times now stand, I have no liberty or encouragement to deliver my opinion, – only, it will be ominous to London, unto her merchants at sea, to her traffique on land, to her poor, to all sorts of people inhabiting in her or her liberties, by reason of sundry fires and a consuming plague."

In 1651 Lilly published a pamphlet called *Monarchy and no Monarchy* containing one of his famous symbolic woodcuts within which, to quote his autobiography, "[I had] framed an hieroglyphic . . . representing a great sickness and mortality; wherein you may see the representation of people in their winding-sheets, persons digging graves and sepulcures, coffins etc. . . . After the coffins

and pickaxes there is a representation of a great city all in flames of fire."

Lilly was still alive when the plague and fire had happened. So famous and notorious did he become, that the Parliamentary Committee examining the causes of the fire summoned him to give evidence, suggesting that he may have been responsible for starting the fire in order to make his predictions come true. He told the Parliamentarians that his foresight was based purely on astrological skill – an explanation which was accepted.

Andrew Jackson Davis

Davis, the first great American seer, was born in Orange County, New York, in 1826 into an impoverished farming family. From infancy there are records of his visions and the voices he heard – it seems that he was born with the gift of clairvoyance. This may have been refined when, in 1843, a travelling mesmerist visited Davis's community and helped Davis to develop and work on

the ability to enter trance-like states. Soon Davis's parochial fame spread, and he began to travel around the country holding clairvoyant seminars and giving *ad hoc* exhibitions of his divinatory skills.

By 1845 he was publishing books which were dictated while he was entranced – almost speaking in tongues. The view at the time was that the subjects of his books were of such an erudite and esoteric mixture of material that it was impossible that the words came from the relatively uneducated Davis. He would discourse, for example, on advanced medical theories which challenged even the most up-to-date knowledge of research physicians, and one of his specialities was to diagnose and cure disease, without ever having received any formal training.

His books also contained fantastical prophecies of things unheard of and unenvisaged at the time. Having seen him lecture, the visionary writer Edgar Allen Poe became a follower, and was convinced of the veracity of his foresight. Others have not been so sure, and one body of critics has always been highly suspicious of Davis's work and his motives – no more so than when, in later years, Davis became emersed in the Spiritualist movement, which at that time was riddled with con-men and charlatans. Nevertheless, Davis stands head and shoulders above his contemporaries in terms of the accuracy of what he predicted: his words were written, recorded, and published at the time, and, as can be seen clearly from the quoted highlights here, there is no disputing their accuracy.

Left : *In 1651 Lilly predicted the Great Fire of London which devastated the city in 1666; he saw it as following a period of grief and sickness – the Black Death. This prophecy was proved true within his lifetime – and he was regarded with great suspicion.*

Left : *Hailed as one of the great American prophets, Andrew Jackson Davis soon established a strong reputation for prediction through the publication of his books and while conducting lecture tours around the country.*

The Predictions of Andrew Jackson Davis

In 1856, on the Railway:
Cars may be constructed so that no accident or even collision would be dangerous to either passengers or baggage . . . Instead of the present gallery-looking cars, we will have spacious saloons, almost portable dwellings, moving with such speed that perhaps there will be advertisements – "Through to California in four days!"

In 1856, on motor vehicles:
Carriages and travelling saloons [will move along] country roads – sans horse, sans steam, sans any visible motive power, moving with greater speed and safety than at present. Carriages will be moved by a strange and beautiful and simple admixture of aqueous and atmospheric gases – so easily condensed, so simply ignited, and so imparted by a machine . . . as to be entirely concealed between the forward wheels.

In 1856, on air travel:
It will not only [be] the locomotive on the rail, and the carriage on the country road, but aerial cars, also, which will move through the sky from country to country.

A b o v e: *One of the Oracles of Delphi in a frenzied, trance-like state which would enable her to pronounce on the future of those who consulted her.*

R i g h t: *Socrates, the great Greek philosopher, drinking hemlock after being found guilty of impious behaviour towards the gods, in spite of having been declared the wisest man alive by the Oracle.*

The Oracle and Croesus

The fabulously wealthy Croesus, King of Lydia, wished to consult an Oracle about a threat from his neighbour, King Cyrus of Persia. Before committing to a particular temple, he wished to test their accuracy, sending messengers to no less than six. Delphi told the messengers that at the precise moment of the consultation, Croesus was boiling a tortoise and lamb together in a copper pot. On their return home, they found that this bizarre prophecy was precisely true.

Overjoyed by this proof, Croesus sent great riches back to the Oracle, together with a question about what action he should take against Persia. The Oracle declared that if he marched against Cyrus, a great empire would be destroyed. Hearing, in the enigmatic announcement, what he chose to hear, Croesus marched: but it was the downfall of his own empire that the Oracle had foretold, and he was destroyed.

The Oracle at Delphi

This is not one seer, but hundreds: the Oracles – usually young women, called sibyls – who maintained the oracular tradition at the temples of Greece for hundreds of years. Of these temples the most famous and revered was at Delphi, and the sibyl at Delphi was always called Pythia.

People would travel for weeks to get to the Oracle and ask a question. The Oracle would normally appear only once every month, and the fees charged were enormous, meaning that only the rich and aristocratic could make use of the service. Once paid, the Oracle would enter a frenzied trance state, in which she would become a link for the voices of the gods. It is claimed that to aid the trance Pythia used drugs: possibly a mixture of the sacred waters of Cassotis, crushed bay leaf and a natural gas emanating from the rock crevices surrounding the site.

This was genuinely a case of speaking in tongues: the messages were histrionic, garbled, and colourful, providing, like the later quatrains of Nostradamus, a medium for the message rather than the message itself. The last stage in the process was the interpretation of the Oracle's enigmatic pronouncements.

The Oracle and Socrates

The Oracle at Delphi, asked who was the wisest man alive, pronounced that it was Socrates. As the Oracle could not be wrong, this was accepted as fact, and it was this elevation of Socrates among his brethren in those democratic times that first set his countrymen against him, and resulted, eventually, in his forced suicide.

B e l o w : *The remains of the Temple of Apollo in Delphi, Greece. Situated high on a hillside in an isolated area of the Greek mainland, the site still retains its rich atmosphere of mystery.*

BIBLIOGRAPHY

There are many hundreds of books available on all aspects of prediction, divination and the esoteric in general. Some are scholarly and sound; others are far less so. It is strongly recommended that the interested reader wanting to explore any particular subject in more detail use several books rather than depending on the views of just one.

Because of the high availability and constant change of books on astrology, Tarot and other related subjects the more general works are listed here. The following are all highly recommended.

Cavendish, Richard, *The Magical Arts: Western Occultism and Occultists*; Routledge, 1967; Arkana, 1984.

Cavendish, Richard, *A History of Magic*; Weidenfeld & Nicolson, 1987; Arkana, 1990.

Cavendish, Richard (ed.), *Encyclopedia of the Unexplained: Magic, Occultism and Parapsychology*; Routledge & Kegan Paul, 1974; Arkana, 1989.

Chetwynd, Tom, *A Dictionary of Symbols*, Paladin, 1982.

Cooper, JC, *The Aquarian Dictionary of Festivals*; Aquarian, 1990.

Cotterell, Arthur, *A Dictionary of World Mythology*; Oxford University Press, 1986.

Cotterell, Arthur, *The Illustrated Encyclopedia of Myths and Legends*; Cassell, 1991.

Durdin-Robertson, Lawrence, *The Year of the Goddess*; Aquarian, 1990.

Grant, John, *Dreamers: A Geography of Dreamland*; Ashgrove Press, 1984; Grafton, 1986.

Jung, CG, *Dreams*; Princeton University Press, 1974; Ark/Routledge & Kegan Paul, 1985.

Kightly, Charles, *The Perpetual Almanack of Folklore*; Thames & Hudson, 1987.

MacKenzie, Norman, *Dreams and Dreaming*; Aldus Books, 1965; Bloomsbury Books 1989.

McIntosh, Christopher, *The Astrologers and their Creed*; Hutchinson, 1969.

MacNeice, Louis, *Astrology*; Aldus Books, 1964; Bloomsbury Books, 1989.

Matthews, Caitlín & John, *The Western Way: A Practical Guide to the Western Mystery Tradition* (two volumes); Arkana, 1985 & 1986.

Pennick, Nigel, *Practical Magic in the Northern Tradition*; Aquarian, 1989.

Pennick, Nigel, *The Secret Lore of Runes and other Ancient Alphabets*; Rider, 1991.

Pollack, Rachel, *The New Tarot*; Aquarian, 1989.

Van Over, Raymond, *I Ching*; New American Library, 1971.

Wilhelm, Richard (trans. Baynes, Cary F), *I Ching or Book of Changes*; Routledge & Kegan Paul, 1951; Arkana, 1989.

Wing, RL, *The Illustrated I Ching*; Dolphin/Doubleday, 1982; Aquarian, 1987.

ACKNOWLEDGEMENTS

Grateful thanks to *Chris Bell* and *Pat Silver*, and to *Renna Nezos* of the College of Graphology.

None of these people is responsible for the opinions and emphases in this book.

The publishers and author would like to thank the following for their co-operation in providing pictures for use in this publication. Full effort has been made to locate the copyright owners of every photograph; we apologize for any omissions which will be rectified in future editions.

Charles Walker Collection, Images Colour Library; page 2; 8–9; 12 (above right, below right); 13 (below right); 15; 16 (above left & right); 17 (bottom); 21 (above left); 27 (below right); 31 (bottom); 32 (above left); 33 (above right, below left); 34 (above left & right); 35 (above left); 36 (top); 37 (right); 38; 39 (bottom); 40 (below right); 42 (above left & right); 44 (bottom); 49; 50 (right); 51 (below left); 53 (top); 54 (above right); 56 (left); 58 (below right); 61 (bottom); 63 (below right); 64 (bottom); 67 (top); 68 (below right); 69 (top); 71; 72 (top); 73 (right); 74 (top & bottom); 76 (top & bottom); 77 (top); 78 (right & left); 79 (top & bottom); 80 (top & bottom); 81 (top); 82 (above right, below left); 83 (top & bottom); 84 (top); 85; 88 (above right); 90 (above left); 102 (below right); 104 (above left); 105 (below left); 106 (above left); 107 (below right); 108–9 (top & bottom); 110 (below left); 111 (above right); 114 (below right); 115 (above right); 116 (above right, below left); 117 (top & bottom); 119 (top & bottom); 120; 121; 124 (right & left); 125; 126; 127; 129; 131; 132 (top); 133; 134; 135 (right & left); 137 (top & bottom); 138; 139 (right & left); 140 (above left & right); 142 (top); 144 (right & above left); 145 (top & bottom); 146 (above & below left, & right); 147 (right); 148 (top & bottom); 149 (left); 150 (right); 151 (top & bottom); 152; 154; 155 (right & left); 157; 159; 160 (right); 161 (bottom); 162; 163 (top & bottom); 166; 167; 168; 169 (bottom); 170; 171; 172; 173 (top & bottom); 174 (top & bottom); 175; 176–7; 178 (bottom); 179; 181; 182; 184 (top); 185 (top); 186 (left); 192–3; 194 (left); 195; 196 (right); 198 (top); 199; 200 (bottom); 200–201 (right); 202; 203; 204; 205 (top); 206 (above left & right); 207 (above left & right); 210 (right & left); 211 (top & bottom); 212 (below right); 213; 215; 216; 217 (top & bottom); 219 (below right); 223; 233; 241 (top); 246 (top); 247 (right); 248–9; 256.

Visual Arts Library: page 11; 14 (top); 45; 47 (top); 52 (top); 58 (top); 59 (bottom); 65 (below left); 66 (top); 69 (bottom).

David V Barrett: page 102 (above left); 189.

US Games Systems, Inc: page 44 (top); 56 (right); 77 (bottom); 81 (bottom); 86 (left & right); 87 (above left); 88 (far left, top & bottom); 89 (above right); 92 (top left & right, & bottom); 93 (right); 95 (below left & right); 97 (top, & below right); 100; 101; 161 (top).

Nicolaas CJ van Beek: page 87 (centre left); 91 (above left & right); 99 (centre left).

Amanda Barlow, published by Eddison Sadd: page 112 (above left); 113; 180.

Rachel Pollack, published by Droemersche Verlagsanstalt Th. Knaur Nachf., Munich: page 88 (centre left & bottom); 89 (above left).

Osvaldo Menegazzi: page 87 (below right, top card); 89 (bottom); 90 (above right); 97 (above left); 98 (below left & right).

Index